ULTIMATE
Dive Sites

ULTIMATE
Dive Sites

TODD THIMIOS

Hardie Grant
EXPLORE

Introduction — vi
Kinds of diving — ix
Diver safety — xiv
Ethical encounters with marine life — xv
Best of the best — xvi
Map of the world — xviii

AUSTRALIA, AOTEAROA NEW ZEALAND AND ANTARCTICA

Rapid Bay, SA, Australia — 2
Great Barrier Reef, Queensland, Australia — 6
Lord Howe Island, NSW, Australia — 12
Ningaloo Reef, WA, Australia — 19
Byron Bay, NSW, Australia — 23
SS Yongala, Queensland, Australia — 26
Port Lincoln, SA, Australia — 30
The Rowley Shoals, WA, Australia — 36
Whyalla, SA, Australia — 40
Milford Sound, Aotearoa New Zealand — 44
Antarctica — 49

AMERICAS

Grand Bahama, The Bahamas — 56
Bonito, Brazil — 60
Malpelo Island, Colombia — 64
Cocos Island, Costa Rica — 68
Gardens of the Queen (Jardines de la Reina), Cuba — 74
The Silver Bank, Dominican Republic — 78
Dominica, The Caribbean — 83
Santa Catalina Island, USA — 87
Magdalena Bay, Mexico — 90
White Cave System (Sistema Sac Actun), Mexico — 95
Banco Chinchorro, Mexico — 99

Above Galapagos whaler patrols the shallow reefs of Lord Howe Island, Australia

EUROPE AND UNITED KINGDOM

Northern Norway (Arctic Circle)	104
The White Sea, Russia	111
Silfra Fissure, Iceland	115
Medes Islands, Spain	119
The Hebrides, Scotland	123
Scapa Flow, Scotland	127
Lundy, Devon, England	130

ASIA

Similan Islands, Thailand	136
Mergui (Myeik) Archipelago, Myanmar	143
Misool, Raja Ampat, Indonesia	149
Waigeo, Raja Ampat, Indonesia	153
Lembeh Strait, Indonesia	158
Sipadan Island, Malaysian Borneo	165
Tubbataha, Philippines	169
Anilao, Philippines	172

PACIFIC

Rock Islands, Palau	178
The Tuamotus, French Polynesia	182
Vava'u, Tonga	187
The Coolidge, Santo, Vanuatu	190
Vatu-i-Ra, Fiji	194
Beqa Lagoon, Fiji	199
Wolf and Darwin Islands, Galápagos	202
Tufi, Papua New Guinea	208

INDIAN OCEAN AND AFRICA

Fuvahmulah, Maldives	214
Baa Atoll, Maldives	218
Trincomalee, Sri Lanka	223
KwaZulu-Natal coast, South Africa	227
Southern Red Sea, Egypt	231

Index	236
About the author	240
Acknowledgements	241

Introduction

While writing this book, I travelled to Vanuatu to photograph a wreck I hadn't dived in 20 years. At my guesthouse, I read this Melanesian proverb:

> All men are torn between two needs
>
> The need for the canoe
>
> And the need for the tree
>
> And men wander constantly between these two needs, yielding to one and then the other
>
> Until the day they understand that the canoe is made from the tree

For me, diving is the vessel that transports me to faraway places, and it is also the roots of my identity. While diving connects me with a great community at home, it also connects me with a global community. The sea brings a sense of familiarity; whether I'm teaching my daughters to snorkel in the local rock pool, or travelling on a liveaboard in Myanmar, I always feel at home when I'm underwater.

As a kid, I dreamt of diving my way around the world, and so becoming a dive instructor at age 20 kicked off the journey. What I didn't consider, at the time, was how differently I would encounter the world as a result of being a diver.

During my 20s I worked as a dive guide in Vanuatu and Lord Howe Island. Together with the local staff, we'd spend our days underwater, and on our days off we'd hike hidden trails and drink kava into the night with the villagers. Our mutual love for diving broke down barriers. And by living in dive destinations, I'd get to do the same dive over and over. My favourite underwater activity became staying in one place, sometimes for an hour at a time, just watching, observing.

When I began sailing the world on private yachts in my 30s, taking clients to the world's best dive sites, I still relished any opportunity for stillness underwater (though, most clients were 'go go go', wanting to see it all). Whether I was hovering above a reef wall for an hour in the Galápagos, waiting for a hammerhead shoal to appear, or looking for a pygmy seahorse on a gorgonian fan in Indonesia, it felt meditative to just dial my focus to one event. I'd find myself no longer observing individual things but noticing how they all worked together. Seeing this interconnectivity, you become so aware of the fragility of the ecosystem. A pressing urgency emerges, to help protect this space that you love so much.

Perhaps one of the most astounding things about the sea is how little we know about it. Over 80% of the ocean has never been seen, or even mapped, by humans. In this way, divers are explorers and there are endless opportunities to discover the undiscovered. The more you advance your training, the more you'll see. You might get into cold water diving, or cave diving, or learn to use a rebreather so you can dive deeper and longer. You may desire to go as deep as you can and do submersible training. I vividly remember when I piloted a sub down to 1000m (3200ft) in a remote part of the Bahamas and parked on the ocean floor, turning off the floodlights. In that moment, sitting behind the console in the darkness within a toy-sized sub, I'd never felt so small in my life.

While writing this book, I went back through 25 years of dive logbooks, photos and footage. I flew to destinations, old and new, passing through in my figurative canoe. In curating a list of 'ultimate' dive sites, I found myself pondering how I, the dive traveller, could be the ultimate guest. The ultimate ocean steward. How I could teach my daughters to love their local rock pool as much as the idea of an exotic reef. Because, ultimately, both ecosystems are equally important. I hope this book helps you guide your canoe to some incredible dive sites, near and far, and inspires you to sink deeper into your identity as a diver.

Opposite Author and family at Ningaloo Reef, Australia

Introduction   vii

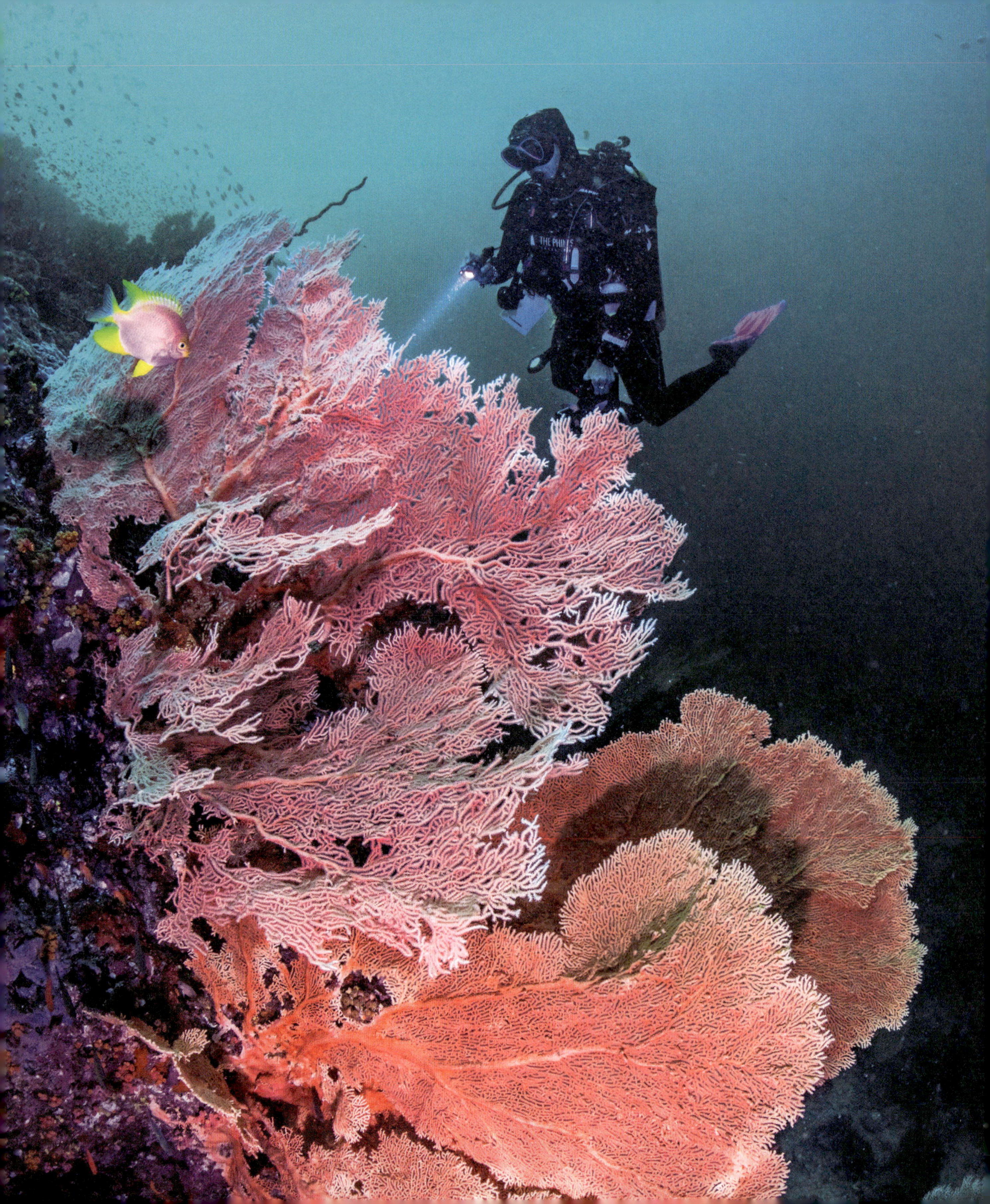

Kinds of diving

Whether it's due to a growing desire for exploration, advancements in technology or even human performance, there's no denying that diving in its many forms is growing in popularity, exponentially. While the main focus of the diving in this book is SCUBA, sometimes a different approach is needed or preferred. Here are the three styles of diving that I've covered in the pages following:

1. Freediving

Freediving has exploded in popularity in recent years and new records are constantly being set with freedivers finning themselves 120+ metres (394+ feet) down the line. Freediving is useful for dives that require a more agile and quick approach, such as jumping into the water with fast-moving orca pods (*see* p. 107)). Freediving can be dangerous and has claimed lives. In recent years, PADI and SSI have formulated specific courses and certifications, solely aimed at teaching skills for safer freediving experiences. There aren't many other sports where humans not only push their limits, but purposefully ignore their bodies' physiological warning signs to stay down longer. Still, freediving will always be the original, rawest and most liberating form of diving. All you need is your mask and the sea.

Freediving gear
- Weight belt
- Freediving fins, which are longer than your typical dive fins and made of a lightweight material
- A freediving mask, which is similar to a scuba diving mask, but has a much smaller profile.

2. Scuba

Self Contained Underwater Breathing Apparatus. There are a few different organisations that offer SCUBA certifications, with PADI and SSI being the most well-known. Beyond being Open Water Certified, I've detailed a few useful certifications below, which I recommend to anyone wanting to go deeper, stay underwater for longer or specialise in a particular kind of diving. From PADI's bubble maker course (from age eight, maximum 2m/6.5ft) to becoming a dive instructor, there are now speciality courses catering to almost all ages and interests.

Open water diver
If you're reading this book, it's likely you're already an accredited open water diver. You've done the theory, you've completed skills with an instructor in a pool, and you've done some open water dives down to a maximum of 18m (60ft). Congratulations on getting this far! Interested in taking your training further? Read on.

Advanced open water diver
Want to go deeper, try night diving, or just become more confident in the water? It's time to upskill. In getting your advanced certification, you'll fine-tune your buoyancy skills, dive to a maximum of 30m (98ft), learn about navigation and choose three areas to focus on for a 'taster', for example underwater naturalist, night and wreck diving. You can then continue training in one of those specialties, if you enjoyed it.

Dive Master diver
After you've logged enough dives and done the required prerequisites, including Rescue Diver relevant safety certifications, you can gain a professional level of dive skills and begin your journey of working in the dive industry. Guiding or helping instructors on courses, this dive course is the beginning of a professional career in diving.

Scuba gear
- Scuba cylinder (tank)
- BCD (buoyancy control device)
- Regulator (delivers air to the diver from the tank at an ambient pressure)
- Dive computer (calculates no decompression limits, depth and dive time)

Opposite The grand coral fans of the Similan Islands, Thailand

Instructor

To get to this level, you've not only dived a great deal and in an array of different environments, but you have also learnt the importance of safety underwater through practical experience and the art of teaching. You can now guide dives, teach courses and (hopefully) dive the world.

Specialty - Drysuit

Some of the planet's best dives are in freezing water, such as ice diving in Russia (*see* p. 111) or diving alongside leopard seals in Antarctica (*see* p. 50). Drysuits are essential for such dives. Your drysuit allows you to wear warm undergarments, like a jumper and tracksuit pants underneath, and the best part is they stay dry. But controlling your buoyancy is tricky and you'll learn all about this in your training.

Specialty - Nitrox

Quick science lesson: the air we breathe is made up of 21% oxygen and 78% nitrogen, with the remaining 1% a combination of other numerous gasses. The body absorbs and releases nitrogen differently under pressure; this is the reason we can't ascend quickly when we scuba dive. Slow ascents and allocated dive times ensure that the nitrogen absorbed in our bodies is released at a safe rate. Without these safety measures a diver would suffer from decompression sickness, aka 'the bends', which is the formation of nitrogen bubbles in the tissues of the body. A typical nitrox blend is 32% or 36% oxygen and, subsequently, less nitrogen. This means the body absorbs less nitrogen, allowing for longer dive times and shorter surface intervals.

Nitrox does not allow you to go deeper, as it has a higher oxygen percentage and oxygen becomes toxic at depth. You will learn more about oxygen and its partial pressure as you continue your dive courses.

Tec Diving - Rebreather

I love using a rebreather; I feel like there's no better tool for helping you capture the shot underwater. Traditionally used by commercial divers, these days rebreathers are becoming more popular with recreational divers, particularly photographers, cinematographers and cave divers.

Rebreathers are vastly different from scuba, requiring extensive specialised training. With scuba, used air is expelled into the water, while rebreathers are closed circuit, recycling air through a constant loop. Air circulates, CO_2 is absorbed and eliminated, and oxygen is added in its place. Divers tend to experiment with different mixed gasses on their rebreathers, accentuating the need for expert training and safety protocols.

Specialty - Cave Diver

Cave divers are a unique breed of divers, as we discover on page 95 in the Sistema Sac Actun. Typically, cave diving is done in a water filled cave (usually involving confined spaces) with an overhead environment that prohibits an ascent to the surface. More often than not, it is done in an exploratory or investigative nature.

Cave diving differs from cavern diving; in cave diving, divers may penetrate a system for hundreds of meters, whereas in cavern diving, divers don't venture far and the entrance is always in sight.

Gear: drysuits
There are many different drysuit options, but the principle is the same. I have a drysuit that has neck and wrist seals. This means I need to add both gloves and a hood to my suit.

- Drysuits require the use of extra weights, more than you'd normally use with a wetsuit

Gear: rebreather
A Closed-Circuit Rebreather (CCR) - this is an underwater breathing apparatus which has a closed loop that typically see the diver's CO_2 eliminated and O_2 added in its place

Cave-diving gear
Professional cave divers tend to opt for using CCR. Along with this:

- Short, stiff fins to reduce the chance of stirring up sediment with fin kicks
- Dive lights
- Navigation reels
- Reserve dive cylinders (bailout tanks)

Opposite top Preparing to dive at Milford Sound, Aotearoa New Zealand *Opposite bottom* Reef mantas in Hanifaru Bay, Baa Atoll, Maldives

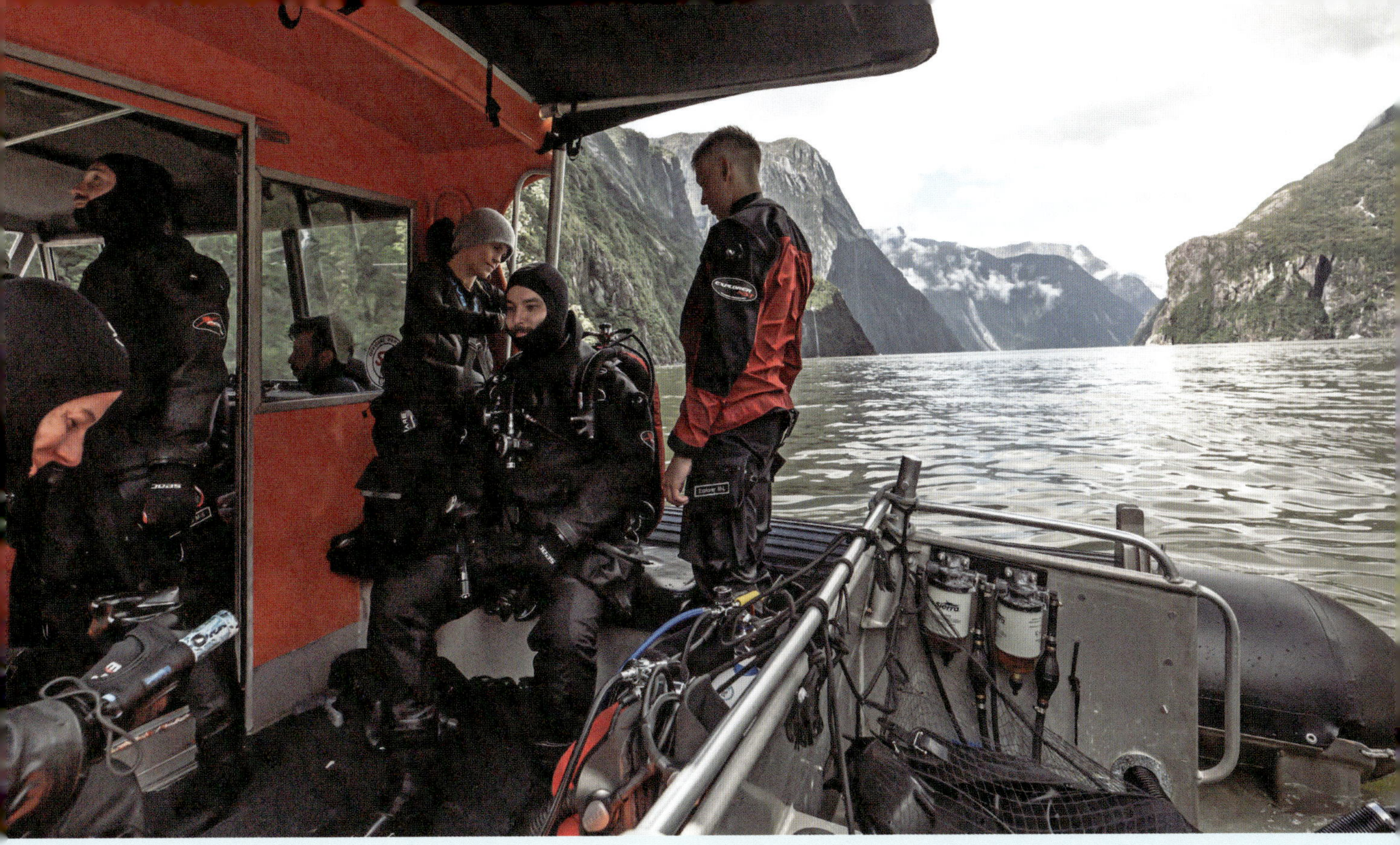

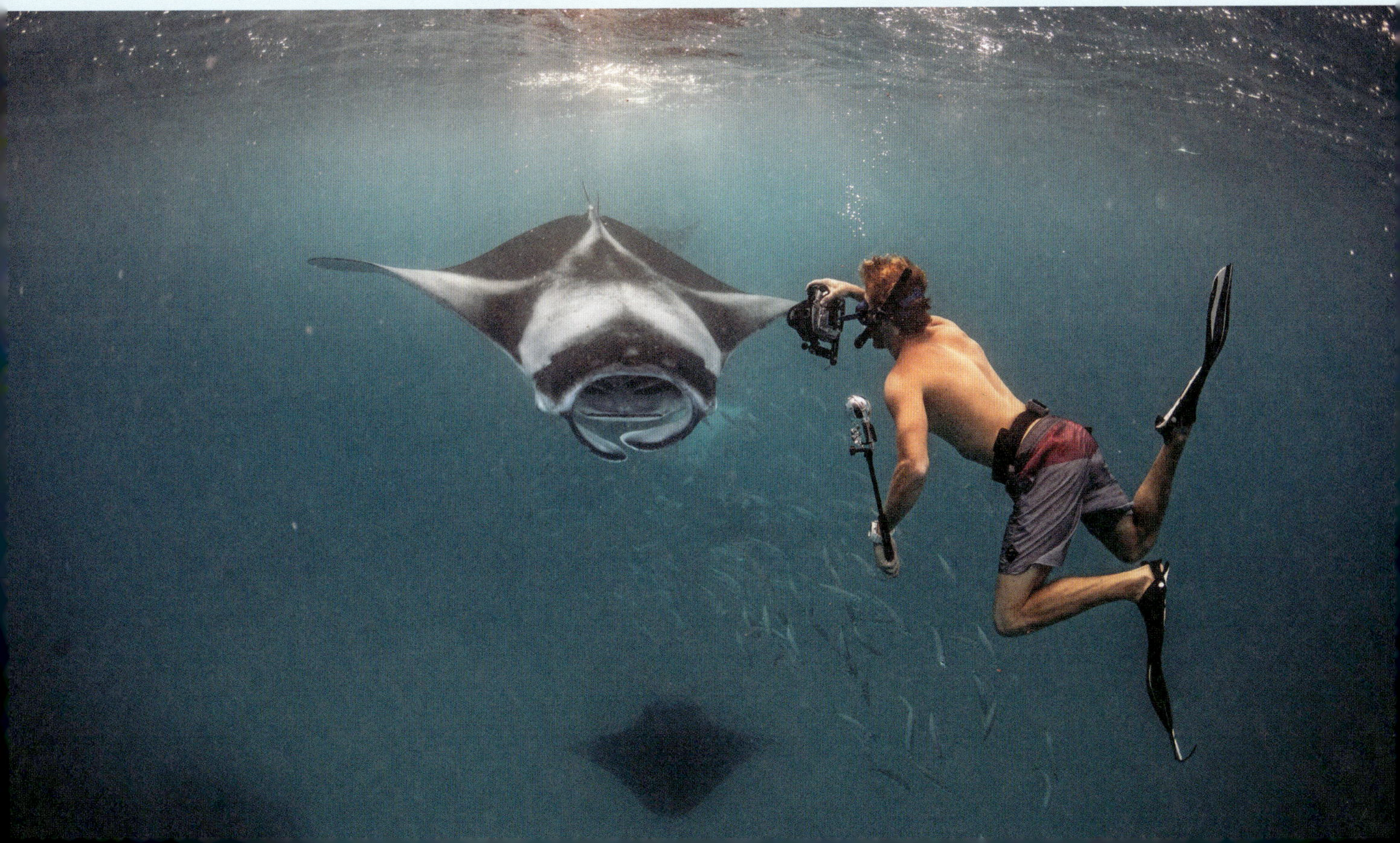

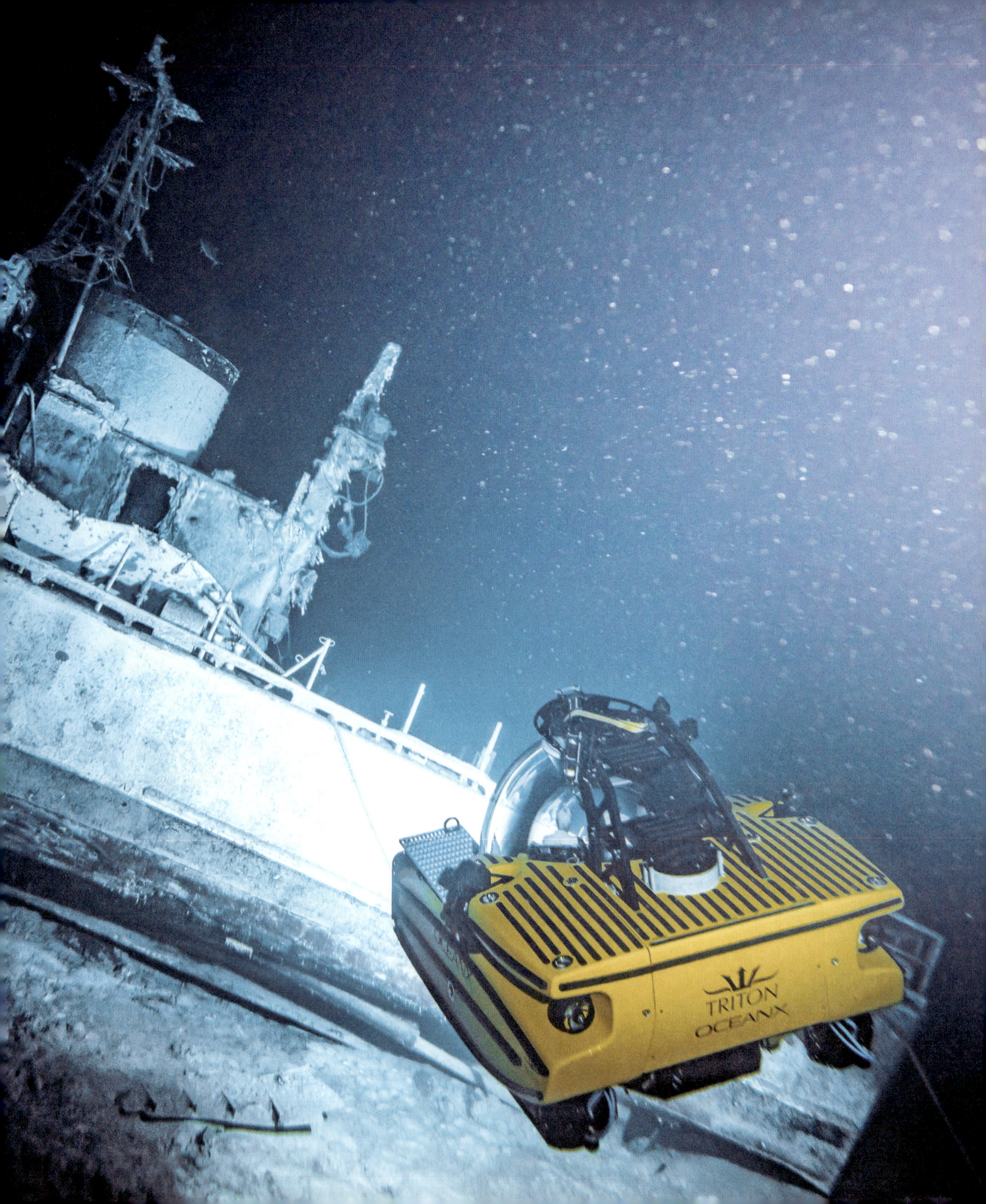
TRITON
OCEANX

3. Submersible

Manned submersibles are one of the most exciting advancements in the world of diving, and they are now regularly being purchased by private yacht owners as well as commercial cruise operators. A manned submersible is an underwater vehicle that communicates with a surface support team. Most submersibles can carry anywhere between two and nine passengers and have a maximum depth of no deeper than 1000m/3200ft (trust me, that feels deep enough). As the submersible's cabin is sealed, its passengers are not subjected to outside pressure whilst at depth. I did a lot of my training through SEAmagine Hydrospace over a number of years, piloting two to three manned submersibles to depths of 1000m/3200ft. Basically, you're sitting inside a tiny bubble, kind of like being inside a goldfish bowl, with an acrylic dome around you, giving you an almost 360-degree view of the marine world around you. SEAmagine's training program was initially developed in the '90s for the US Coast Guard, but nowadays it's become the leading training program for submersible pilots and topside crews within the industry for both private and commercial yachting, as well as the defence force. This kind of training is not cheap (I was lucky to have my employer sponsor me through the program), but if you're able to explore this incredibly unique opportunity, you'll be amongst a small group of people on the planet with this skill.

Opposite A triton submersible illuminates a wreck in the Bahamas once thought out of reach for divers *Below* Diving the clear waters of the Bahamas from a Triton submersible

Kinds of diving

Diver safety

What happens when you find yourself alone on a dive? Or maybe your gear fails at depth? Or, what if you've resurfaced from your dive to find your boat nowhere in sight, like I did in Sipadan (*see* p. 165). Or, you show signs of an illness or injury after a dive. Like most adventurous activities, diving carries risk. Below are a few practices that can reduce this risk.

Remember your training

Safety starts with comprehensive diver training and a solid understanding of emergency procedures. Remarkably, most dive fatalities occur to divers who have ended up alone – a scenario we are told to avoid early in our training. Ultimately, on top of training it's the time spent in the water that instils confidence and awareness. An expert diver is one who can recognise a risk well before it raises its ugly head, and this only comes with time in the water.

Understand your environment

Prior to any dive outing, especially a trip to a remote location, a diver should ensure they are fit and healthy enough to dive. Diving places a variety of stresses on our bodies, especially our hearts, and it's important to ensure we can cope with these. This is particularly relevant to older divers who often have cardiac disease, which they may not be aware of. Those over 45 years old are well advised to be checked for fitness-to-dive by a diving doctor.

Prior to any dive, divers should complete a comprehensive pre-dive briefing, gaining a solid understanding of local marine life, currents, potential hazards and recommended depths and times, from someone who dives the site regularly. This builds confidence and minimises risk.

Embrace recommendations

Sometimes the company we keep is our greatest safety measure. Choosing a reputable operator enhances safety by ensuring adherence to industry standards and regulations. Verified operators prioritise diver safety through properly maintained equipment, experienced guides and time in the field. Competent operators should also have suitable oxygen and first aid equipment (and a sufficient oxygen supply), appropriately trained staff, and an Emergency Management Plan to deal with serious incidents under their watch. This is especially true to operators in places more remote from good medical care.

If travelling to dive internationally, ensure you have an appropriate insurance(s) to deal with any diving accident or travel problem.

Plan your dive, dive your plan.

Ethical encounters with marine life

As divers, we are given a unique opportunity to encounter marine life in a way that most people will never experience. Our tourism dollars can influence practices set up by local governments and countries, as they realise that they can make more money from animals that are alive. The establishment of the Bahamas shark sanctuary (*see* p. 59) is a good example of this.

It's a privilege to dive alongside creatures big and small and the way we act, including the third party operators that we support, makes all the difference in the continued existence of these species, and the fragile ecosystem they form a part of.

Selecting ethical operators

It's important to throw your support behind the operators who are committed to ethical practices that uphold responsible tourism practices, thereby minimising impact and safeguarding the wellbeing of animals and the marine environment.

Here are a few questions to ask operators:

- Are they a licensed operator with relevant permits (if applicable)?
- Does their crew include a specialist guide and how many years' experience do they have in this field?
- Is there a cap on the number of people in the water with an animal at a time?
- Will the captain approach the animals slowly and follow current distance and operation regulations?

Minimising disturbance

- Enter the water quietly.
- Maintain a minimum distance. This varies depending on the animal. But it's always important to allow the animal to dictate the interaction, for example, let the animal swim to you. Observe the animal's behaviour and proceed accordingly.
- Don't dive down toward a resting whale, a resting pod of dolphins – or a resting turtle for that matter.
- Vessels must not box wildlife in, cut off their path or herd or chase them.
- Vessels must minimise boat and other noise, eg. gear shifting.

Avoid Physical Contact

- Some animals may react defensively.
- Wait for them to approach and observe from a distance.
- Be cautious around protective mothers. Give them space.
- Never, ever touch

Best of the best

Best cold-water dives
Antarctica, *see* p. 49
The White Sea, Russia, *see* p. 111
Northern Norway (Arctic Circle), *see* p. 104
Milford Sound, Aotearoa New Zealand, *see* p. 44

Best coral reefs
Vatu-i-Ra, Fiji, *see* p. 194
Great Barrier Reef, Queensland, Australia, *see* p. 6
Misool and Waigeo, Raja Ampat, Indonesia, *see* pp. 149 and 153
Similan Islands, Thailand, *see* p. 136
Southern Red Sea, Egypt, *see* p. 231

Best shark dives
Grand Bahama, The Bahamas, *see* p. 56
Malpelo Island, Colombia, *see* p. 64
Cocos Island, Costa Rica, *see* p. 68
Wolf and Darwin Islands, Galápagos, *see* p. 202
Port Lincoln, SA, Australia, *see* p. 30
Beqa Lagoon, Fiji, *see* p. 199

Best macro dives
Misool and Waigeo, Raja Ampat, Indonesia, *see* pp. 149 and 153
Lembeh Strait, Indonesia, *see* p. 158
Anilao, Philippines, *see* p. 172
Tufi, Papua New Guinea, *see* p. 208

Best for beginners
Gardens of the Queen (Jardines de la Reina), Cuba, *see* p. 74
Great Barrier Reef, Queensland, Australia, *see* p. 6
Similan Islands, Thailand, *see* p. 136
Byron Bay, NSW, Australia, *see* p. 23
Medes Islands, Spain, *see* p. 119

Best Wrecks
SS Yongala, Queensland, Australia, *see* p. 26
Scapa Flow, Scotland, *see* p. 127
Rock Islands, Palau, *see* p. 178
The Coolidge, Santo (Vanuatu), *see* p. 190
Tufi, Papua New Guinea, *see* p. 208

Opposite Mother and calf inspect me up close in the Norwegian Arctic

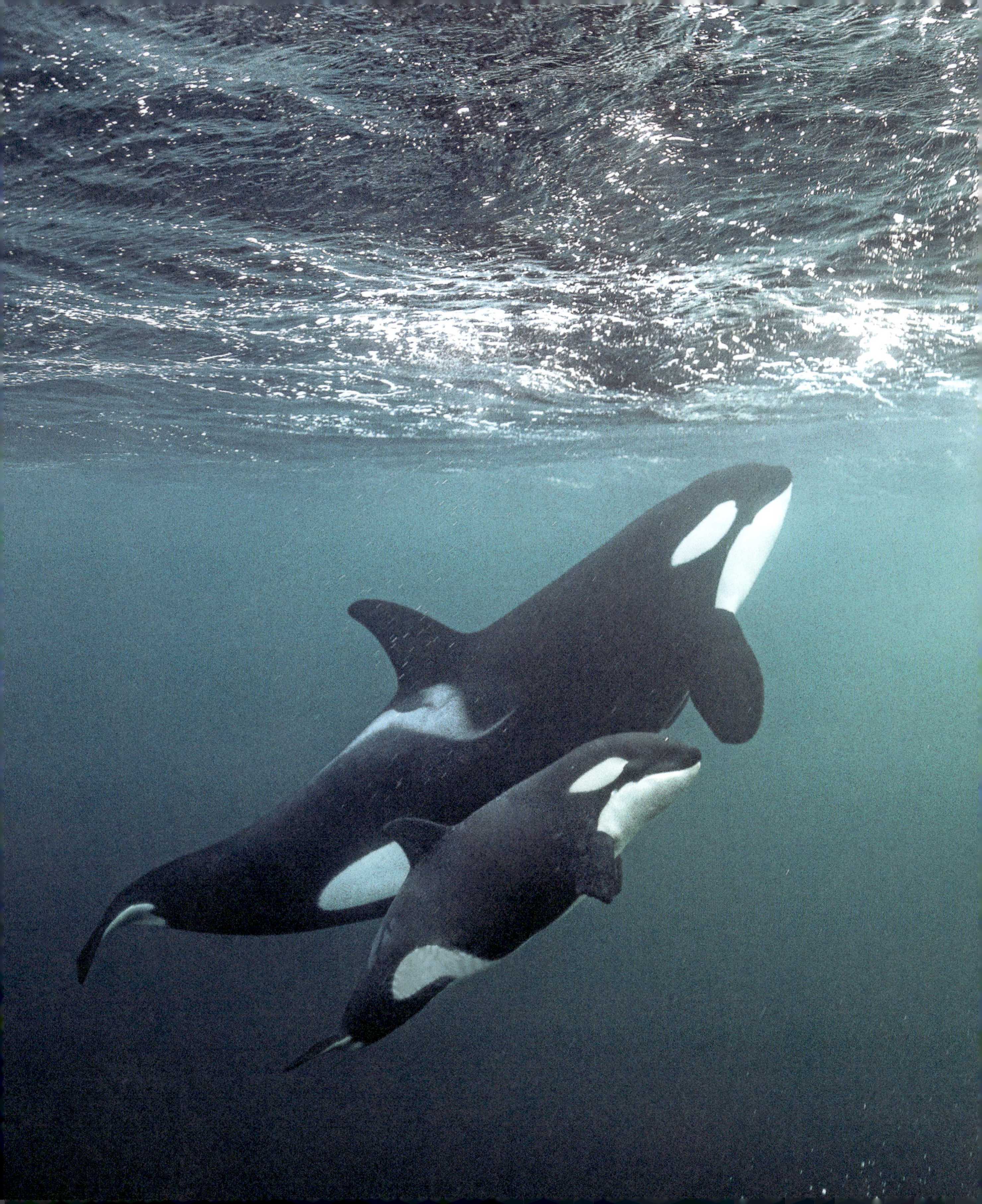

Map of the world

Australia, Aotearoa New Zealand and Antarctica

1. Rapid Bay, SA, Australia 2
2. Great Barrier Reef, Queensland, Australia 6
3. Lord Howe Island, NSW, Australia 12
4. Ningaloo Reef, WA, Australia 19
5. Byron Bay, NSW, Australia 23
6. *SS Yongala*, Queensland, Australia............... 26
7. Port Lincoln, SA, Australia............................... 30
8. The Rowley Shoals, WA, Australia 36
9. Whyalla, SA, Australia 40
10. Milford Sound, Aotearoa New Zealand 44
11. Antarctica... 49

Americas

12. Grand Bahama, The Bahamas 56
13. Bonito, Brazil 60
14. Malpelo Island, Colombia 64
15. Cocos Island, Costa Rica 68
16. Gardens of the Queen (Jardines de la Reina), Cuba 74
17. The Silver Bank, Dominican Republic 78
18. Dominica, The Caribbean 83
19. Santa Catalina Island, USA............................. 87
20. Magdalena Bay, Mexico 90
21. White Cave System (Sistema Sac Actun), Mexico...................... 95
22. Banco Chinchorro, Mexico 99

Europe and United Kingdom

23. Northern Norway (Arctic Circle) 104
24. The White Sea, Russia 111
25. Silfra Fissure, Iceland 115
26. Medes Islands, Spain 119
27. The Hebrides, Scotland 123
28. Scapa Flow, Scotland 127
29. Lundy, Devon, England 130

Asia

30. Similan Islands, Thailand 136
31. Mergui (Myeik) Archipelago, Myanmar 143
32. Misool, Raja Ampat, Indonesia 149
33. Waigeo, Raja Ampat, Indonesia 153
34. Lembeh Strait, Indonesia 158
35. Sipadan Island, Malaysian Borneo 165
36. Tubbataha, Philippines 169
37. Anilao, Philippines 172

Pacific

38. Rock Islands, Palau...................................... 178
39. The Tuamotus, French Polynesia................. 182
40. Vava'u, Tonga 187
41. The Coolidge, Santo (Vanuatu) 190
42. Vatu-i-Ra, Fiji 194
43. Beqa Lagoon, Fiji 199
44. Wolf and Darwin Islands, Galápagos 202
45. Tufi, Papua New Guinea................................208

Indian Ocean and Africa

46. Fuvahmulah, Maldives.................................. 214
47. Baa Atoll, Maldives 218
48. Trincomalee, Sri Lanka 223
49. KwaZulu-Natal coast, South Africa............... 227
50. Southern Red Sea, Egypt 231

Map of the world   xix

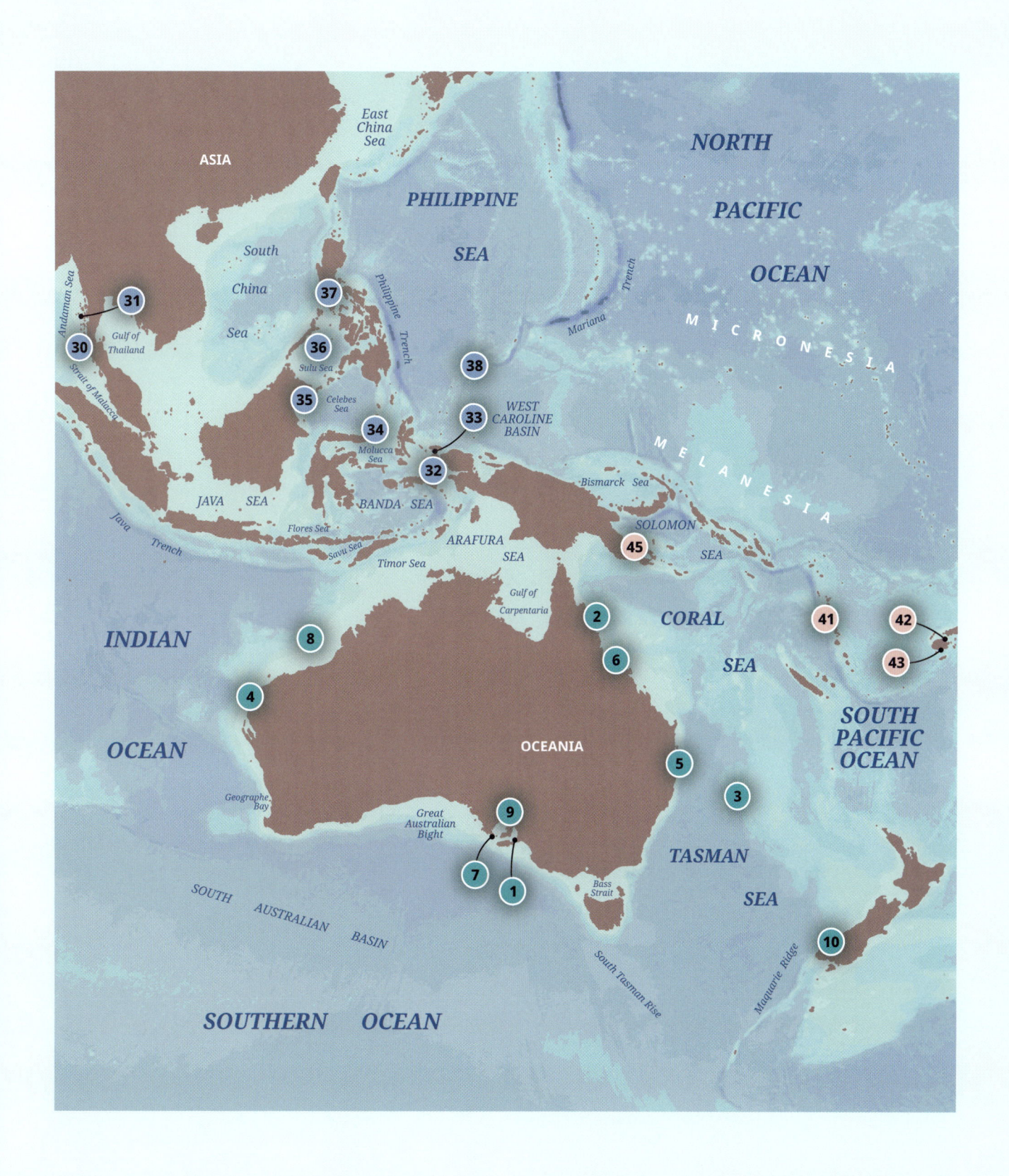

NORTH AMERICA
NORTH PACIFIC OCEAN
19
Cedros Trench
Hawaiian Ridge
Hawaiian Islands
KAMEHAMEHA BASIN
20
21
22
Gulf of Mexico
12
16
17
18
Sargasso Sea
Caribbean Sea
Guatemala Basin
15
14
44
Galápagos Islands
POLYNESIA
Marquesas Islands/
Îles de Marquises
SOUTH AMERICA
40
Society Islands
39
Tuamotu Archipelago/
Archipel des Tuamotu
Cook Islands
Tonga Trench
Austral Islands
Kermadec Trench
LOUISVILLE RIDGE
PERU BASIN
Nazca Ridge
Peru-Chile Trench
13
Easter Island/
Rapa Nui
Salas y Gómez Ridge
CHILE BASIN
SOUTH PACIFIC OCEAN
SOUTH-WEST PACIFIC BASIN
Chatham Islands
SOUTH-EAST PACIFIC BASIN
Patagonian Shelf
Falkland Islands
Chile Trench
DRAKE PASSAGE
Scotia Sea
11
SOUTHERN OCEAN
Marguerite Bay
Bellingshausen Sea
Wrigley Gulf
Amundsen Sea
Ross Sea
ANTARCTICA

Map of the world xxi

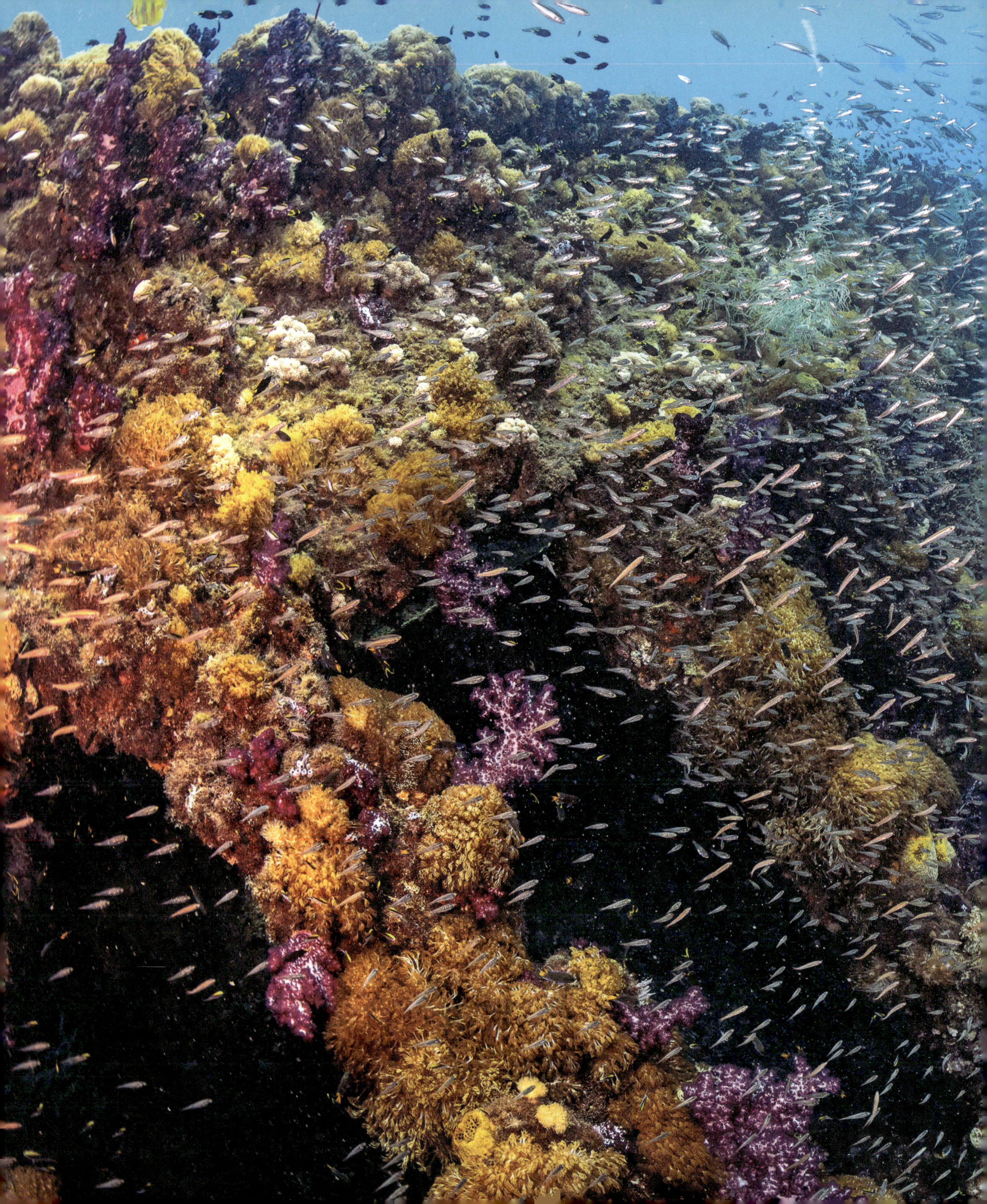

Australia, Aotearoa New Zealand and Antarctica

1. Rapid Bay, South Australia 2
2. Great Barrier Reef, Queensland, Australia 6
3. Lord Howe Island, NSW, Australia 12
4. Ningaloo Reef, Western Australia 19
5. Byron Bay, NSW, Australia 23
6. SS Yongala, Queensland, Australia 26
7. Port Lincoln, South Australia . . 30
8. The Rowley Shoals, Western Australia 36
9. Whyalla, South Australia. 40
10. Milford Sound, Aotearoa New Zealand 44
11. Antarctica 49

Rapid Bay, SA, Australia

Seaweed or sea dragon? You'll need a good eye to see this dragon!

Why it's special

The leafy sea dragon is one of the ocean's prettiest inhabitants, but few people will ever see one. Living only in the cooler waters of southern Australia, there are just a handful of spots where they are reliably encountered. In South Australia, where the leafy is the state's official marine emblem, the Bluff at Victor Harbor, Kangaroo Island, the Eyre Peninsula's Tumby Bay jetty and a few spots on the Yorke Peninsula are known for them, but the most popular place is the old jetty at Rapid Bay. Known as Yatagolanga, Patparno or Patpangga, the Traditional Land of the Kaurna People, Rapid Bay is just an hour and a half by road from Adelaide/Tarntanya. As I learned first-hand, it takes patience and persistence to find a leafy, so this is one trip not to be rushed.

Best time to dive

While you can dive here year-round, summer months are not only warmer, but the weather is also more stable, allowing for more frequent dive days and comfortable camping (if you're sleeping at the seaside campground). Also, from September to February, leafies are more active and tend to be more visible in their weedy environments.

Gear
- 5mm wetsuit in summer and 7mm in winter
- Gloves and hood
- If you've got one, you wouldn't look out of place if you wanted to don a drysuit in winter
- Sea Dragon Dive Lodge in Second Valley offers a filling station for your air tanks, plus accommodation and valuable local advice
- If you like camping, bring gear to stay at the seaside campground near the jetty

Photography tip

Leafies are full of intricate detail. For my trip, I packed a 100mm lens. It has a nice focal distance, which allows you to be positioned a good metre away from the leafy, so as not to disturb them.

In terms of strobes, leafies tend to shy away from lights, so have your strobes set to low and don't spend too long on the one subject.

Qualification
- Open water

Due to the incredibly fragile nature of leafy sea dragons and their habitat, an excellent level of buoyancy control is paramount.

Getting there

Rapid Bay is a 1.5-hour drive down the scenic Fleurieu Peninsula, departing from Adelaide.

Opposite Rapid Bay Jetty, South Australia. Top tip: bring a trolley to wheel your gear down Rapid Bay's 240m (787ft) long jetty
Previous My brother and favourite dive buddy, Toby Thimios, diving the Yongala

Australia, Aotearoa New Zealand and Antarctica

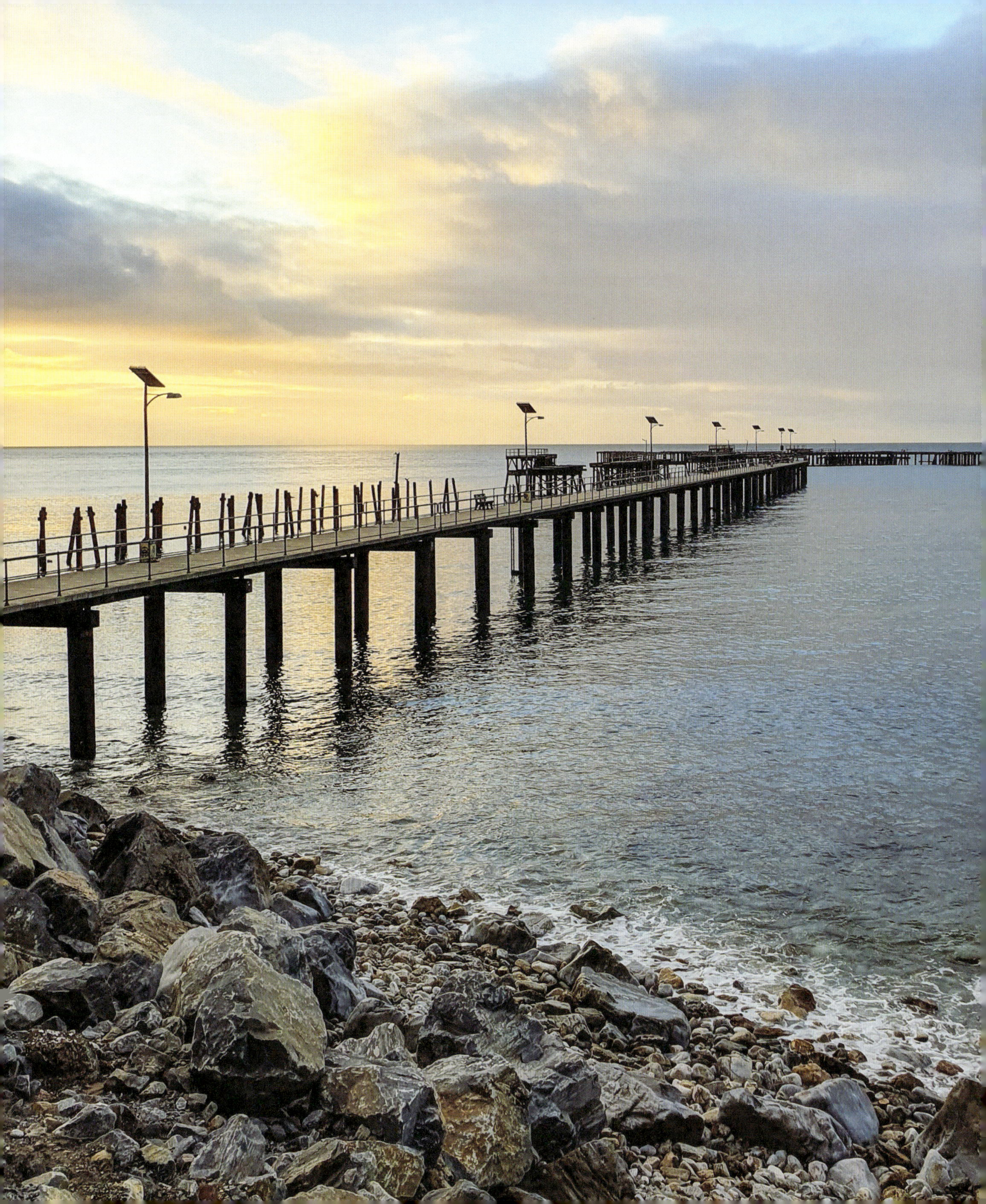

Australia, Aotearoa New Zealand and Antarctica

Dive in

Have you ever seen a dragon? For years I dreamt of seeing one, and on my mission to Fleurieu Peninsula, after many hours hovering under Rapid Bay's jetty, they remained as elusive as their mythical namesakes. For the time and money spent on flights and car hire, I learned one main lesson: just because you've come to the dragon's den, doesn't meet it will appear. Sometimes they'll show themselves, but sometimes they just want you to leaf them alone. But either way, patience is the name of the game.

The jetty at Rapid Bay is renowned as one of South Australia's premier shore dives. The allure lies not only in the convenience of its location (an easy step off the jetty) but also in the rich marine life that thrives in the cold, temperate water. It's here, among the pylons and weedy kelp of Rapid Bay's old jetty, that you have the best chance of finding an Australian leafy (Glauert's) sea dragon – one of the prettiest creatures in the sea, in my opinion.

Endemic to the southern waters of Australia, this delicate sea dragon has leaf-shaped appendages draping off its head, body and tail, making it easily mistakable for seaweed and allowing it to easily camouflage into a seagrass meadow. Coming from the family Syngnathidae, which includes pipefishes and seahorses, leafy sea dragons enjoy coastal waters with temperatures of 13–19°C (55–66°F). Usually, they can be found drifting anywhere between the water's surface down to 30m (98ft).

Floating gracefully and solitarily, the leafy's masterful camouflage protects it from predators and, frustratingly, makes spotting one a real challenge. Not to be confused with the bigger and more colourful weedy sea dragon (also found at Rapid Bay), the leafy can reach up to 35cm (14in) in length. Mimicking its surrounding environment of seaweed and kelp, the leafy is one of the few animals in the world that hides by moving. Its tiny, translucent fins along the side of its head help it steer and turn, plus two rows of dorsal fins along its spine help it move through the water.

Admittingly, I have a mild obsession with leafy sea dragons, perhaps driven by their elusiveness. While writing this book, I travelled to Rapid Bay mid-winter, enthusiastic and over-confident about seeing my first leafy. In the carpark, locals suited up from the back of their cars and loaded their dive gear into trollies – something that I later realised was a great idea to avoid lugging the heavy equipment down the 240m (790ft) long jetty. Anyway, walking down the new jetty with my gear and stepping off the platform, I finned across to the longer old jetty that runs adjacent. Built in 1940 for the nearby limestone and dolomite mine, this jetty has now been decommissioned, but is a popular spot for leafies, as well as nudibranchs, sea stars, pufferfish, the odd bull ray, and lovely soft corals on the jetty's pylons. The T-section at the end is especially noteworthy for big schools of fish and your best chances of locating a leafy.

After days of waiting out bad weather, and with excitement levels at an all-time high, I patiently scoured the underwater scene during several dives over three days, being extra careful to control my buoyancy so that I wouldn't disturb a leafy or its fragile environment. After three days of mind trickery, where every piece of seaweed was considered for leafy potential, I didn't spot a single dragon. With unfavourable weather forecast for coming days, I abandoned the mission and pledged to return one day.

The warmer months of spring and summer are a delight on the Fleurieu Peninsula, and Rapid Bay's oceanside campground is a favourite escape for Adelaide's residents. The turquoise water beckons you in for a swim and there's an interesting cave to explore further down the beach. I plan to return in the summer, together with my wife and daughters, to spend a week or three by the sea. And, fingers crossed, I'll finally see a leafy.

Opposite The delicate features of a leafy sea dragon
Above Ornate cowfish

Great Barrier Reef, Queensland, Australia
A reef so great, you can see it from space!

Why it's special

One of the seven wonders of the natural world, the Great Barrier Reef needs no introduction. This incredible reef, which is comprised of over 3000 separate reef systems, is every bit as 'great' as its name suggests. There are several jump-off points to visit the reef along its 2000km (1200mi) length, including Port Douglas, Cairns, Townsville and the Whitsundays. In the Southern Great Barrier Reef, the best Reef experiences can be found at Heron Island and Lady Elliot Island. You can expect to see different underwater worlds at each of these locations. In the tropical north, Cairns and Port Douglas offer the closest access points, and each has a wide variety of day trips to choose from. It can get busy with tourist boats and locals (should you come across a boat named Billy Buoy, say g'day, that'll be the Thimios family, who head out to the reef anytime the winds are favourable). For a next-level experience however, you need to spend several nights on a liveaboard, visiting the Reef's northern reaches. From mantas, minkes and giant potato cod at the Ribbon Reefs to the giant seamounts of Osprey, Holmes and Bougainville Reefs in the Coral Sea. This remote part of the Reef is pristine, uncrowded and as good as it gets.

Best time to dive

Though the Great Barrier Reef is in a tropical location, it is largely affected by two seasons. April to August is windy with SE trade winds, while October to March have more stable weather and lighter winds. In the north, late summer is also rainy season, the wettest month being March. The months of October and November are locally known as 'the doldrums' when winds are typically low, and seas are glassy. The winter months of June and July offer the best visibility and best opportunity to encounter dwarf minke whales on the Ribbon Reefs, and at the Reef's southern tip, manta trains on Lady Elliot Island. Also in the south, January to March offer calm seas, warm water and turtle hatchlings.

Gear
- In the northern reaches of the Reef, 3mm suit for the summer months and 5mm wetsuit over winter
- In the southern Great Barrier Reef, water can get as cool as 21°C (69.8 °F) so a 6mm semi-dry is recommended
- Standard scuba gear of BCD, regulator, computer and mask and fins
- November to April is 'stinger season' in the north so stinger suits are recommended. Full length leggings and long sleeve rash shirt will provide sufficient protection
- Reef safe sunscreen

Photography tip
Pack a wide-angle lens to capture those vibrant coloured reefscapes and large pelagic schools. There are also some incredible macro-opportunities, so if you have the chance to shoot macro, go for it. Remember strobes are vital on the reef. Colours are quickly absorbed by the density of water (red first), so by using strobes you are illuminating and displaying the true colours of the reef.

Qualification
- An open water certification is suitable for most of the Ribbon Reefs, but if you want to enjoy the deeper open ocean sites in the Coral Sea require a minimum Advanced Open Water qualification.

Getting there
The Great Barrier Reef can be accessed via a liveaboard from Cairns.

Opposite A coral cod hunts on a bommie on the northern Ribbon Reefs

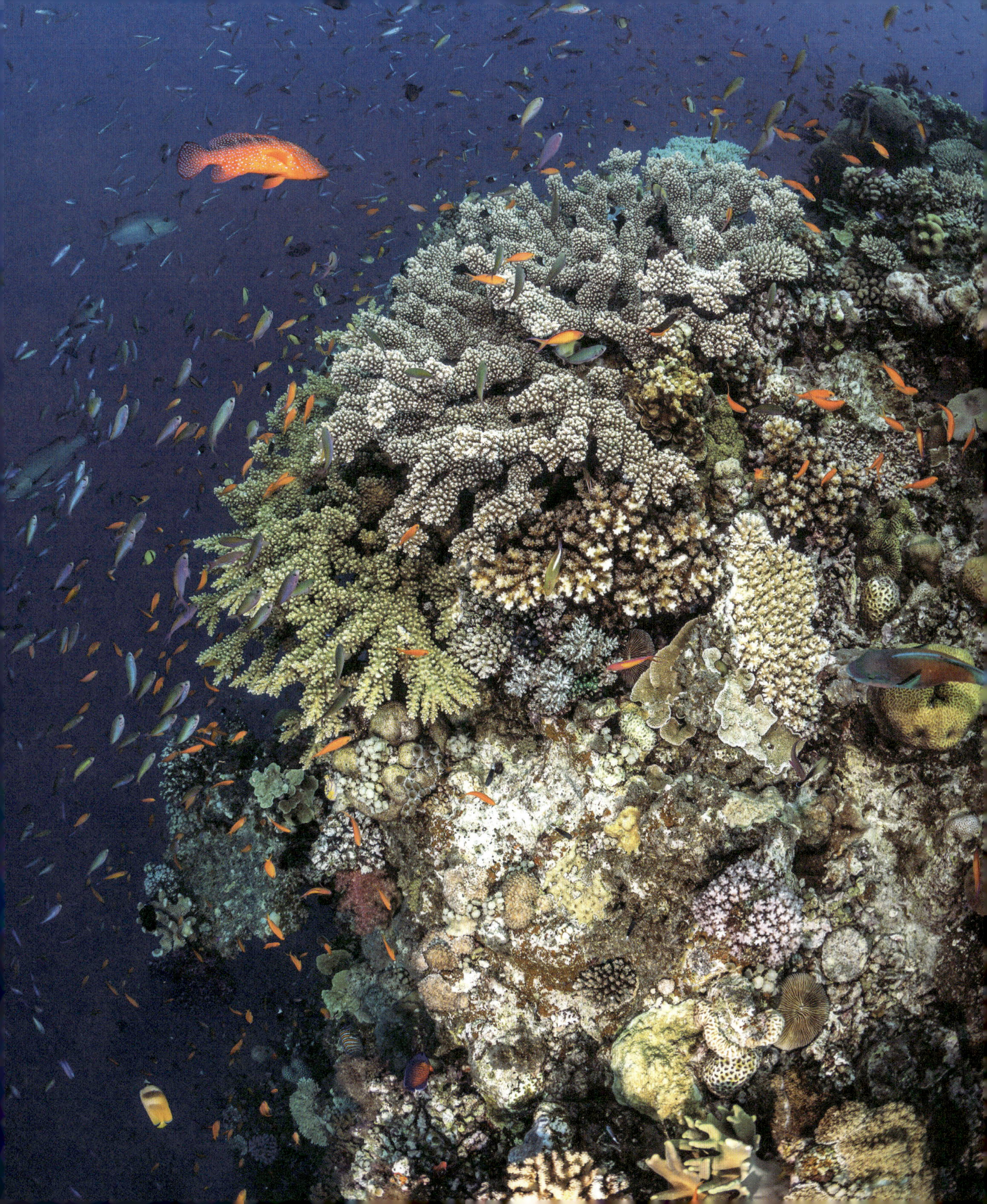

Australia, Aotearoa New Zealand and Antarctica

Dive in

Should you ever find yourself floating in outer space, looking back at Earth, you'll no doubt be rapt to see the outline of the world's most iconic reef. The king of all dive locations, and my personal favourite for sentimental reasons, The Great Barrier Reef (GBR) is the planet's biggest structure that's been built entirely by living organisms. And boy is it beautiful.

The world's largest coral reef system, the GBR is a whopping 2300km (1430mi) long, roughly the size of Italy or Japan. Comprised of thousands of individual reefs and islands, this reef is of immense ecological and environmental significance. Being so big, there's a great deal of variation between its northern and southern ends, and it's often hard for divers to decide which part to explore. As a Cairns kid who spent my childhood diving and fishing the more accessible parts of the reef on my family's boat, I often dreamt of the remote, northern reaches of the reef, particularly the Ribbon Reefs and Osprey Reef.

The Ribbon Reefs are a series of reefs north-east of Cooktown in far north Queensland, stretching 100km (62mi) from Ribbon Reef #1 through to Ribbon Reef #10. Acting as long, fringing barriers dividing the Great Barrier Reef and the Coral Sea, these reefs have an endless array of dive sites to choose from. In the protection of these ribbon reefs, many small isolated reefs (bommies) rise to the surface like coral-studded pinnacles. This is coral reef diving at its best; imagine hard and soft corals, an abundance of tropical fish and inquisitive megafauna including mantas, large sharks and dwarf minke whales. Some of the GBR's most famous sites are located within this stretch of the Ribbons including Cod Hole, Steve's Bommie, Flare Point and Pixie Pinnacle. It's not uncommon to encounter large schools of trevally, mackerel and fusiliers, numerous turtle species, and all of the stars from *Finding Nemo* (the film was based on these very reefs).

The winter months (June/July is prime), herald the arrival of dwarf minke whales on their northern migration from subantarctic waters, and this is the only place in the world where you can have an in-water encounter with them. Minkes are a favourite with divers and snorkellers, as they're known to seek out human interaction and to stick around for a while, sometimes hours on end, when you're in the water with them.

Osprey Reef, on the other hand, is a different beast altogether. Located 350km (217mi) north-east of Cairns, this isolated seamount is the remnant of an ancient volcano and a real

Opposite (clockwise) Grey reef sharks; vibrant anemonefish; hard coral *Below* A sheltered mooring on the Great Barrier Reef

highlight of the Coral Sea Marine Park. Incredible soft corals and gorgonian fans, plummeting walls that disappear two kilometres (one mile) down into the abyss, along with 30m (98ft) visibility make this one of the best dive sites in the world. Sitting so far offshore, Osprey sits smack-bang in the middle of the South Equatorial Current, so it hosts a huge variety of marine life. Expect large predator species like silvertip and grey reef sharks, the occasional hammerhead, tuna, and the majestic oceanic manta ray. At Osprey's North Horn, there is a well-established shark feeding site, where you can sit in a natural coral amphitheatre and watch a grey shark feeding frenzy.

I recommend watching David Attenborough's *Great Barrier Reef*, episode two, to learn more about this beautiful part of the GBR. Attenborough travels to Osprey Reef aboard Alucia, a research vessel that I once worked on, and he dives deep in a Triton (a small submersible). From within the three-passenger sub, Attenborough peers out through the glass dome with a 360-degree view of the surrounding reef, spotting sharks and turtles as they motor along. The 3D maps of the ancient sea floor at around the five to six minute mark are especially interesting.

The Ribbon Reefs and Coral Sea are accessible via liveaboard Cairns, with two boats operating three, four and seven night trips every week, Spirit of Freedom and Mike Ball's Spoilsport. Both operators have a long history operating in the region, with Mike Ball (now retired) renowned as one of the pioneers of dive tourism. Both boats offer the same three, four and seven-day trips, but in reverse of the other, so the boats rarely cross paths. Three and four-day trips start or end with a low-level scenic flight from/to Lizard Island, located at the southern tip of the Ribbon Reefs, while seven-day trips are Cairns to Cairns. Throughout the year, both operators also provide special exploratory and expeditionary trips, to Raine Island in the Far North, the far eastern reefs of the Coral Sea, and south to the wreck of the Yongala.

Conservation

Citizen Science and Coral Nurturing

The most significant threat facing the Great Barrier Reef, along with coral reefs globally, is climate change, causing an increase in tropical cyclones, and warming seas – an effect of which is a phenomenon known as coral bleaching. When corals are subjected to warmer water than they are used to, for extended periods, they expel their symbiotic algae (zooxanthellae) that provide them with their vibrant colours and a source of food. During this process, the stressed corals fluoresce, then turn white . Prolonged bleaching events can lead to coral death. The Great Barrier Reef has experienced numerous, and more frequent mass bleaching events in recent years. If you'd like to help, be part of the solution, there are several reef nurturing and citizen science projects you can contribute to.

These include the Reef Restoration Foundation (rrf.org.au), which manages coral nurseries to help repopulate damaged reefs, the Coral Nurture Program (coralnurtureprogram.org) which aims to boost resilience at high value reefs, and Citizens of the Great Barrier Reef, which aims to educate and involve the world in saving the Reef. By becoming 'Citizen' subscribers are asked to take a pledge to save the reef with one simple action – use less single-use plastic, cycle to work instead of drive, turn the lights out when you leave a room – anything you can do to help lower your carbon footprint and combat climate change. Citizens are also encouraged to take photos of the Reef when they visit and upload them to a global database using the Eye on the Reef app. Can't visit the Reef? You can still help this citizen science program by analysing some of the thousands of images already uploaded, using a recently developed AI-assisted app (citizensgbr.org).

Another great way to help save the Reef is to visit it. Visit, and learn more about it, on a guided tour with a Master Reef Guide. Master Reef Guides are highly trained master story tellers, able to explain the Reef's intricacies in a way that make you fall in love it and determined to save it! (gbrmpa.gov.au/learn/master-reef-guides)

Damselfish swim amongst healthy staghorn coral

Lord Howe Island, NSW, Australia

Rare clownfish and glowing mushrooms are just part of the magic of this ancient volcano

Why it's special

This World Heritage-listed island hosts the planet's southernmost coral reef, thanks to its position at the tail end of the warm East Australian Current (EAC). Endemic species like the McCulloch's anemonefish, three-striped butterfly fish and the odd looking double-header wrasse all call this remote rock home. The topside views are incredible; steep mountains crowded with kentia palms rise abruptly from the sea, the remnants of an ancient volcanic mountain range. The magic of Lord Howe Island is omnipresent; from mushrooms glowing in the forests to sprawling soft coral gardens and old volcanic reefs under the waves. Speaking from experience, I can also add that it's a fantastic place to elope! Despite it being only a two-hour flight from Sydney, amazingly, Lord Howe remains relatively unknown to the outside world. Maybe that's part of its charm, and why it's worthy of being named one of the world's ultimate dive spots.

Best time to dive

With a limit of 400 visitors on the island at any time (plus the island's permanent population of 380), Lord Howe's dive sites remain uncrowded year-round. The high season runs from October to April, with water temperatures at their warmest from January to March (reaching up to 26°C/78.8 °F in March). The island's only dive centre closes from the 1st of June to the 31st of August, when the water temperature is at its coldest, and high winds often limit diving opportunities.

Gear
- 5mm wetsuit year-round
- 5mm neoprene hood (in winter)
- 3mm vest (if you really feel the cold)

Pack light! You'll be flying on a small Dash 8 to Lord Howe Island, with a strict 14kg (30lb) weight limit, plus 7kg (15lb) of hand luggage.

Photography tip
Lord Howe is a mixed bag when it comes to underwater photography. Both a macro and a wide lens will have their place here on the island, but if your flight's restricted baggage allowance limits you to take just one, go wide.

Qualification
- With a good variety of dive sites, Lord Howe is suitable for all dive certifications and an ideal place to learn to dive.
- More challenging sites such as Balls Pyramid will require Advanced Open Water and experience diving in current.

Getting there
Qantas offers a two hour, direct flight from Sydney to Lord Howe, or alternatively Eastern Air Services offer direct flights from Port Macquarie, the Gold Coast and Newcastle.

Opposite Lord Howe Island, with Balls Pyramid just visible to the south

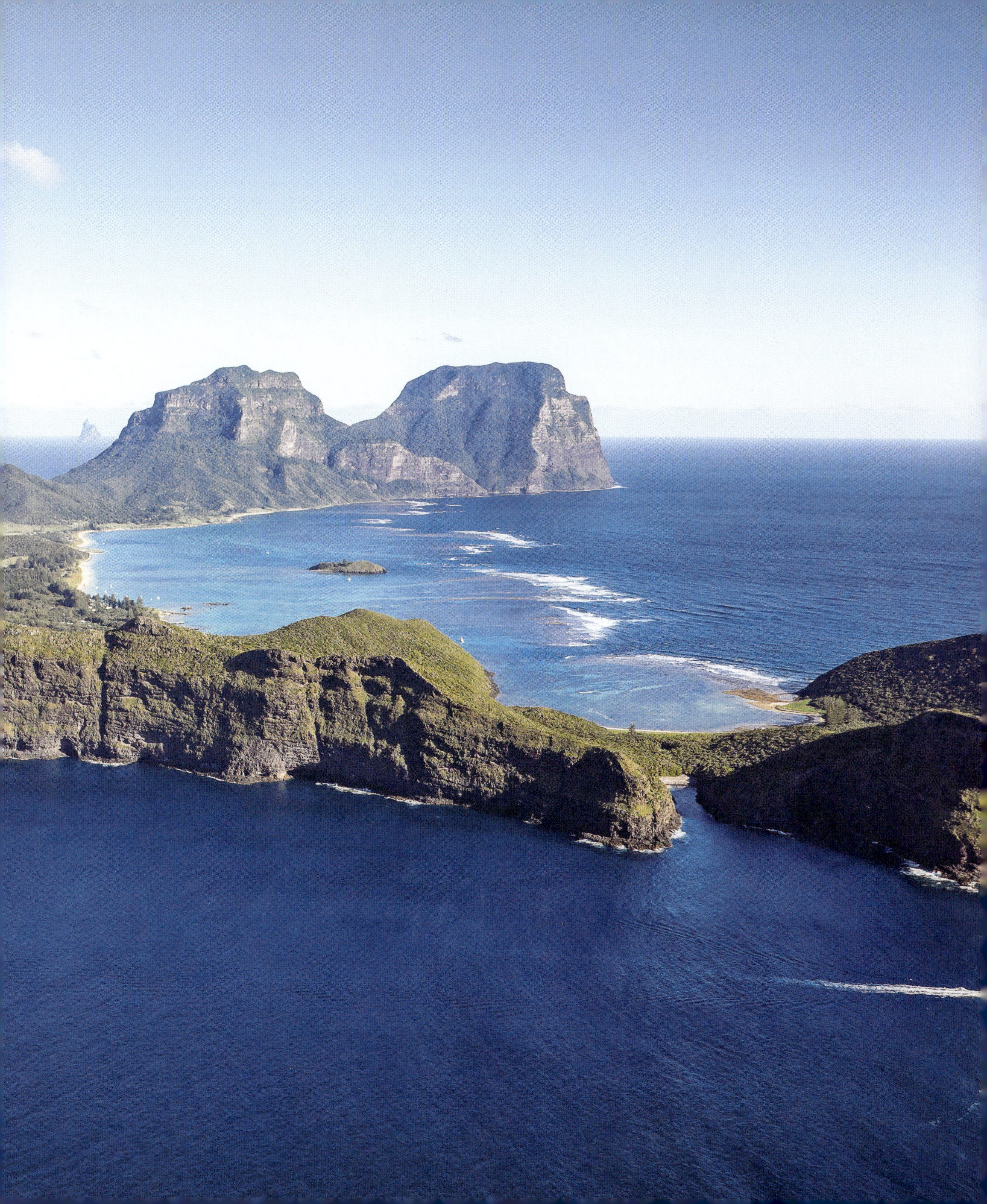

Australia, Aotearoa New Zealand and Antarctica

Dive in

I was fortunate to work on Lord Howe Island as a dive instructor for most of my 20s, but it wasn't until I later started travelling the world that I understood how unique Lord Howe's diving is. Considering its temperate location, it may seem strange to call it a tropical island. The island's warm water and tropical fish species can be attributed to the East Australian Current (EAC). Made famous in the film *Finding Nemo*, the EAC continuously moves warm tropical water from the Great Barrier Reef southward all the way to Lord Howe Island, the world's southernmost coral reef.

The EAC is just one of the five major ocean currents that intersect at Lord Howe, resulting in an incredible diversity of tropical and cold-water marine species mixed together. Sharks, rays, sea turtles and shoals of fish thrive amongst temperate green sea grasses and colourful hard and soft tropical corals. There's also an abundance of rare and endemic marine life here. Add that to the volcanic terrain of caves, overhangs and trenches, plus the local ban on commercial fishing, and you'll find that this is a marine environment unlike anywhere else on the planet.

Dive Lord Howe is the sole operator. For this reason, I recommend booking ahead if you're visiting during the busier months of December to March. With over 100 amazing dive sites surrounding the island, you'll be spoilt for choice. The following are my must-do's:

The lagoon

The island's fringing lagoon is perfect for that first dive after arriving on the island. It's also a calmer option for days when it's rough offshore. Within the lagoon are plenty of soft corals and tropical fish, such as three-stripe butterfly fish, silver drummers and double-headed wrasse. You may also encounter turtles and small Galapagos whaler sharks, whose curiosity and sleek silhouette make them favourites amongst photographers. Being 5–10m (16–32ft) deep, the lagoon is loved by both snorkellers and freedivers. I recommend renting a kayak from one of the boatsheds, asking staff to point out some lagoon classics like Erscotts Hole, Comets Hole or The Potholes.

Bluewater dive with Galapagos Whalers

During my instructing years with Howea Divers, we consistently floated ideas for new experiences to offer divers. It was always a thrill to encounter Galapagos whaler sharks, and, out in the blue water, we were amazed to often find them naturally aggregating in large numbers. Dive Lord Howe now offers a fantastic sunset dive with these sharks. Done as a drift dive, you'll drift through open blue water with the ocean floor nowhere in sight. If you're lucky, you may find yourself surrounded by up to a hundred of these curious sharks. Though small (usually under two metres), it's an overwhelming experience to encounter so many together.

The Admiralty Islands

Only a 15 minute boat ride north of Lord Howe Island, visible from the shores of Neds Beach, lie the Admiralty Islands. These eight volcanic islets are ideal for all divers, with depths ranging from 12–40m (39–131ft). Here you'll find great patches of soft corals, colourful nudibranchs and schools of tropical fish, such as the rare half-banded angelfish. Notable sites include North Rock, Tenth of June, Rupert's Reef and the incredible swim-through of the Eye of Roach.

Balls Pyramid

The pinnacle of all of Lord Howe Island's dive sites is Balls Pyramid. Towering 562m (1840ft) above sea level, this is the world's tallest sea stack. There's a saying amongst the dive staff that 'whatever you find around the island, you will always find more of, but bigger, at Balls Pyramid'. Resembling a massive shark fin freestanding in the middle of the ocean, the waters surrounding the pyramid are home to a variety of creatures including dolphins, mantas, whale sharks and the occasional great white. If you're lucky, you may even see a Ballina angelfish. Usually found elsewhere at around 100m (328ft) deep, you can spot them here at about ten metres, making this the only place in the world where you can dive with them. The pyramid never fails to delight and surprise even the most seasoned divers. It's worth noting that a trip to the pyramid involves at least half a day on the water, as it lies 16 nautical miles south of Lord Howe, so it's usually off limits during bad weather.

Opposite Galapagos whaler sharks patrol the lagoon

Warming seas

The enemy of anemones

The hottest topic on the planet today is climate change, and one marine animal affected by rising ocean temperatures is the anemone. Offering an early indication of warming seas, anemones are known to discharge the algae that they rely on for survival if water temperatures rise even slightly. When this happens, they lose their colour. This is known as anemone bleaching. When anemones die, unfortunately, so also do the anemonefish that call them home. In Lord Howe Island's lagoon, which is home to the planet's largest population of McCulloch's anemonefish, an annual survey has been underway since 2009. Marine scientists have combined forces with local tour operators, marine park staff and school kids to count anemonefish and their host anemones on selected patches of reef. So far, the survey has revealed that there has been a downturn in numbers since 2011. Now is the time to act, in order to save Lord Howe's endemic McCulloch's anemonefish.

Juvenile McCullochs anemonefish, endemic to the waters of Lord Howe Island

Lord Howe Island, NSW, Australia 17

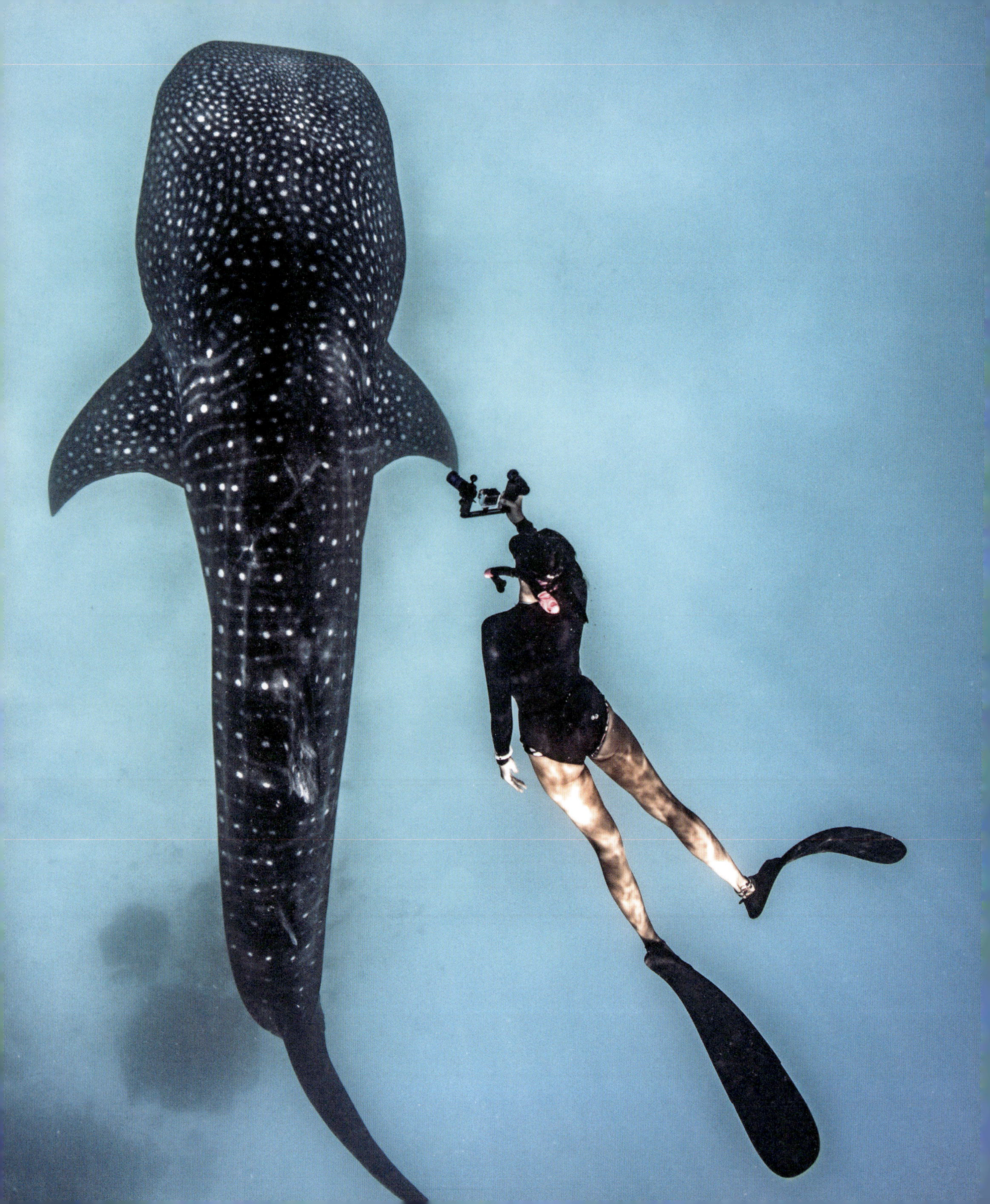

Ningaloo Reef, WA, Australia

Swim straight off the beach and into Australia's largest fringing coral reef

Why it's special

Drive 13 hours north of Perth and you'll arrive at one of Australia's most remote towns, Exmouth, gateway to Ningaloo Reef, or Nyinggulu in the language of the Traditional Owners, the Baiyungu, Thalanyji and Yinigurdira People. Here on Australia's Coral Coast, where desert meets reef, all the action happens in the sea. There's a boat in every second driveway (when the winds are up) and the town has very few shops. From March to October, this town of 3000 doubles in population as travellers descend upon Ningaloo to swim with its most well-known annual visitor. This is where the world's largest documented aggregation of whale sharks happens every year. I saw my first whale shark at Ningaloo and I intend to bring my daughters back here, one day, to see their first as well. It's also on the migratory path of over 40,000 humpbacks a year and, out here, the land is so quiet that you can hear them breathing from the beach at night.

Best time to dive

Whale sharks arrive after the coral spawn, usually in March or April and disappear again by August. For your best chance of seeing them, visit in May or June. These are comfortable months to visit, with average air temperatures in the mid to high 20s in Celsius (low 80s in Fahrenheit). This is ideal as opposed to summertime when temperatures can soar into the 40s (low 100s). When planning your visit, check on Australia's school holiday dates, when this small town packs a crowd and accommodation books out. Humpbacks visit from July to October and mantas are found year-round.

Gear
- 3mm wetsuit
- Reef safe sunscreen
- Sun protective clothing
- If you like camping, bring gear to stay at one of the cheap seaside campgrounds run by national parks

There is almost zero shade on the beaches here. BYO beach umbrella or buy one from a tourist shop in town on your first day. You'll use it a lot.

Photography tip

Ningaloo is home to some of Australia's grandest megafauna. Your go-to lens is something wide like 24mm.

Strobes will have little use here, unless you're diving the Navy Pier (which is a must for photographers).

Qualification
- Snorkellers, freedivers, and scuba divers of all levels

Getting there

There are daily direct flights (two hours) from Perth into Learmonth Airport, which is 20 minutes south of Exmouth's CBD. Coral Bay is a 1.5-hour drive south.

Opposite Freediver and whale shark on Ningaloo Reef. Every whale shark has a unique pattern of spots and stripes which can be used as unique identifers

Dive in

At the northern tip of the 260km (161mi) World-Heritage-listed Ningaloo Marine Park, you'll find the towns of Exmouth and Coral Bay. The beaches along this stretch are deserted, apart from the odd wandering emu, the land is uninhabited. But step into the sea and you're greeted with a very different scene. There are colourful coral bommies just metres from the beach and the fringing reef is high in biodiversity (over 500 species of fish, over 300 coral species, 155 species of sponges ... the list goes on), thanks to the influence of the warm Leeuwin current and the cooler Ningaloo current. There are turtles galore (including loggerhead, hawksbill and green), dolphins, sharks and mantas, then, just beyond the reef, there's the show-stealers that appear each year – whale sharks and humpbacks.

The real beauty of Ningaloo (Nyinggulu in the language of Baiyungu, Thalanyji and Yinigurdira peoples, the Traditional Owners of the land)) is how wild and underdeveloped the whole scene is. Fish will swim right up to your mask and the rawness of the experience is magnified by the surrounding ancient limestone landscape.

With such accessible marine encounters and some of the world's best diving, one could wonder why this region is so underpopulated. For many, the arid landscape of the desert, sweltering summer heat, cyclones, flies, and isolation are all deterrents. Shady trees are a dime a dozen and there are no freshwater creeks or waterfalls to wash off the salt and dust. But for long-time locals, such as novelist Tim Winton, there's nowhere they'd rather be. Winton's documentary *Ningaloo Nyinggulu* is a must-see for anyone travelling to the region, offering a local's perspective on this incredible corner of the continent.

The Navy Pier

Within Exmouth's Naval Communications Station is one of the Australia's best shore dives. Soft corals and sponges cling to the jetty's pylons attracting nudibranchs and various species of reef fish like butterfly, angel, Moorish idol and parrotfish. Thick schools of Mangrove jacks are commonly found overhead, while sea snakes, octopuses and the occasional grey nurse shark can be found below. A giant grouper, nicknamed the BFG, lingers at around 15m, though he can tend to creep up on you since visibility ranges between 3–10m (10–32ft). Dive times very much revolve around the tides here. The only way to dive the Navy Pier is with Dive Ningaloo and you'll need to verify your identity with the Australian Federal Police on arrival. Book as soon as you arrive in Exmouth, or better still, before you arrive.

The lagoon

Ningaloo is a freediver's paradise; with the fringing reef running parallel to the coastline, there's a long lagoon that averages about two to four metres (7-13ft) deep with coral bommies and all kinds of marine life including dugongs, dolphins, sharks and turtles. Oyster Stacks is a good place to start as the action begins straight off the beach, but it can be crowded. If you want a patch of reef to yourself, your best bet is to hire a kayak and paddle to a kayak mooring at Tantabiddi or Osprey Sanctuary Zone. If you're hoping to spot dolphins or a tiger shark, hire a boat for half a day from one of the local rental companies. Be sure to check the wind forecast prior to booking and bring a beach umbrella for shade inside your dinghy. For bargain beachside camping, pre-book a Cape Range campsite via the Department of Parks and Wildlife (exploreparks.dbca.wa.gov.au).

Manta Rays at Coral Bay

Drive an hour and a half south of Exmouth and you'll arrive at the coastal oasis of Coral Bay, consisting of a couple of caravan parks, a convenience store and a handful of tour operators. Year-round, you can find manta rays in the pristine waters surrounding Coral Bay. Manta, meaning 'blanket' in Spanish, is a fitting name for these creatures, as their wing spans can reach up to eight metres (26ft) wide and, if you happen to be freediving beneath one as it passes overhead, it will block out the sun. Your best bet for finding them is by jumping on a half or full day boat tour.

Megafauna beyond the reef

If you want to swim with a humpback or whale shark, you'll need to book with a tour operator, but be prepared as day trips (six to eight hours) can be pricey. Pilots in spotter-planes fly overhead and locate animals, then the tour boats race to the location to get everyone into the water and in the path of the oncoming whale shark or humpback. There's no scuba involved; just snorkelling and freediving. Though it's a bucket list item that lures travellers to Ningaloo each year, it can feel like a very manufactured tourism experience. But, if you're wanting to get up-close with one of these majestic animals, Ningaloo is the place to do it and the industry is well regulated for the protection of the animals, with only ten people allowed in the water at a time, and strict rules regarding the distance you keep from them. A tip: spend more for a boat that takes less people, especially if you want to maximise your time in the water.

Opposite top Desert meets reef *Opposite bottom* Bottlenose dolphins in Ningaloo's lagoon

Ningaloo Reef, Western Australia

Australia, Aotearoa New Zealand and Antarctica

Byron Bay, NSW, Australia

Sharks, mantas and turtles at the Australian mainland's most easterly point

Why it's special

The laid-back, coastal town of Byron Bay, the Traditional Land of the Bundjalung of Byron Bay Arakwal People, the Minjungbal and Widjabul People, is well known for its beaches, hippies and eco-ethos (though most of the hippies moved to the hinterland many moons ago, replaced by fashionably wealthy sea-changers). It's hard to imagine the town's former days as a whaling station, as whale watching is now a major tourist attraction. While the local beaches offer great snorkelling, with turtles and the odd ray, it's the small, rocky outcrop of Julian Rocks that lures divers offshore. Here you'll find leopard sharks, wobbegongs, mantas, kingfish and turtles aplenty. It's one of only a handful of habitats for the critically endangered grey nurse shark along the east coast of Australia, making it an awesome shark diving location during winter.

Best time to dive

Summer (February is my favourite) sees the arrival of many warm water species making their way south from the Great Barrier Reef, like blue water leopard sharks and mantas. Meanwhile, the cooler winter months of June, July and August are prime for grey nurse sharks and the arrival of the annual humpback whale migration.

Gear
- 5mm wetsuit in winter, 3mm in summer
- Reef safe sunscreen

Photography tip
A 50mm lens would suit most subjects here, with a wider lens for sharks and rays.

Being a reasonably contained environment, this is a great site for experimentation. With great natural lighting, strobes are optional for shallower depths, but try experimenting with or without for some more artistic shots.

Qualification
- Open Water
- Julian Rocks is a great place to learn to dive, with depths ranging from 6-24m (19-79ft).

Getting there
Ballina Airport is a one-hour flight from Sydney, and then it's a 1.5-hour drive to get to Byron Bay. Alternatively, Byron is just over 2 hours' drive from Brisbane Airport.

Opposite A humpback whale passes by Byron Bay, Australia. From June to September you may be lucky enough to spot whales from your dive boat

Dive in

Byron Bay's underwater world is a distinct mix of tropical species in a subtropical temperate environment. Known as Australia's most easterly point (though, technically, Flat Rock half an hour south of Byron and right near my house is the most easterly on a low tide), Cape Byron has a unique geographical location, and its surrounding waters enjoy a broad mix of vibrant marine life year-round. The East Australia Current (made famous by Nemo's dad) runs very close to shore near Byron Bay, creating a marine environment that is quite special, with a mix of tropical and temperate species that varies greatly throughout the year.

Over the winter months, Humpback whales migrate north to their breeding grounds in tropical north Queensland. Passing close to shore, you can spot whales from the beach or from Byron Bay's lighthouse. This is also a great time of year for diving with grey nurse sharks, a threatened species whose numbers have dwindled due to commercial fishing. These placid creatures also had a bad run during the '50s and '60s when spearfishermen targeted them using explosive-headed spears. Numbering less than 2000 today, they're labelled 'critically endangered' on the IUCN Red List and can only be found at a few safeguarded locations along the coast. At just 2.5km (1.5mi) from shore, Julian Rocks is one of a very few places they can be reliably encountered each winter. Declared a marine reserve in 2002 and later a sanctuary zone in 2006, Julian Rocks Nguthungulli Nature Reserve consists of a group of small islets that are home to over 1000 marine species. It's a beloved spot for locals and tourists alike, but for the land's Traditional Owners, the Bundjalung-Arakwal, it's a place of deep cultural significance known as Nguthungulli meaning 'father of the world'. There's certainly a powerful, yet peaceful feeling in the waters surrounding this rocky outcrop.

Apart from grey nurse sharks, you may also encounter hawksbill and loggerhead turtles, dolphins, leopard sharks and eagle rays here. Depths range between 6–24m (19–79ft), catering for both freedivers and SCUBA at the six main dive sites around the rocks. The Nursery is the most popular spot, with depths from 6–12m (20–39ft) and plenty of fish and turtles to be seen, plus leopard sharks (in the warmer months of December–April) and Wobbegongs. On the southern end of the rocks, The Needles is a great spot for photography due to its shallow depths of 9–15m (29–49ft) and large bommies which are popular haunts for turtles and rays, and in summer, leopard sharks and mantas. Photographically, the two trenches at Hugo's Trench are great for capturing grey nurse sharks in the winter months when they swim between the narrow gaps in the walls, offering some really nice framing for photos. You can also spot turtles and rays here. When the winds are from the south, which is a lot of the time, the Cod Hole is an incredible dive, with its resident jewfish, trevally and grey nurses over winter.

There are regular trips out to Julian Rocks with local dive operators. Sundive is one of Byron's longest running dive centres and provides a quick, ten minute trip from the closest launch point, The Pass (a novelty in itself). As one of Australia's most popular surf spots, it's certainly an interesting place to begin/end your dive excursion, dodging set waves and long boards. Residing nearby, Julian Rocks has become my local go to dive and I feel incredibly privileged to have such a beautiful dive site on my door step.

Opposite Grey nurse sharks fill the gutters of Julian Rocks in the winter months *Above left* A spotted eagle ray and a leopard shark swim in tandem at Julian Rocks *Above right* There are six main dive sites around Julian Rocks Nguthungulli Nature Reserve

SS Yongala, Queensland, Australia
A passenger steamship that disappeared in 1911 is now a diver's wonderland

Why it's special

The SS Yongala, aka 'Aussie Titanic' is one of the world's biggest intact shipwrecks and has rightfully earned a reputation as one of the world's best wreck dives, visited by up to 10,000 divers a year. This passenger steamship disappeared in 1911 when a category five cyclone raged around her, while other ships received a radio signal and took shelter. Ironically, a brand-new ship's radio awaited her in Cairns, ready to be installed for her 100th voyage. Items from the ship including the body of the racehorse 'Moonshine' washed up on nearby beaches and in creeks, but the Yongala's whereabouts remained a mystery until the Navy accidentally located her three decades later. Now covered in marine life, the Yongala is a very fun dive, especially for fit divers who can handle strong currents.

Best time to dive

Due to its incredible amount of biomass, there really is no wrong time to dive the Yongala. The best thing to take into consideration is the weather in the region. Due to the Yongala's resting place being so exposed to the weather, it is not uncommon to have dives cancelled or postponed because of strong winds. In summer months there are lighter winds and clearer waters, but cyclones are a possibility. Meanwhile, winter has more consistently windy days with continued south-east trade winds.

Gear
- With water temperatures ranging from 22-25°C (71.6-77°F) from June to September and 26-31°C (78.8-87.8°F) in summer, a 3-5 mm suit is perfect for winter and a 2mm suit ideal for summer

Photography tip
The Yongala is buzzing with life, so any wide-angle lens with a zoom (like a 16-35mm or 11-24mm) would be excellent. Strobes are a must, to really illuminate the life - and colours - of the wreck.

Qualification
- Advanced Open Water
- A good level of fitness and ability, for possible strong currents
- Having your advanced ticket would also be beneficial, allowing you to venture a little deeper

Getting there
Day trips depart from Alva Beach near the town of Ayr, which is 1 hour's drive south of Townsville. You can fly directly into Townsville from Brisbane, Darwin, Melbourne and a handful of other Australian airports.

Opposite Coral trout preys on glass fish on the Yongala

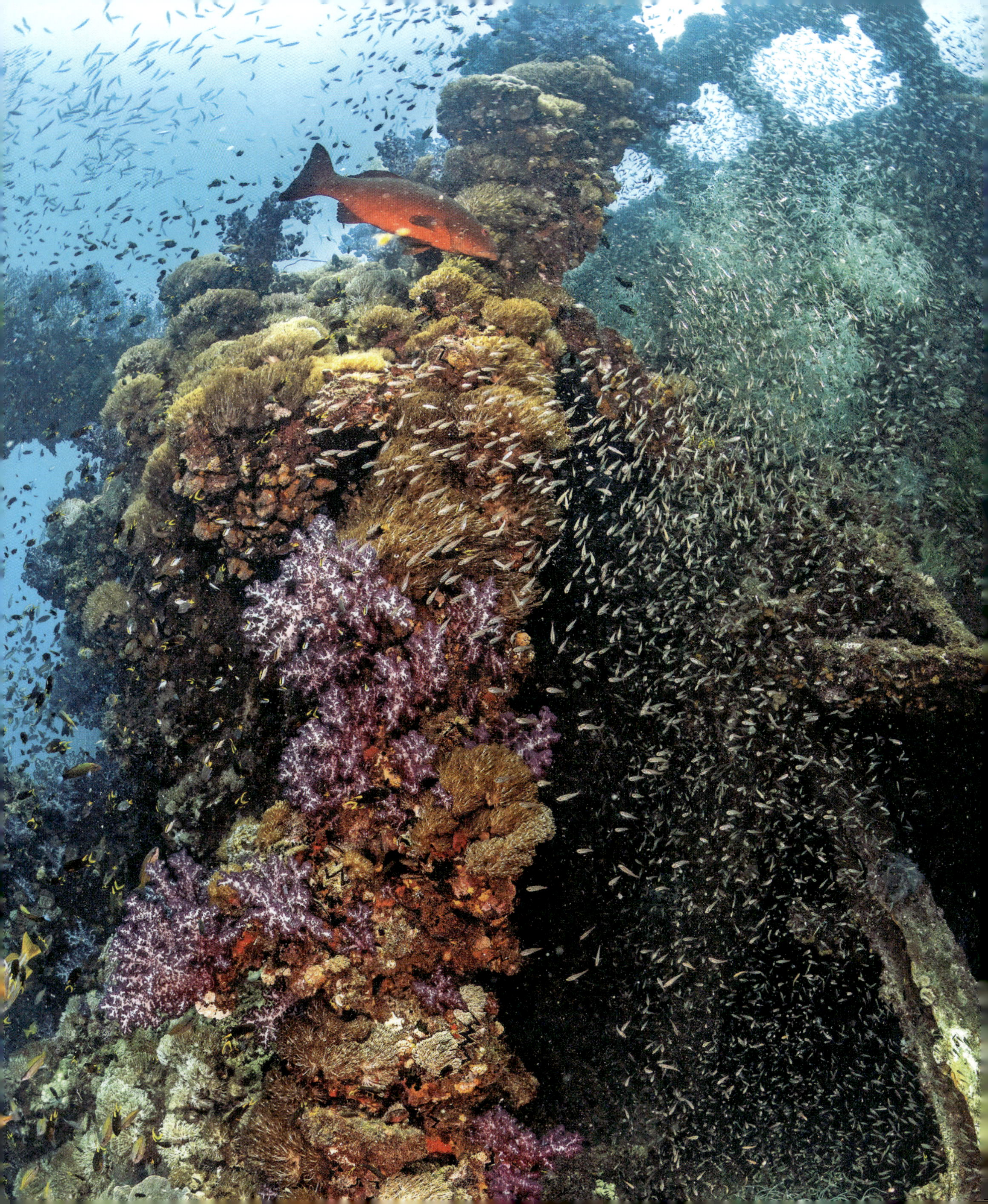

Australia, Aotearoa New Zealand and Antarctica

Dive in

About 48 nautical miles south-east of Townsville, within the Great Barrier Reef Marine Park, lies the wreck of the SS *Yongala*. Despite its close location to my hometown of Cairns, I had never dived it until researching this book (bad weather stopped me numerous times in the past). But eventually I got there and a weekend in Townsville with my brother Toby turned out to be one of the most fun dive trips I've ever done.

Built in England in 1903 for the Adelaide Steamship Company, this majestic ship was named after the town of Yongala, South Australia. In the language of the Ngadjuri People, the Traditional Owners of the land, Yongala has several interpretations, including broad water, broad, wide watering place and good water. At just over 100m (328ft) and reaching a speed of up to 17 knots, SS *Yongala* was one of the fastest ships of her kind at that time in Australia. Accommodating 110 first-class and 130 second-class passengers, she provided a transport link between Fremantle (Western Australia) and Sydney/Warrang during Australia's gold rush and then in 1906 her summer route was extended to Cairns, Queensland. Unfortunately, venturing into northern waters was to be her undoing.

In 1911, the Yongala struck tragedy when her northward journey from Melbourne/Naarm coincided with a category five cyclone. Warnings were sent to the ship by a signal station near Mackay, but the captain didn't receive them, and continued on his course. She was last seen by a lighthouse keeper as she steamed through the Whitsunday Passage before she disappeared, remaining buried beneath the waves for several decades. The cyclone claimed the lives of everyone on board, including a racehorse called Moonshine. The official count of passengers and crew was thought to be 122, marking it one of Australia's worst maritime disasters on record.

In the 1940s the Australian Navy encountered the wreck and believed it to be the Yongala. Then in 1958 a local fisherman, Bill Kirkpatrick, discovered it, eventually leading a team of divers to the site, where they recovered a cabin safe with a partial serial number that was used to identify the wreck. In the '90s, after a foreign diver decided to take home a human femur bone from the wreck as a souvenir, the site became protected under the Historic Shipwrecks Act and divers were no longer permitted to enter inside.

Opposite (clockwise) The very unique beach launch to dive the Yongala; Yongala's bow now thrives with sea life; diver Toby Thimios returns from the bow of the Yongala

Now acting as an artificial reef, Yongala provides a home to a diverse range of marine creatures like coral trout, napoleon wrasse, schools of trevally, olive sea snakes and several species of sharks and rays. In my years of diving the world, the Yongala stands out as the wreck with the most abundantly rich marine life I've ever come across. I'd argue that there is more life per square metre on this wreck than I've ever seen before. Resting on her starboard side at a depth of about 30m (98ft), with the upper parts of the wreck just 16m (52ft) below the surface, the wreck has retained much of its structural integrity, despite the region being hit by another category five cyclone in 2011, exactly one century after she was originally sunk. Cyclone Yasi completely stripped the wreck of its thick encrusting corals and hosting habitat but, incredibly, in just a few years this covering of life returned.

Sadly, the wreck made headlines in 2003 when American woman, Tina Watson, drowned while diving with her husband on their honeymoon. It was initially believed to be an accident as Tina was a novice diver, but her husband was later convicted of manslaughter – a charge that was subsequently dropped due to lack of evidence. In 2016 the Yongala almost claimed another life when local diver, Alan Griffiths, went on a solo mission to dive the wreck. Swept away by a current, he spent 14 hours at sea before being rescued 50km (31mi) away. For anyone considering diving the Yongala, it's important to consider that currents can get strong here. Therefore, the wreck is ultimately best suited to competent/advanced divers, accompanied by a local dive operator.

Yongala Dive (yongaladive.com.au) run daily dives from Alva Beach near the town of Ayr, where they also have a dive centre and accommodation. Due to its unique location, Yongala Dive use large tractors to launch the dive vessels straight into the surf, and from there it's just under an hour to get to the wreck (or half an hour if you get glassy conditions). Cairns-based liveaboards Spoilsport (mikeball.com.au) and Spirit of Freedom (spiritoffreedom.com.au) periodically relocate to Townsville to run seven night trips to the Yongala and nearby reefs.

Port Lincoln, SA, Australia
Eyeball Jaws in the chilly waters of the Neptune Islands

Why it's special

Great white sharks have a fearsome reputation, and rightly so. Growing up to six metres (20ft) they have 300 sharp teeth, their bodies are counter shaded to make them less visible, they can sense a drop of blood from up to half a kilometre away, and they use the element of surprise to hunt. Their sea lion victims don't know what's hit them when they suddenly find themselves in the jaws of these apex predators. They are incredible animals, and they are also a vital part of the ocean's ecosystem. To get up-close with a white pointer is an exhilarating and unforgettable experience, and in the frigid waters of Australia's Southern Ocean you can do just that … from the confines of a shark cage.

Best time to dive

October to March brings nicer weather and longer daylight hours. This is also the most reliable time for seeing sharks. Autumn and winter heralds the arrival of bigger sharks, with April to June an ideal time for spotting large female great whites. Longer liveaboard trips of four to seven nights' duration are ideal for this period of unpredictable weather and shorter daylight hours.

Gear
- A 7mm semi dry wetsuit for the 15°C (59°F) water temperature in winter
- From December to May, water temperature can reach between 18°C to 19°C (64.4°F to 66.2°F) so a 5mm will suffice

Photography tip
There are two options when cage diving in the Neptune Islands, surface cage or ocean floor cage. Strobes can be beneficial at depth but are not necessary (and can prove cumbersome) on the surface.

Lens wise, remembering that great whites can reach a whooping six metres (20ft), a wide angle is best. Try a 16-35mm, if possible, as the reach on this lens may allow for some great portraits.

Qualification
- No dive certification is needed for the surface cage as you can breathe with a hooka system
- For the ocean floor cage, an Open Water dive certification is needed

Getting there
Port Lincoln is a 7.5-hour drive from Adelaide or a one hour flight with QantasLink. The road trip takes you past Whyalla, so if you're travelling in winter, it's worth diving with the cuttlefish, too (see p. 40).

Opposite A great white shark rises from the depths to appear metres in front of me. Its countershading offers it great camouflage

Port Lincoln, South Australia

Australia, Aotearoa New Zealand and Antarctica

Dive in

I've always enjoyed diving with sharks. I love how they move through the water with ease and, often, how they somehow manage to appear from nowhere. Nothing could have prepared me for my first face-to-face encounter with a great white in the Neptune Islands. Inside a shark cage with three other divers, we were lowered beneath the surface and, like canaries in a cage waiting for a cat to appear, we anxiously watched.

Acclimatising to the shock of the cold water, I evaluated the underwater landscape. The clear blue water hosted an environment of rock, kelp and prolific fish life. Then suddenly there was a great white right in front of me. Its girth was enormous, seemingly as wide as it was long, with giant wing-like pectoral fins. I was totally blown away. How did this 5m (16ft) shark just appear from nowhere? Casually cruising, it showed minimal interest in me and my fellow cage occupants. What followed this introduction was one of the best liveaboard dive experiences of my life; an unforgettable few days diving, filming and learning about great whites in the remote Neptune Islands of South Australia.

Long known for their remoteness and hostility, the Neptune Islands have also been an important habitat for great white sharks. The islands are also the breeding ground for Australia's biggest colony of long nose fur seals – a tasty treat for a great white. There's no better place for divers to experience the awe, fascination and sheer adrenaline that comes with being face-to-face with a white pointer. In the past, South Africa's Cape Town and the Mexican Island of Guadeloupe were also hotspots for diving with great whites, but in recent years these locations have reduced their shark diving operations, thus making the Neptunes the world's premier destination for great white diving (and the only place that you can have an encounter on the sea floor).

At the helm of the Neptunes' shark diving scene is the Fox family, led by Rodney and son Andrew (rodneyfox.com.au). Rodney Fox pioneered the industry of shark cage diving in Australia and has been instrumental in educating the public to better understand these magnificent but widely feared creatures. It's an interesting path to follow for Rodney who, back in 1963, survived being bitten by a great white while spearfishing. After the incident, Rodney became fascinated by sharks, and he's dedicated his life to advocating for the protection of great whites.

Opposite A large shark hits the bait as my Uncle Terry Thimios watches on

Port Lincoln, South Australia

Rodney's invention of the first ever shark diving cage opened a window of opportunity for both filming and behavioural observation. He captured some of the underwater scenes in *Jaws* (though, this film unfortunately amplified the general public's fear of sharks). Today, Rodney offers three-to-five-night liveaboard trips to the Neptunes, where divers can descend in a cage to the ocean floor, about 20m (66ft) down, and non-divers can jump into the cage for a surface-level experience, breathing through a regulator hooked up to a central air hose. These trips also act as research expeditions, where important data is collected by staff and passengers and given to scientists and shark researchers to help further knowledge of these apex creatures.

There's also a day trip option with Calypso Star Charters (sharkcagediving.com.au), departing from Port Lincoln at 6am out to the Neptunes (about three hours away by boat), returning between 6–9pm. Calypso offer a surface level cage experience (no dive qualification is needed) for up to eight people at a time. With a capacity of up to 45 people on their boat, shark cage experiences are rotated between passengers and, all-up, you hopefully get about 30 minutes in the cage (hot tip: go in winter as people get cold quickly so you may get more time in the water). Like Rodney Fox's trips, Calypso use bait and burley to attract sharks and to keep them close. While this by no means guarantees that you're going to see a shark, it certainly increases your chances.

Opposite top South Australia's rugged coastline *Right* Australian sea lions play in the shallows

Australian Sea Lions
Puppies of the Sea

A real highlight of diving in this region is the chance to swim with endangered Australian sea lions. Of course, in waters that are renowned for great whites, it's natural to question the sanity of jumping into the ocean with their primary food source. But, while white pointers dominate the deeper waters surrounding the Neptune Islands, these sea lion encounters take place further inshore, close to the mainland and away from the sharks.

Sea lion interactions offer a stark contrast to the adrenaline of cage diving with great whites, but they are a pure delight. These adorable 'puppies of the sea' are playful and inquisitive, and often you'll find yourself smiling underwater, forgetting about the apex predators lurking further offshore. Most Rodney Fox and Calypso tours will incorporate a sea lion dive during their shark trips; just enquire prior to booking.

The Rowley Shoals, WA, Australia
Holy Rowley! Are these shoals the dive world's best kept secret?

Why it's special

In a part of Australia that (on the map) looks too remote and arid to be populated, is the resort town of Broome, the Traditional Land of the Yawuru People, who call the area Rubibi. Also known as 'the port of pearls', Broome is where my wife grew up. A keen diver herself, Melissa insists that this is Australia's greatest liveaboard dive spot. Broome serves as the departure point for a handful of local cruise operators, who each set aside two months per year to take divers to this well-kept secret, 260km (161mi) out to sea. After an overnight steam, you'll wake up to some of the planet's best wall diving on the edge of three huge, pear-shaped coral atolls known as the Rowley Shoals. Within each of the Shoals – Mermaid, Clerke and Imperieuse – are glassy lagoons resembling giant aquariums. The water's warm, the diving is out of this world and it's likely your boat will be the only one there.

Best time to dive

The small handful of dive operators that visit the Shoals each year do so between the months of September and November a period known as the 'doldrums', when the trade winds are light, and the sea is calm. Boats depart from Broome in northwestern Australia and it's an overnight affair to get there.

Gear
- A 3mm wetsuit for water temperatures averaging 28°C (82.4°F)
- Sun protective clothing for tender excursions under the hot north Australian sun
- Reef smart sunscreen

As these boats normally operate adventure cruises along the Kimberley Coast, any dive gear required will need to be hired in advance. Diverse Watersports in Broome offer dive gear rentals.

If you're prone to sea sickness, pack tablets for the open sea journey to/from the Shoals.

Photography tip
If you're savvy with a drone, bring one. Aerial photography at the Shoals is incredible and it's the only way you'll get to see a bird's eye view, offering an overall perspective of the places you're diving.

Qualification
- Open Water
- Advanced Open Water certification is recommended so that you can do some night dives, and you'll need to be comfortable diving in strong currents

If you intend just to snorkel and freedive at the Shoals, you won't miss out, the visibility is out of this world. Just ensure you are freediving with safe practices in mind and never dive alone.

Getting there
There are daily direct flights to Broome from Perth or Darwin, and then it's 260km/161mi - (an overnight steam) from Broome's port.

Opposite Glassy conditions in the middle of the sea, on the edge of the Australian continental shelf

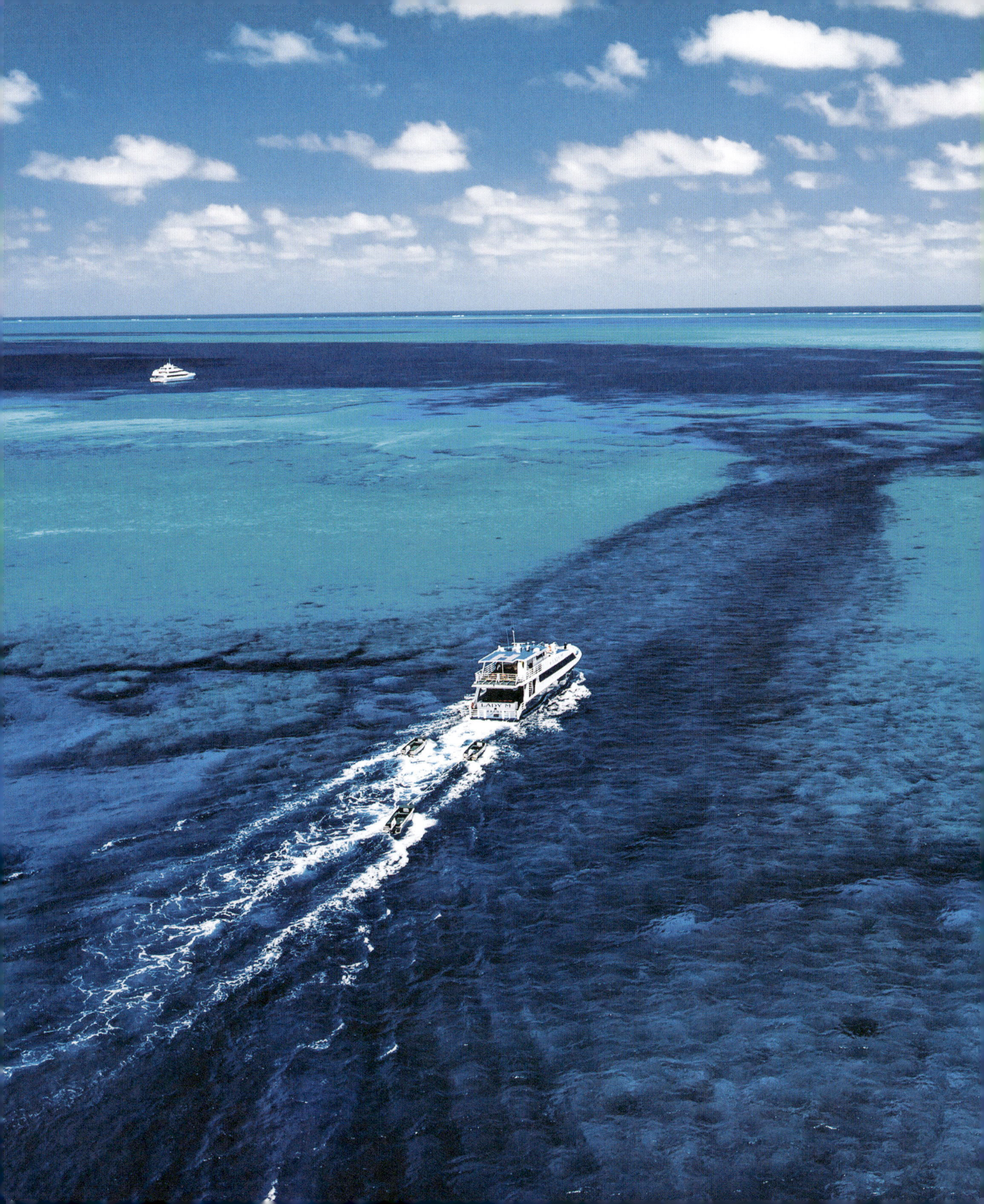

Australia, Aotearoa New Zealand and Antarctica

38

Dive in

What a sight it must've been for Captain Rowley when he first spotted Imperieuse Reef while sailing these waters on the HMS Imperieuse in 1800. Long before snorkels and SCUBA were invented (and even the glass aquarium), crystal-clear, shallow water teeming with fish would've been a welcome sight to hungry sailors. Back then, the Rowley Shoals were known as Pulau Pulo Dhaoh to the Indonesians who fished here for sea cucumbers, turtle shell, trochus shell and shark fin. These days, the three giant coral atolls that make up the Rowley Shoals Marine Park and Mermaid Reef Marine Park are known for their world-class snorkelling and diving. Very few people have heard of them and even fewer visit them.

Rising 400m (1310ft) from the ocean floor, the Shoals are Australia's best examples of shelf atolls. Within each atoll are enormous shallow lagoons resembling giant swimming pools in the middle of the sea, crowded with colourful fish, giant clams and sea stars. The tropical tidal range of up to 5m (16ft) has shaped some interesting coral landscapes and there are great opportunities for high-speed drifts, such as 'Jimmy goes to China', so named for its ability to whisk you away if you're not careful. On an outgoing tide, you'll find yourself gliding past pecking parrotfish, gorgeous gorgonian fans and green turtles hitching a ride with the current. Thanks to the huge tides, plenty of nutrients are washed in and out of the reefs every six hours, so you'll find that the corals and fish here are healthy and oversized.

You may be asking, 'if it's so great, why haven't I heard of it?' Well, getting here is tricky, due to its remote location. About 260km (162mi) west of Broome in the Indian Ocean, on the edge of the continental shelf, only a small handful of commercial operators are licensed to visit the Shoals each year, and only for a few weeks when the doldrums create glassy conditions. Amongst these few operators, even fewer offer scuba (most just offer snorkelling). The expense and effort of flying to here deters many divers, and then there's the problem of availability, with the few scuba trips on offer usually booked out a year or so in advance.

But for the die-hard divers that do make it here, underwater utopia awaits. Just imagine the most incredible walls of hard and soft corals, and visibility of 50+m (165+ft). Imagine over 200 species of coral, plus more than 600 fish species including potato cod, groupers, Maori wrasse and pelagics like mackerel, tuna and trevally. And then there's hammerheads, humpbacks, mantas, bottlenose and spinner dolphins and even the odd orca spotted here. But perhaps the greatest thing about the Shoals are the pristine conditions.

If you like your water balmy, the water temperature ranges from 28°C to 30°C (82.4–86°F); there's no need to pack a thick wetsuit for this trip (unless you go night diving). On this holiday you'll be on a strict routine of sleep, eat, dive, repeat. And when you're starting to feel waterlogged, there's a white sand cay called Bedwell Island at the northern end of Clerke Reef, which is great for sunset snacks and beachcombing, and is also a resting stop for seabirds migrating from as far away as Siberia.

The Rowley Shoals are one to add to your tropical dive wish list, but don't wait too long as it's now starting to hit the radar of Youtube-ing sailors and larger cruise operators. Odyssey Expeditions (odysseyexpeditions.com.au) and MV Great Escape (greatescapecruises.com.au) run weekly dive trips each season, while a few larger luxury cruise lines such as True North and Coral Expeditions have one or two trips each year that include Rowley Shoals. See kimberleycruises.com for more dive operators (owned by my parents-in-law. Tell them I sent you!)

Opposite top The pristine sand cay of Bedwell Island *Opposite bottom* Diver exploring the remote reefs of Rowley Shoals Marine Park

Whyalla, South Australia

Step off the rocks and into a cuttlefish lovefest as thousands of cephalopods get jiggy with it

Why it's special

For an animal with three hearts and a name that sounds like 'cuddle fish', what's not to love about these colour-changing sea chameleons? Seeing one giant cuttlefish is cool, but each winter in Whyalla you can scuba dive and freedive with tens of thousands of them. For underwater photographers, the reliability of the encounter and the shallow depth (with plenty of sunlight) makes for a dream scenario. And anyone that loves the natural world will be captivated when coming face-to-face with thousands of cuttlefish, who are all here for the same reason – reproduction. Whyalla's Stony Point and Black Point offer the easiest access to the action. Point Lowly is good, too, though the currents may be stronger here. If you're travelling via campervan, the area also offers bargain beachside camping.

Best time to dive

Cuttlefish begin to arrive in May, but the best time is June or early-July when the love-fest is in full swing. Check the weather forecast prior to coming as sunny days and light winds make for a much more enjoyable experience, while strong onshore winds will keep you out of the water. If you're after a cheap campsite at the nearby Point Lowly, avoid South Australian school holidays.

Gear
- 7mm semi-dry wetsuit and hood
- 3-5mm gloves
- Wetsuit socks
- If snorkelling/freediving, you will want a bit of weight on your belt

Photography tip
To showcase the vibrant colours of the cuttlefish, I recommend anything from 50-100mm lens
Strobes are also essential

Qualification
- Open Water scuba
- Or, optionally, freedive/snorkel (no qualification needed)

Getting there
From Adelaide Airport, it's a 4.5-hour drive to the coastline of False Bay on the Eyre Peninsula. Alternately, Whyalla is a 55-minute flight from Adelaide. Head to Stony Point, Black Point or Point Lowly to get amongst the cuttley action.

Opposite Stony Point offers easy access to the cuttlefish action

Whyalla, South Australia

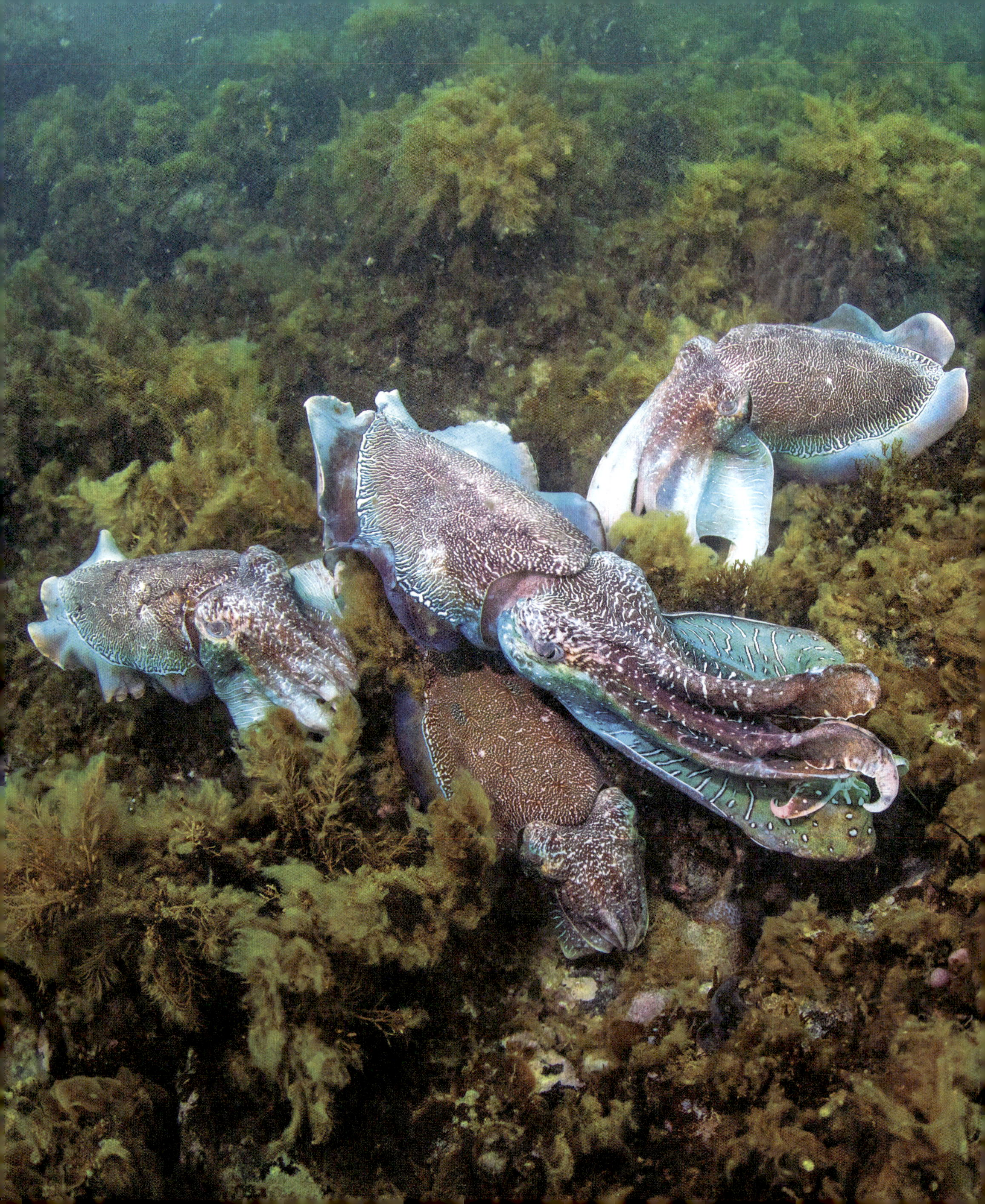

Dive in

In the frigid waters of South Australia's Eyre Peninsula, the Traditional Land and waters of the Barngarla People, there's a rocky reef that hosts a flamboyant underwater party every May to July. The weedy, shallow waters of the Northern Spencer Gulf is the heart of the action, between Fitzgerald Bay and False Bay (Whyalla), where tens of thousands of Australian Giant Cuttlefish (Sepia apama) come to breed and then hide their eggs under rocks.

Usually known to be solitary creatures, there are over 120 different species of cuttlefish. This variety is the biggest (hence the 'giant' in its name), growing up to 60cm (24in) long and weighing up to six kilograms (13lb). For divers, there aren't many aggregations that happen so close to the shore. The shallow depths, ranging from three to five metres (10-16ft), offer an amazing opportunity to observe these fascinating creatures lit up by the sunlight. Meanwhile, an average visibility of around ten metres (33ft) gives a clear view of all the cuttley action.

The name 'cuttlefish' is deceptive. Just as a killer whale is not a whale, a cuttlefish is not a fish. Rather, it belongs to the intriguing family of cephalopods, the same as an octopus. In Latin/Greek, their name means 'head foot', which is a more apt description as their eight limbs are directly connected to their head. There are also an extra two tentacles that they use for grabbing prey, before consuming it with their beak-like mouth and tooth-lined tongue.

For the male cuttlefish of Whyalla, this annual get-together is serious business, they need to put on their best show to impress the ladies since males outnumber females by up to 11 to one. They try to out-flash each other to increase their chances of securing a mate; their courtship ritual involves vibrant displays of pulsating patterns and a dazzling array of fluorescent colours. These brilliant colour displays are caused by special embedded chromatophore cells (the cells that are responsible for pigment and light reflection). The females also use colour signals to send messages to the males; if she's not interested, she'll flash a white, horizontal stripe along the side of her body, telling the male to 'just keep swimming'.

As is often the case in nature, size does matter. Larger cuttlefish are more attractive to their female counterparts, giving them an advantage, while smaller males are sometimes known to adopt a clever tactic – crossdressing. These 'sneakers' disguise themselves as females, altering their colour and pulling in their longer tentacles to mimic a female shape. When the larger males are distracted, the little guys seize the opportunity to sneak in and mate. Apparently, this cunning strategy has a success rate of 60%.

The ability to quickly shapeshift and colour-change surely makes cuttlefish the superheroes of the underwater world. And, with one of the largest brain-to-body size ratios among invertebrates, they are also extremely intelligent. Yet, few folks know much about these intriguing creatures, or about the aggregation that happens each year in Whyalla. Even fewer will come to see it in full swing.

For recreational and commercial fishers, the masses of cuttlefish are an easy target. In 2013 their numbers dropped to just 13,000, after which the state government banned fishing for them in the Spencer Gulf, allowing their population to skyrocket to 240,000 by 2020. This area, known as the Cuttlefish Coast Sanctuary Zone, has now been placed on the National Heritage List, though other threats still exist such as live-fire training at a nearby military training ground (studies have shown that cuttlefish may be sensitive to shockwaves travelling through water).

For a creature that only lives to one or two years old, the time spent in their Whyalla breeding ground is significant. In fact, this is their final hurrah, as they die shortly after their eggs hatch. The Whyalla aggregation offers an opportunity to witness one of nature's most intriguing courtship rituals, for anyone willing to wade into the 12–15°C (53.6–59°F) water. Whether you're a photographer, a seasoned diver or just plain curious to see something different, Whyalla's colourful cuttlefest is the place to be.

Opposite A giant female cuttlefish is pursued by optimistic males

Milford Sound, Aotearoa New Zealand

Dive below mountains and waterfalls into an environment you'd usually find 200 metres deeper

Why it's special

Aotearoa New Zealand's South Island is world-renowned for its dramatic mountainous scenery, and there are few places more dramatic than the Milford Sound. For divers, black coral (which is actually white) is the main attraction, but the Sound has much more to offer, and the magic all begins with the drive in. While many foreigners flock here to be herded together onto a big tourist boat, as a diver you'll experience its raw beauty from water level with just a small group. Zipping around the Sound in a customised dive boat, you'll feel a bit like James Bond. The whole experience is exhilarating, and it will make you feel very small, in a good way. Imagine sky-high waterfalls spilling down mountains and into the sea right in front of you, creating rainbows aplenty. Then, there's the fantastic wall diving and a world of unique marine creatures waiting in the depths below.

Best time to dive

October to April is the diving season, and I dived just on the tail end of the season in March. My dive trip was delayed by three days due to a storm rolling in, though this ultimately rewarded us with spectacular topside scenery as thousands of ephemeral waterfalls spilled down the fjords. Descend Diving is currently the sole operator.

Gear
- A drysuit (some local divers will opt for a 7mm semi dry wetsuit over the peak summer days)
- Gloves
- Hood
- Socks
- Thick undergarments
- Dive light

Cold winds are not pleasant after diving, so bring a heavy duty coat, a beanie and gloves for your time on the tender.

Photography tip

Showcasing the landscape both above and below the surface was my main focus when I visited Milford, so I felt that shooting wide was the best option. I used a 11-24mm zoom. This yielded good results of both marine life and divers amongst Milford's cold-water reefs. Ensure your strobes are reliable, as even though visibility can be good, it gets dark real fast.

Qualification
- Open water
- Drysuit Certification

Due to extremely cold water temperatures, completing a drysuit certification is mandatory.

Getting there

Dive day tours begin at the Deepwater Basin Road boat ramp in the Milford Sound, which is a 4-hour drive from Queenstown.

Opposite Milford's mountainous landscape is even grander from the water

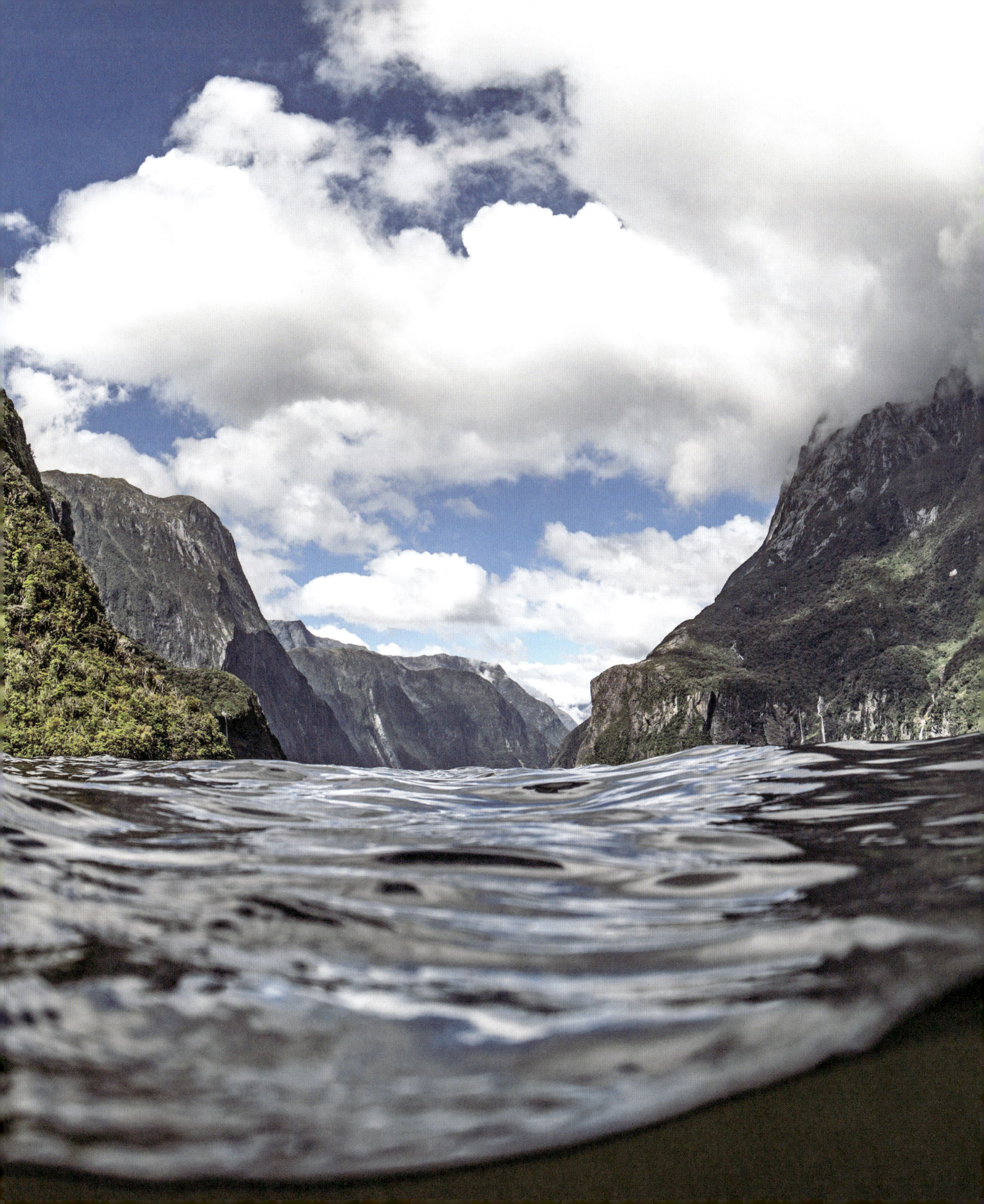

Dive in

According to Māori legend, Aotearoa New Zealand's fjordlands were carved out by the demi-god Tu-te-raki-whanoa, who, upon reaching Piopiotahi (the Milford Sound), did his best work before ending his journey. Undoubtedly, this is one of the prettiest landscapes on Earth. But if you think the landscape of Milford Sound is otherworldly, wait 'til you see what's below.

While the technical diving and discomfort of wearing a drysuit deters many divers, the fun of exploring the ethereal world beneath the fjords is absolutely worth the effort. Known as Aotearoa New Zealand's 'coral capital', some of the interesting coral trees that you'll find here are that of red and black corals. Despite their name, black corals are actually white in appearance, thanks to millions of miniscule white polyps in a thin layer of tissue covering the coral's black skeleton. Finding these usually-deepwater corals in shallow water is a novelty, made possible by the murky surface layer of freshwater run-off, blocking out sunlight. This existence of usually deep water animals surviving at shallower depths is called 'deep water emergence'.

With over 6800mm (267in) of annual rainfall, this is one of the wettest places on Earth. As the rain falls onto the mountains, it pulls nutrients from the forest floor down into the sea, creating a blanket effect on the water's surface. The result of this murky, tannin-stained water is an incredible marine environment that is starved of light; in summary, an ecosystem typical of 200m (656ft) depth, is found within only 10–20m (32–65ft) of water. There's an eerie feeling for the first few metres as you descend into the murkiness, but once you've reached the bottom of that freshwater blanket, the visibility and scenery opens up to dramatic walls hosting large branches of snow-white coral, stingrays, octopuses, nudibranchs, dog or carpet sharks, and clusters of crayfish, all enjoying the protection of the 690ha (1705ac) Piopiotahi/Milford Sound marine reserve. If you're lucky (I haven't been, so far) you may spot a New Zealand fur seal or some bottlenose dolphins.

A day with Descend Diving will have you zipping through the Sound and out to the Tasman Sea, with scenic stops for waterfalls and wildlife spotting. Two dives are offered and those without prior drysuit experience can pay extra to get training and a certification while on the tour. If you're used to the freedom of diving in tropical waters, donning a drysuit for the first time can be an uncomfortable experience. The comfort of keeping your skin dry (and toasty warm) comes with sacrifice, extra weights and constant buoyancy control. But at the end of the day, you'll remember the exhilarating feeling of diving a spot that few have dived, rather than the discomfort of the cold water and the bulky drysuit.

With the dive boat setting off from the boat ramp at 9am, I recommend that you stay close by, rather than driving the winding road (which is prone to rockfalls) in the dark. There are chalets and a campground at Milford Sound Lodge (milfordlodge.com), but they book out far in advance. If you can't stay there, the next option is the town of Te Anau 118km (73mi) away; allow about an hour and a half for the drive as the 1.2km (0.8mi) Homer Tunnel can get congested sometimes. If you're driving a campervan, there are also some great, cheap Department of Conservation (DOC) campsites, which are positioned in scenic locations along the drive in (doc.govt.nz).

Opposite Black coral exists in surprisingly shallow water here, thanks to the murky surface layer blocking out the sun *Below* A red rock lobster seeks shelter amongst a black coral tree

Milford Sound, Aotearoa New Zealand

Australia, Aotearoa New Zealand and Antarctica

Antarctica
Chill like krill in the sub-zero waters of the southern continent

Why it's special

In the vast, icy desert that is Antarctica, divers can encounter one of the white continent's most formidable characters; the leopard seal. These polar predators, with their serpentine bodies and deceptive smiles can reach speeds of up to 40km/hr (25mi/hr), propelled by their large fore-flippers. Few people will ever dive with leopard seals and, given the icy conditions, this one's best suited to seasoned divers with plenty of drysuit experience. But diving in Antarctica is not just about watching an apex predator in action, it's the thrill of diving one of Earth's last wild frontiers surrounded by towering icebergs, in crystal-clear water, with endless hours of daylight.

Best time to dive

The best time to visit Antarctica is over the southern hemisphere's summer, between November and March. During this time temperatures are warmer; days are longer and the sea ice melts. This is also the best time for ocean cruising and for crossing the infamous Drake Passage, with a better chance of a 'Drake Lake' than a 'Drake Shake'. Summer water temperatures (let's be honest, it's always going to be extremely cold) are around −1°C (30.2°F) and there tends to be clearer visibility, with the bonus of seeing young penguins, which attract leopard seals.

Gear
- A drysuit is essential to keep warm in the frigid waters
- Specialised dry gloves, or thick dive gloves
- 9mm neoprene hood, at least. The brand *Waterproof* sells a great 10mm hood. Don't underestimate the heat loss from your head
- Thick specialised undergarments
- A regulator specifically designed for extremely cold temperatures

Photography tip

Underwater photographers need to adapt their equipment for operation with thick gloves and ensure camera housing can handle the freezing temperatures. Shoot wide-angle to take in Antarctica's grandeur.

Qualification
- Advanced Open Water Diver
- Drysuit Certification
- Previous cold water diving experience

Due to extremely cold temperatures, drysuit training is mandatory. Divers should have good buoyancy control and be well prepared, both mentally and physically, for the full force of the cold.

Getting there

Depending on the sea conditions, your voyage from Ushuaia to Antarctica will take about 48 hours via the Drake Passage.

Opposite An expedition tender explores Antarctica's landscape of icebergs, glaciers and ice

Dive in

Antarctica is a place of stark, unspoiled beauty. It's a realm where massive icebergs, some as big as cities, float in deep blue water, creating a surreal landscape both above and below the surface. The landscape has an ethereal atmosphere unlike anywhere else on the planet, and the wind and water surrounding this continent contribute a crucial link to the 'ocean conveyor belt' which circulates water around the planet.

During the Austral summer, Antarctica's ocean temperature hovers at around −1°C (30.2°F), but since saltwater has a lower freezing point than fresh, it doesn't freeze. For this reason, it's possible to dive here, in what's likely to be the coldest water you'll ever dive in (unless you visit the White Sea, see p. 111), in the most incredible seascape you could ever imagine. Early in the season, prior to the rich plankton blooms, the water can be crystal clear, with some days offering visibility of over 20m (66ft).

Photographers delight in Antarctica's incredible lighting and sculptured ice formations, while divers are often surprised by the marine biodiversity. Algae and phytoplankton flourish here and Antarctic krill is so abundant that it can turn the ocean red/brown. There's kelp, jellyfish, soft corals, sea butterflies and anemones, including one anemone species that lives within the ice. There's Antarctica's most famous residents, penguins, which survive in the cold climate thanks to a layer of air in their feathers that helps add insulation. Above water, they're cute and cuddly, waddling around the ice, but below the surface they're little torpedos, shooting past you and accelerating to launch themselves metres into the air and onto an ice floe. Then there's the bigger guys like orcas, whales, fur seals and the most enigmatic of them all – the leopard seal.

Growing up to 450kg (992lb) and four metres (13ft) long, leopard seals are Antarctica's top predator, alongside orcas. Their long, sharp teeth are perfect for munching on penguins and fish, while serrations in their teeth also allow them to feed on krill, which makes up almost half of their diet. With orcas as their only predator, they rule Antarctica's waters sporting a somewhat permanent grin, and can live up to 26 years. In recent years, diving with these solitary creatures has become possible, with more and more tourists coming each year (105,000 visited in the 2022/23 season) and many expedition boats now including diving in their programs. Encounters are unpredictable; sometimes you'll just catch a glimpse of a leopard seal lounging on an ice floe, other times you may be lucky enough to see one hunting a penguin. They chase their prey with incredible speed (up to 40km/hr/25mi/hr), often leaving a massive wake in the water. For the most part, leopard seals are curious about divers, though there have been instances where they've have shown aggression towards humans, therefore divers should always act with caution, letting the seal dictate the interaction and avoiding obstructing their path.

Due to the extremely challenging conditions, Antarctic diving is best suited to seasoned divers with cold-water experience and solid buoyancy control when donning a drysuit. Dives are generally done at depths of under 20m (66ft), as there's no decompression chamber anywhere nearby and you're very far from help should anything go wrong. Antarctica's chill factor is unimaginable; in 2010 a satellite recorded an air temperature of −93.2°C (−135.76 °F) here, the coldest ever captured on Earth. Add the force of the katabatic winds, and the air feels even colder! Diving in water that's colder than the inside of a fridge, you exert more energy and consume air faster. Your head goes numb and your hands ache, making it hard to remove your gear after diving. Make no mistake – diving Antarctica is hardcore.

The journey here is a feat also unto itself, beginning with the sea crossing from Ushuaia, aka 'the end of the world', and crossing the notoriously rough Drake Passage. But the opportunity to dive in such an unspoiled environment is a privilege that few will ever experience, and one that will stay with your forever.

Above A leopard seal inspects its reflection in the glass of the dome camera housing, Antarctica

Submersibles

Submarining the white continent

With some cruise operators carrying their own submersibles, there's now another (much warmer) way to dive the white continent, allowing you to venture deep into the lower epipelagic zones (100m/328ft). While I haven't personally piloted any submersible trips in Antarctica, my Uncle and Aunt, who recently did a sub trip during their voyage, spoke highly of this once-in-a-lifetime experience. Unlike a submarine, which can act as an independent watercraft, a submersible relies on a support vessel. So, the adventure begins with your sub being towed away from your cruise ship by a small boat until it's positioned above the desired descent location. This first step is weather dependent, as your sub can't launch safely in rough seas. You'll then get ferried across to the sub in a Zodiac before stepping through a hatch and clambering down a ladder into what feels like the inside of a fishbowl. After some safety checks, your descent begins. That moment when you lose sight of the world above and are completely engulfed by water is strange the first time that you experience it! Another strange feeling is the daylight disappearing until you're floating in pitch black. Soon, your sub's floodlights will be turned on and you'll be illuminating all kinds of creatures, like sea star and sponges, krill (oh so much krill) or you may even be lucky enough to spot something rarer such as a giant phantom jellyfish. Beyond tourism offerings, these subs offer great opportunities for scientists to gain new information about species in Antarctica that they haven't previously been able to study. There's also the opportunity for guests to become 'citizen scientists' by relaying sightings to organisations like The Polar Collective.

Triton 1000/2 carried out the first ever manned submersible mission to Antarctica

Antarctica 53

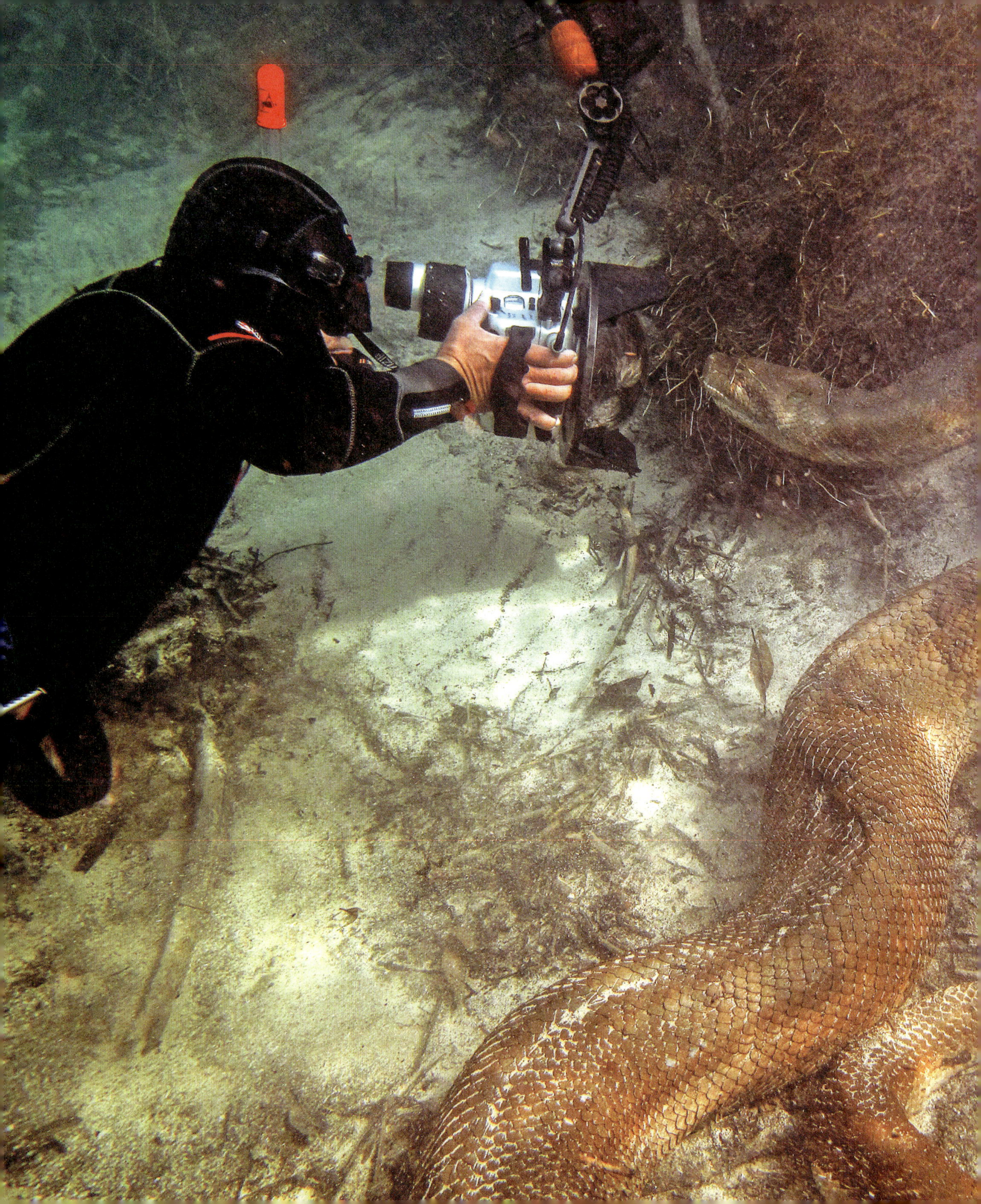

Americas

1. Grand Bahama, The Bahamas . 56
2. Bonito, Brazil. 60
3. Malpelo Island, Colombia 64
4. Cocos Island, Costa Rica. 68
5. Gardens of the Queen
   (Jardines de la Reina), Cuba . . . 74
6. The Silver Bank,
   Dominican Republic 78
7. Dominica, The Caribbean 83
8. Santa Catalina Island, USA. . . . 87
9. Magdalena Bay, Mexico 90
10. White Cave System
    (Sistema Sac Actun), Mexico . . 95
11. Banco Chinchorro, Mexico 99

Grand Bahama, The Bahamas

Look into the eye of a tiger (shark) on a shallow sandbank in the northern Bahamas

Why it's special

With over 40 species of sharks inside the protection of a 630,000km² (240,000mi²) marine sanctuary, the Bahamas is one of the world's premier spots for shark diving. Back in 2010, when a seafood company declared its plans to export shark meat to Asia, environmentalists campaigned and thus the Atlantic Ocean's first shark sanctuary was established. In the northern Bahamas, the islands of Grand Bahama and Bimini draw thousands of divers every year for one thing shark diving. On a shallow sandbank known as Tiger Beach off Grand Bahama you can dive with tiger sharks, and you may also see some of the Bahamas' other 40-odd shark species including nurse, lemon, great hammerhead and bull sharks. Just south of Grand Bahama is Bimini which is especially known for its great hammerheads; combine the two spots for the ultimate shark diving trip.

Best time to dive

While it's a year-round diving destination, June to November is hurricane season. Sharks are best seen in the winter months, when water temperatures drop to 22–25°C (71.6–77°F). The prime season for Tiger Beach is October to January for tigers and January to March to see great hammerheads. Prime time for great hammerheads at Bimini is December to March.

Gear
- 2mm wetsuit in summer when the water is 30°C (86°F), or 5mm in winter when the water is 25°C (77°F)

Photography tip
Photographing huge Tigers and Hammerheads up-close means you've got five or so metres (16ft) of shark and a whole lot of teeth that need to be in the frame and sharp with detail. For this reason, I like shooting with a fish eye lens (it's super wide and also has the ability to focus on really close subjects). Alternatively, any quality wide angle will work.

Strobes are optional at Tiger Beach as it's such a shallow dive with good ambient light. Remember, if using strobes your frame rate is reduced, which is not ideal for action photography.

Qualification
- Open water

Previous experience diving with sharks is definitely helpful, but not mandatory. Just tell your guide it's your first time, and your nerves are racing.

Getting there
American Airlines have direct, one hour flights from Miami to Freeport, Grand Bahama. Both Tiger Beach and Bimini can be accessed via dive boat from Grand Bahama. Silver Airways operate a direct, 45-minute flight from Fort Lauderdale to Bimini.

Opposite Tiger shark in the crystal-clear waters of the Bahamas
Previous During the dry season the waterways near Bonito become clear, offering good visibility for an anaconda dive

Grand Bahama, The Bahamas

Americas

Dive in

The Bahamas may be a playground for the rich and the famous and also, strangely, for some sunburned swimming pigs, but for divers the crystal-clear waters of this archipelago of 700 islands offer incredible experiences, such as coming face-to-face with tiger sharks and great hammerheads (nowhere near the swimming pigs).

Over the past two decades, Tiger Beach has gained worldwide recognition as one of the best places to dive cage-free with tiger sharks. About 30km (19mi) west from Grand Bahama's town of West End, Tiger Beach is not actually a beach, but rather a shallow sandbank close to a deep drop-off. While the region has a year-round presence of tiger sharks (plus lemon, nurse and Caribbean reef sharks), it was the practice of divers taking bait boxes into the water here in 2003 that saw these sharks become regulars around the sandbank.

Formerly known to locals as Dry Bank, Tiger Beach is located on the Little Bahama Bank, with nutrient rich waters being pumped through from the deep oceanic Gulf Stream creating the perfect pelagic playground. Tiger Beach is pretty well-known among shark enthusiasts these days, as it's one of the few places on the planet where you can get so close to tigers reliably and for long sessions. It's also accessible as a day trip from West End on Grand Bahama (or, part of a longer liveaboard, if you prefer). Back in 2012, the yacht I worked on docked in Nassau for a few weeks and some of our crew flew across to Grand Bahama. I jumped in on the action and found myself in the presence of half a dozen tiger sharks shortly after arriving at the sandbar. On the other hand, I took my employer (the yacht's owner), a few days after and we didn't see any (I wasn't very popular after this). For this reason, it's best to schedule a week here to maximise your chances of seeing what you came to see.

While an estimated 100 million sharks are killed every year worldwide, there are no dramas in the Bahamas for the 40+ shark species that hang out here. In 2011 this location was designated the privilege of being the Atlantic Ocean's first shark sanctuary, with 63 million ha designated to safeguarding sharks (go Bahamas!) Prior to this, in 1993, commercial longline fishing – the practice of using a fishing line that has hundreds (or even thousands) of hooks on it had also been banned. Apart from being great for shark populations and overall marine biodiversity, it's been a solid economic move for the nation, whose shark diving industry brings in over $110 millionUSD per year. Unfortunately though, unregulated fishing remains an issue, with spiny lobsters, conches and sharks among targeted illegal catches.

Among the aforementioned 40+ species of sharks in Bahamian waters, you'll find the great hammerhead. The biggest of the hammerhead species, growing up to 6m-long and 230kg (507lb), these beauties, known for their huge dorsal fin, are currently listed as Critically Endangered on the IUCN Red List. Greater conservation efforts and awareness are urgently needed, worldwide, to save this rapidly declining species from extinction. Diving with them is a rare treat and you can do so in the winter months at Bimini (80km/50mi east of Miami) each October to May. This region also offers some wreck diving and snorkelling with friendly bottlenose or Atlantic spotted dolphins. Local operator Epic Diving, with their vessel the M.V. Thresher, offers trips that incorporate both spots – Tiger Beach and Bimini – over several days (epicdiving.com). Grand Bahama and Bimini are also featured on several liveaboard itineraries, such as the Bahamas Aggressor (aggressor.com).

Opposite top The waters of the Bahamas are a protected shark sanctuary *Opposite bottom* The author filming sharks in the Bahamas

Bonito, Brazil
Dive with giant serpents in the wetlands of southern Brazil

Americas

Why it's special
Of the four species of anaconda that exist, three can be found in Brazil. The largest of these is the green anaconda, the world's heaviest snake, which can grow up to 250kg (550lb). While sliding into the water with one of these serpents may not be every diver's dream, it's certainly a unique experience and, with a knowledgeable guide, less risky than you might think. The waterways surrounding the remote town of Bonito in Brazil is where all the action takes place, with the rivers becoming clear enough during the dry season to jump in and spot these river monsters underwater.

Best time to dive
Water visibility is best in the dry season between May and November, after the wet season rains (and associated muddy run-off) are long gone. During the dry, anacondas come out of their hibernation to feed and, between July to September, to mate. These three months are the best time to find them.

Gear
- 3-5mm wetsuit for 22-24°C (71.6-75.2°F) year-round river temperatures. Most dives are at a shallow depth of under four metres (13ft)
- Plenty of weight on your belt, so you've got no problems staying put and composed whilst staring at an anaconda head-on

Your expedition guide will provide dive gear, including tanks and weight belts.

Photography tip
Obviously, an anaconda is huge so you'll want to shoot relatively wide. With that said, it's difficult to guess how much of the anaconda will be visible in advance, so I recommend a wide lens that has a good zoom on it. This allows for the possibility of a nice portrait close up. Something like a 16-35mm.

Qualification
- For this dive, beyond a formal dive certification, you really just need a wealth of experience being in the water with marine megafauna. The quality of your experience is going to be a reflection of how comfortable you are with the anaconda.

Getting there
Bonito is a 4-hour drive from Brazil's Campo Grande international Airport. Your tour operator may include an airport transfer.

Opposite Green anacondas can spend up to ten minutes underwater before resurfacing

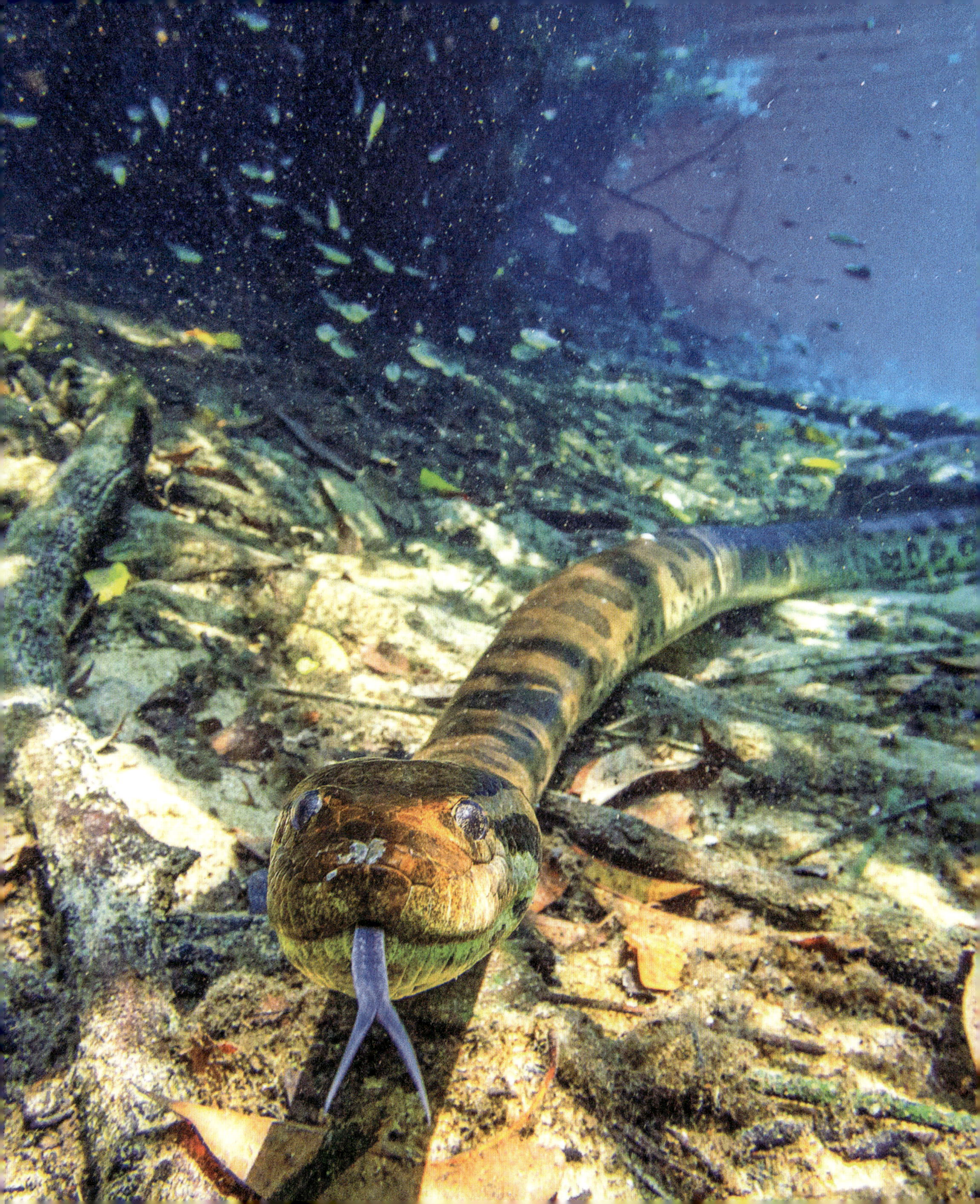

Americas

Dive in

The Pantanal in Southwest Brazil is the world's largest tropical wetland area, and a wildlife watcher's dream. Blue macaws, giant anteaters, jaguars, and capuchin monkeys are just a few of the animals you can see here. Though the Amazon is more well-known, the open, savannah landscape of the Pantanal make for better wildlife viewing. Each wet season (December to March), the Pantanal turns into a giant floodplain as torrential rains bucket down on the thirsty countryside and then, by the time mid-year rolls around, the swollen rivers have reduced in size, lagoons have shrunk, and fields are dry enough for animals to graze again. In the absence of dirty run-off, water visibility is at its best for spotting marine life. During this time, you can come face-to-face in the water with the world's heaviest snake, the green anaconda. Yep, you read that correctly.

The remote town of Bonito is the gateway to the action a four-hour drive from the Campo Grande Airport. The waterways near Bonito, which interconnect with the Pantanal wetlands, are where you can reliably find green anacondas. Not only can you see them but, with the help of an experienced guide, you can dive with them the only place on the planet where you can do so. In other places they habit, the water is simply too murky to see them. Native to South America, giant anaconda, or 'sucuri' as they are called in Brazil, can measure up to nine metres (30ft) long and weigh up to a whopping 250kg (550lb). Being semiaquatic, they prefer to hang out in swamps, marshes and streams, where they're much more agile than they are on land, and therefore more efficient hunting prey.

Despite their intimidating size, there are very few documented human deaths by anaconda. The last incident covered by mainstream media was in 2007, when an anaconda began to swallow an eight-year-old boy headfirst, before his granddad saved him. Go pops! As boa constrictors, these non-venomous snakes crush or suffocate their prey and then stretch their mouth wide to swallow it whole. Admittedly, it's a gruesome way to go. After polishing off a sizey creature, like a tapir or wild boar, an anaconda can spend weeks digesting it. Therefore, straight after a meal is the best time to jump into the water with one when it's immobile.

Patience and a great local guide are necessary for this mission, as anacondas' excellent camouflage makes them hard to spot and they're usually quick to disappear after sensing you. Once underwater, they can spend up to ten minutes below before resurfacing for another breath. Since they're easily spooked by noise, your boat ride through the wetlands will involve motoring quietly and speaking in whispers. Ideally, you'll spot one on the riverbank sunning itself, and then when it slides into the water, you'll quickly follow it in. In the shallow depth of between one to four metres (13ft), you can SCUBA or snorkel, usually with several metres of visibility. Topside, there's plenty to see while you're motoring along, like caimans and river otters, though ultimately you need to prepare for long, tiring days under the sun.

These trips are highly specialised, as they were originally only organised for film crews, but they've now hit the radar of underwater photographers. In the process of writing this book, I spent a year and a half researching and reaching out to the few operators that advertise this experience, eventually getting hold of a bilingual guide and biology graduate named Marcos Violante. Marcos, who has worked as a naturalist guide in the Pantanal since 1996, is at the forefront of Bonito's anaconda scene, offering trips for small groups (maximum five) between July and September. Marcos' tour packages are seven days, with five of those days being out on the field. The aim is to find a big, female anaconda which Marcos says is by no means guaranteed, though there's a very good chance you'll find an anaconda, even if it's a smaller male. They are long days from 8.30am until sunset, with the best time to spot anacondas being between 11am and 4pm.

At around $10,000USD per person (for two people travelling together), the price reflects the exclusive nature of the trip. For a group of four, the price drops to around $7,000USD per person. It's also worth sticking around Bonito after your tour to see other attractions like the underground cave and blue waters of Anhumas Abyss (there's some great diving here).

Unfortunately, I didn't make it to Bonito as planned, as the arrival of my second daughter paused some of our travel plans. So, I thank Marcos for all of the information that he provided and also his friend, Daniel de Granville, for his amazing imagery. You can connect with Marcos via his email mviolante99@gmail.com. Daniel also offers wildlife expeditions via his company Photo In Natura (photoinnatura.com).

Opposite top Your guides have well-trained eyes for spotting anacondas before they slip into the water *Opposite bottom* An anaconda can spend weeks digesting prey

Malpelo Island, Colombia
Pelagic magic on the eastern edge of the Hammerhead Triangle

Why it's special
A solitary volcanic formation in the Pacific, the remote Malpelo Island (Isla de Malpelo) is one of the sharkiest dive sites in the world. This is one of the largest no-fishing zones in the Eastern Tropical Pacific Ocean, governed by Colombia and vigilantly guarded by its military. Sitting on the eastern tip of the so-called Hammerhead Triangle, Malpelo's renowned for its dense shark populations and unique species, including the ragged-toothed shark. A 36-hour steam from the island is accessible only by specialised dive charters with a permit from the government. With steep walls, caves and dramatic pinnacles, this is an exciting destination for advanced divers who are confident and fit enough to handle its challenging and unpredictable conditions.

Best time to dive
Prepare for varying conditions as Malpelo's weather can be unpredictable. From January to April, the dry season brings calmer and colder water temperatures (between 16°C to 18°C/60.8°F to 64.4°F). This is an ideal time to see large schools of hammerheads. Alternatively, the wet season from May to December brings warmer waters (around 25°C to 27°C/77°F to 80.6°F) and rain. This time is notable for large schools of silky sharks, particularly in the early months of the wet season, plus whale sharks, Galapagos sharks, and manta rays.

Gear
- 5 mm wetsuit due to cooler water temperatures and occasional thermoclines
- Hood
- Gloves and booties
- A reef hook, if allowed
- A reliable dive computer

Given Malpelo's strong currents and remoteness, a surface marker buoy (SMB), whistle and any other signalling device such as a Personal Locator Beacon (PLB) are crucial.

Your expedition guide can provide dive gear, including tanks and weight belts.

Photography tip
This is a wide-angle shark paradise. The holy grail of imagery here is the shoaling hammerheads (think wide angle, strobes off).

In Malpelo, there's so much life, big and small, it's hard to know what to photograph. I like to focus on the big stuff here. Shoot wide.

Qualification
- Advanced Open Water

Malpelo is best suited to experienced divers due to strong currents, deep water and its remote location. Divers should have a good fitness level and be comfortable with potentially challenging conditions.

Getting there
Columbia Dive Adventures a ten-day liveaboard trip to Malpelo exiting the port of Buenaventura, a 3-4-hour scenic bus ride from Cali Colombia.

Opposite A legendary hammerhead shoal of Malpelo Island, Columbia

Malpelo Island, Colombia

Dive in

Embarking on a journey to Malpelo Island is an adventure into one of the planet's most isolated and extraordinary dive sites. Revered for its ecological importance and schooling sharks, this UNESCO World Heritage Site offers an exclusive experience for advanced divers.

First discovered by the Spanish conquistador Francisco Pizarro back in 1513, the island's extreme isolation and barren environment has kept it from becoming populated. While its isolation is part of its allure it is also, unfortunately, the reason why it's so vulnerable to overfishing. The Colombian military's presence has helped mitigate illegal fishing activities in the area, with a small military post on the island staffed year-round. Nowadays, the only authorised visitors to the island are research vessels and, luckily for divers, one dive liveaboard.

At the time of writing, the sole operator is Columbia Dive Adventures (colombiadiveadventures.com). Beyond being one of the world's best shark diving sites, the Malpelo Fauna and Flora Marine Sanctuary is a critical research site for scientists studying pelagic ecosystems and shark behaviour, contributing valuable information to global marine conservation efforts.

Diving in Malpelo is raw, wild and overwhelming. 500km (310mi) west from Colombia's mainland, getting to Malpelo involves a 36-hour boat ride from the port of Buenaventura. Upon arrival, divers are greeted by the island's stark and dramatic landscape, both above and below the surface, with rocky cliffs plunging down into the water forming steep walls, caves and tunnels that are a magnet for marine life. Malpelo's unique underwater landscape can be credited to its position on the Malpelo Ridge, an extension of the 300km (186mi) Nazca Plate which, in parts, plunges to incredible depths of

4000m (2.5mi). Meanwhile, the huge diversity of species can be credited to the convergence of major oceanic currents and counter-currents running through here.

The waters around the barren island and its rocky outcrops are a pelagic playground hosting several shark species including scalloped hammerheads, silky sharks, and the elusive ragged-toothed shark. Alongside Cocos Island and the Galapagos Islands, Malpelo forms the eastern vertex of the Hammerhead Triangle, a triad of dive locations known for their natural aggregations of hammerheads. The sight of up to 300 sharks swimming together in unison is awe-inspiring and a testament to Malpelo's significance as a global shark sanctuary.

While schooling hammerheads and silky sharks are the main drawcard for divers, the nutrient-rich currents that run past Malpelo attract a myriad of marine species, from huge schools of jacks and tunas to whale sharks, giant groupers and free-swimming moray eels. Meanwhile, the presence of rare fish such as the red-lipped batfish and endemic species like the Malpelo wrasse and the Malpelo barnacle-blenny add to its allure as a biodiversity hotspot.

Dive planning and safety are paramount in Malpelo, given its remote location and challenging dive conditions. Divers are expected to follow strict guidelines to not only minimize their impact on this remote environment, but also to ensure their own safety and guarantee they come home safe. The island's rugged beauty, abundant shark populations, and unique marine biodiversity make it a once-in-a-lifetime diving destination for the most passionate of divers.

Opposite Your view from the water after a 36-hour boat journey
Above One of Malpelo's resident spotted moray eels

Cocos Island, Costa Rica

Hidden treasure and shark-infested waters make this oceanic island legendary

Why it's special

A remote tropical island with soaring cliffs, waterfalls and shark-infested waters is the perfect setting for a classic novel ... and for pirates to bury their treasure. For centuries, Cocos Island has been shrouded in mystery and legend, with a reputed $1billion USD of treasure buried on the island. While it's lured many treasure hunters to its shores, it's what lies just offshore that attracts explorers these days, including myself. Known as 'The Island of Sharks', within the nutrient-rich waters of this UNESCO World Heritage Site you'll find the largest aggregation of hammerhead sharks in the world. These beauties will leave you spellbound and stoked that you made the mammoth effort to get here. The seamounts and bays of Cocos attract 14 different shark species and vortexes of jacks and barracudas. If you love sharks and pelagics, then you'll go loco for the Isla del Coco!

Best time to dive

December to May is considered the dry season (although, it can still rain in these months) and this is the best time for diving in terms of visibility and calmer conditions which make more dive sites accessible. For hammerheads schooling in larger numbers, the rainy months of mid-June to mid-October are best, though the 36-hour sea crossing from the mainland will likely be rougher. June to November are also better for mantas, devil rays and whale sharks, though visibility is cloudier due to plankton.

Opposite Cameraman Ofer Ketter filming scalloped hammerheads

Gear
- 3-5mm wetsuit. While water temperatures range from 24-29°C (75.2-84.2°F) year-round, cool thermoclines can sometimes catch divers off-guard
- Hood
- Booties
- A reef hook, if allowed
- A reliable dive computer

Given Cocos' strong currents and remote location, a surface marker buoy (SMB), whistle and any other signalling device such as a Personal Locator Beacon (PLB) are crucial.

Photography tip
This is a wide-angle shark paradise, with large sharks swarming above and sometimes getting close. Think 16-35 or a 11-24mm.

Strobes on for up close action, strobes off for sharks in the distance.

Qualification
- Advanced Open Water

Although there are a number of shallower sites, Cocos is best suited to experienced divers due to strong currents (five currents converge here), deep water and its remote location. Divers should have a good fitness level and be comfortable with potentially challenging conditions.

Getting there
After flying into San Jose, you can catch a taxi or private transfer to Puntarenas which will take at least 1.5 hours depending on traffic. Your liveaboard's sea crossing from Puntarenas, Costa Rica, takes about 36 hours.

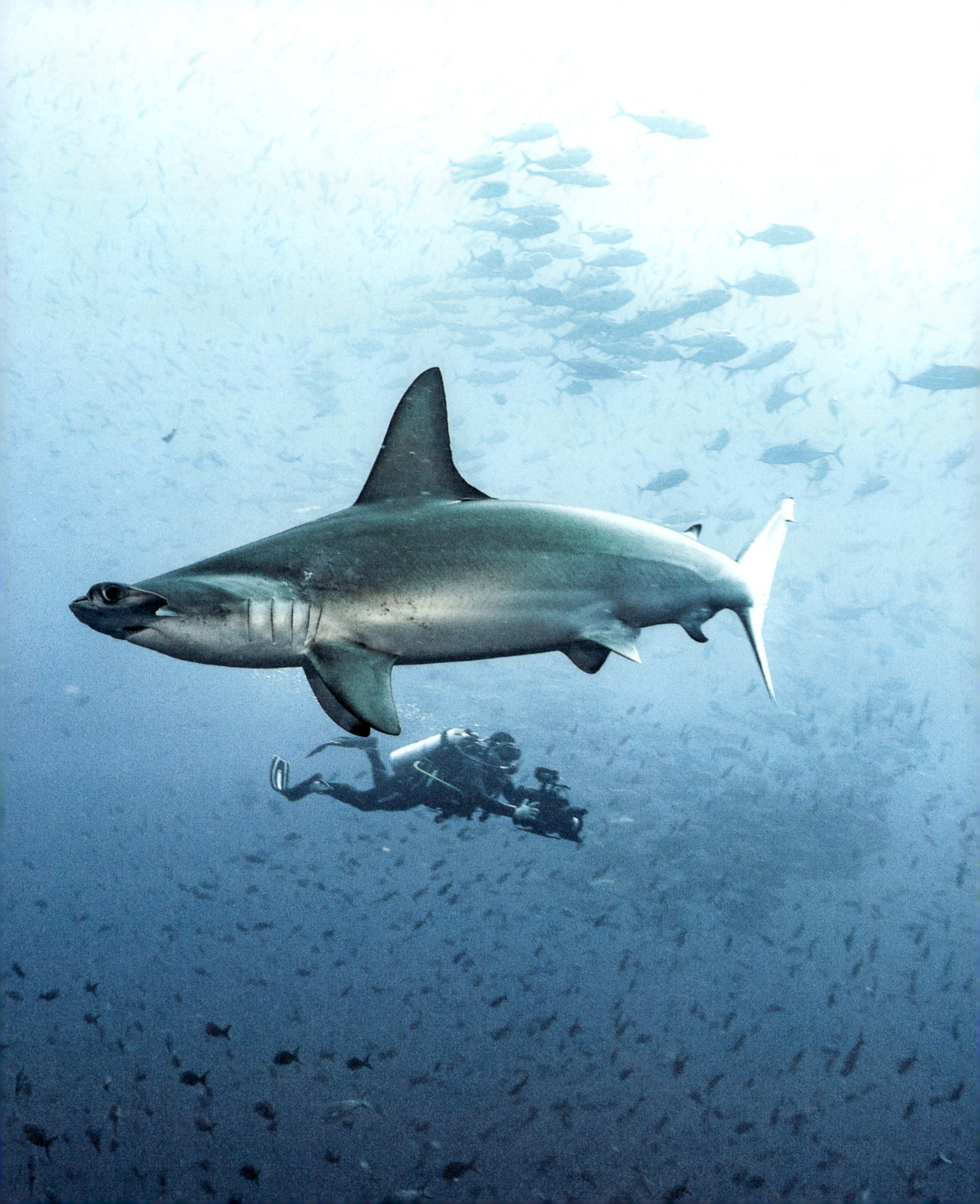

Dive in

About 550km (342mi) off the coast of Costa Rica is the legendary Cocos Island (Isla del Coco), one of the greatest dive spots on the planet. Dubbed 'the most beautiful island in the world' by Jacques Cousteau and used as the film set for Isla Nublar in Jurassic Park, this small, uninhabited island is resplendent with thick rainforest, waterfalls and hidden coves. With large schools of scalloped hammerheads and unparalleled marine biodiversity, Cocos sits high on the wish lists of in-the-know divers, though many will never get there due to the cost involved.

I vividly remember my first trip to Cocos Island. I was working as a dive guide on a private yacht and when we first saw Cocos on the horizon, after the long sea crossing from Puntarenas, I was bursting with excitement for the week ahead. At this super remote, oceanic island it felt like we were lost in time. I could almost hear the Jurassic Park theme song playing across the scene. This was a wild place where anything could happen and where sharks rule the underwater world. Part of my job was itinerary planning – to recommend to my yacht-owner employer the best places in the world to dive with certain marine species, and then to coordinate getting to this location with the ship's captain, whereupon my employer would fly in and meet us. Nicknamed 'the island of sharks', Cocos offers reliable encounters with schooling hammerheads and for my time-poor, shark-loving boss, this was an opportunity to experience something really special in the small window of time that he could get away from running his companies.

Diving at Cocos is all about patience, acting calmly and holding your position/maintaining buoyancy in the current. Then, slowly but surely you could be witnessing hundreds of hammerhead sharks circling gracefully overhead, or, if you're diving shallower waters, seeing them being cleaned by butterflyfish and angelfish. Your remote location means that you'll share this encounter with very few divers, making the experience even more extraordinary.

Despite them being the main attraction, Cocos' underwater scene is not limited to hammerheads. This protected national park and UNESCO World Heritage Site boasts a unique combination of geographical features such as pinnacles, tunnels and sheer walls, plus nutrient rich currents, creating an underwater haven for big marine life. Imagine manta and mobula rays gliding effortlessly through the water; massive schools of jacks and snappers; visiting humpback whales and a wide range of shark species including Galapagos, tiger and silky sharks. Then there's the extraordinary topside scenery and the mystery of buried treasure, some of which was found by park rangers on the beach after a storm in 2016. Strangely, there are very few articles online about the $200 millionUSD find, which consisted of old wooden chests filled with gold and silver, plus an 84kg (185lb) gold statue of the Virgin Mary. The island has various legends of buried treasure, and it's believed to have influenced Robert Louis Stevenson's iconic classic 'Treasure Island'.

Cocos' inaccessibility may have been the reason it was a favourite location for pirates to bury their loot, but its remoteness also means that modern-day explorers need to fork out a small fortune to get here. Unless you're lucky enough to visit via a private yacht, the only option is to join a liveaboard. Liveaboard fleets; Nautilus, Undersea Hunter and Aggressor Adventures run ten-night trips for around $7000USD per person twin share. To preserve the fragile ecosystems of Cocos, the number of divers is limited, and strict regulations are in place, ensuring that future generations of divers can continue to experience the magic of this underwater sanctuary.

Above Chatham Bay, Cocos Island

Americas

Submersibles

Submarining Cocos' Everest

Most of us will never explore outer space, but deep-sea exploration via submersible. is becoming more accessible, with some tourism operators now carrying their own submersibles. One such operator is the Undersea Hunter, taking guests beyond the limits of a scuba tank in the waters surrounding Cocos Island. Undersea Hunter travels with a custom, three person SEAmagine submersible, the same brand of sub that I trained in and have piloted in various locations around the globe. Unlike a submarine, which can act as an independent watercraft, a submersible relies on a support vessel. So, you'll begin by being towed away from your liveaboard 'mother ship' until you're positioned above your desired descent location. In the case of Cocos, the favoured spot is Everest Seamount. Once above Everest, your one-atmosphere 'DeepSee' sub will slowly submerge to a depth of 90m (295ft). The feeling of sitting inside the sub is incredible (albeit a little claustrophobic) – you've got 360 degrees of vision beyond the acrylic bubble dome out to the shelves of coral, rays and sharks swimming around you, all while you stay dry. As you continue to descend, the light quickly disappears and you'll feel your senses on overload as you take in the new, alien environment. If you're lucky, you may spot a prickly shark in deeper waters, or the Aquaumbra klapferi family of coral – a marine species that had never been seen at Cocos before it was discovered during a mission on the DeepSee. And when the sub. parks on the sea floor, you'll experience a feeling of being very, very small in the world. Nothing compares. My time of piloting submersibles has no doubt been some of the most exciting and challenging work of my career.

Opposite Dense schooling fish in the fertile waters of Cocos Island
Above left The welcome sign that greets you on Cocos Island
Above right Mobula ray

Gardens of the Queen (Jardines de la Reina), Cuba
Scuba in Cuba with sharks, crocs and endangered elkhorns

Why it's special

Officially protected since 1996, the Gardens of the Queen (Jardines de la Reina) is one of the Caribbean's most significant marine protected areas (MPAs). Covering about 684,000ha (1,690,000ac), this archipelago of small islands, reefs and mangrove forests sits just off the south coast of Cuba in the Gulf of Ana Maria. Named by Christopher Columbus after Queen Isabella, the Jardines are a no-take sanctuary whose protection can be credited to Fidel Castro's transformation from a fisherman to an environmental steward (stories say one-time friend Jacques Cousteau had some influence). Divers will revel amongst schools of tarpon and snappers, plus giant groupers, and almost-guaranteed shark sightings, including Caribbean reef sharks and silky sharks. A unique experience is the opportunity to dive with American saltwater crocodiles in the relatively clear waters of the Jardines' mangroves, if you're feeling brave.

Best time to dive

Diving here is year-round, but optimal conditions can be found during Cuba's dry season from December to April with calmer seas and improved visibility, though the water temperatures are cooler at around 23–25°C (73.4–77°F). This period promises encounters with a diverse shark population and the awe-inspiring saltwater crocodile. The warmest ocean temperatures occur in August.

Gear
- 3mm wetsuit in summer, all the way to a 5mm in winter for those really long dives
- Reef smart sunscreen

Photography tip
The Jardines are a mixed bag for photographers. Sharks and crocs will have you shooting wide. But don't underestimate the parks' macro opportunities. Take as many lens options that allow.

Qualification
- Open Water

With shallow dive sites, very clear water and minimal currents, this is a great location for all divers. For new divers, it's an ideal location to get some dives logged, while enjoying the Caribbean's best.

Getting there
Liveaboards depart from the port town of Jucaro, which is a 5-hour bus trip from Havana. If transiting through the US, please check your visa requirements.

Opposite Caribbean reef shark cruises above a thriving ecosystem in the Gardens of the Queen

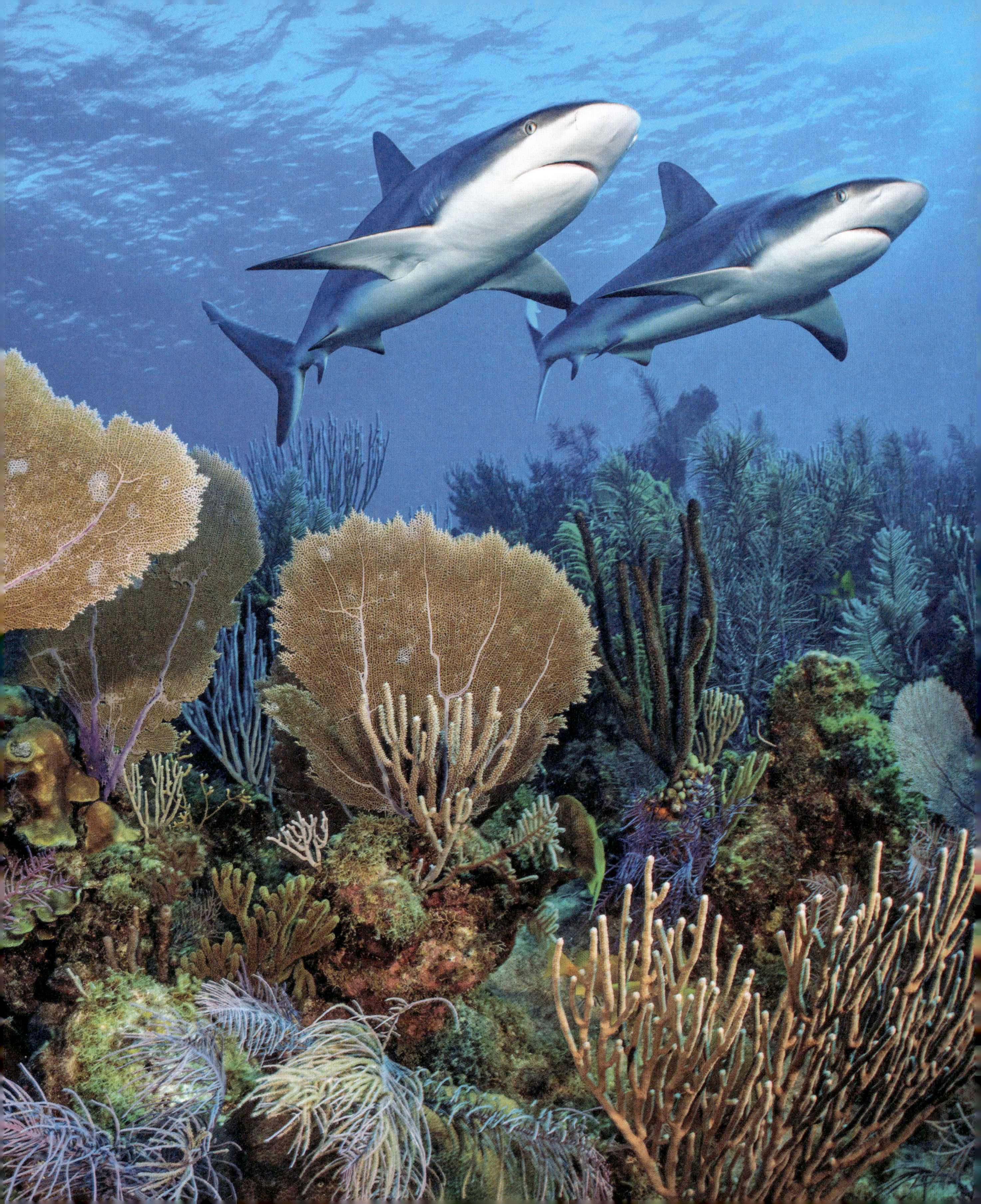

Dive in

Cadillacs and colourful buildings are the quintessential travel snapshots of Cuba. But for divers, this island archipelago offers some of the Caribbean's most pristine seascapes, mainly due to policies put in place by the former dictator who also happened to be a keen diver.

The reefs and wetlands are thriving in Cuba, the only country in the Caribbean with intact coral systems. Nowhere is this more evident than the Jardines de la Reina (Gardens of the Queen). In this flourishing underwater kingdom, you'll find thousands of colonies of elkhorn corals, one of the Caribbean's most vital reef-building species which, elsewhere in the Caribbean, is listed as endangered. Protected since 1996 by policies put in place by Fidel Castro, this 684,000ha (1,690,000ac) marine sanctuary has avoided the damage caused by mass-tourism seen elsewhere in the Caribbean. The Jardines truly feel like a diver's time capsule, where the past is preserved in the vibrant health of the coral and the existence of species that have long died out in other places.

Accessible solely by liveaboards departing from the port town of Jucaro on a five-hour boat trip, the Jardines de la Reina are suitable for all divers, offering serene shallows for novices and intricate terrains for the seasoned. As an added bonus for beginner divers, the absence of strong currents contributes to some relaxed diving. Here in southern Cuba, dive sites teem with French angelfish and snub-nosed darts, while Caribbean reef and silky sharks patrol the reefs with a serene command. Boulder corals, sea fans and gorgonians create a dynamic seascape, while spotted eagle rays soar overhead. Amidst the reefs, you might spot a peacock flounder or an octopus camouflaged against the ocean floor. The nutrient-rich waters also attract schools of creole fish and horse-eye jacks, often enveloping divers in a mass of silver.

A surprising highlight for divers is the Jardines' mangrove forests which, apart from being the habitat of juvenile sea creatures such as baby lobsters, small barracudas, and tiny reef fish, are also the lair of modern-day dinosaurs, American saltwater crocodiles. This presents an incredibly rare opportunity to snorkel with a croc in the saltwater, under the watch of local guides. Where I come from in northern Australia, you'd be called insane if you willingly swam with saltwater crocodiles, which can grow up to seven metres (23ft) on a diet of cattle and kangaroos. But American crocs are different to their Aussie cousins, and they are known to be quite shy. For this reason, in the relatively clear waters and seagrass meadows around the Jardines' mangroves, you can slide into the water with an American croc, which are generally around 2.5m (8.2ft) long, without feeling threatened, despite their commanding presence. Unlike Aussie 'salties', these crocs don't grow as big and they generally like to fill their bellies with turtles, birds and fish. Though of course, just like any wild animal, if they feel threatened, they may still take a bite, as experienced by a Discovery Channel crew member while filming 'Cuba's Secret Shark Lair' in 2018 (the bite was non-fatal).

Being a heavily protected marine reserve, the annual number of divers is limited to 3000 and there are only a handful of liveaboards departing from Jucaro Marina. Avalon Outdoor is the largest local operator, with six dive liveaboards of varying levels of comfort. The newest of these, Avalon III and Avalon IV, launched in 2019 and 2020 respectively, provide the most comfortable offering (cubandivingcenters.com). Another reliable liveaboard operator is the Jardines Aggressor, part of the global Aggressor Fleet (aggressor.com).

Whether you're here for the crocodiles, the sharks or just some relaxing diving, with a choice of over 80 dive sites on vibrant coral reefs, simply teeming with biodiverse marine life, the Jardines de la Reina won't disappoint.

Below Snorkelling with an American saltwater crocodile above a seagrass meadow

Gardens of the Queen (Jardines de la Reina), Cuba

The Silver Bank, Dominican Republic
Vibrate to the sweet serenade of a North Atlantic humpback whale

Why it's special

Each winter, thousands of North Atlantic humpbacks migrate to the warm waters of the Dominican Republic. The Silver Bank, a known aggregation point, is located on an underwater volcanic plateau that has been protected by the Dominican government, with strict rules banning SCUBA diving and limiting visitor numbers to 600 per season. Despite (and perhaps thanks) to these regulations, it's possible to have incredible in-water interactions with whales via a mask and snorkel. Anchored in the middle of the sea, you're right in the middle of the cetacean action. On some days the whales may come right up next to your liveaboard, and other times you'll go on a tender ride to locate them, sometimes joined by bottlenose dolphins riding the wake of your bow. With visibility ranging between 7–30m (23–98ft), each encounter is different. But sometimes it's less about what you can see, and more about what you hear and feel. A whale's song can echo across great distances underwater and last for up to 20 minutes. Feeling these vibrations through your body is one of the greatest experiences you'll ever have in the water.

Best time to dive

December until mid-April is the whale season at Silver Bank, with March being the peak time.

Gear
- 3mm wetsuit for 26-27°C (78.8-80.6°F) water temperatures
- Reef smart sunscreen
- A windbreaker for those late afternoons on the water

Photography tip
Wide is the only way to go! Stick with our favourites of a 16-35, 11-24mm and a fisheye lens. Your strobes are staying home for this trip.

Let the whale control the interaction, never chase it.

Qualification
- None needed

While snorkelling with humpbacks doesn't require certifications, comfort in open water and good swimming abilities are necessary. A good knowledge of cetacean behaviour and local regulations are imperative to ensure a responsible and respectful experience with the whales.

Getting there
Puerto Plata is one and a half hours via a shuttle bus transfer from Cibao International (Santiago) Airport in the Dominican Republic.

Opposite A humpback whale and her calf cruise past at the Silver Bank

The Silver Bank, Dominican Republic

Dive in

Few experiences compare with diving near a singing whale. Their ethereal calls echo through the water and, if you're close enough, you'll feel your chest vibrating. A humpback's melodies and murmurs are used for communication, attracting mates, and even for navigating vast seas. My most memorable whalesong moment was at Silver Bank, when I spent over an hour in the water with a singing male. Suspended head down, he hung motionless with his barnacle-encrusted pectorals spread wide. He was as wide as he was deep. Singing with all his might, he belted out a hauntingly beautiful tune in the hope that a female would be drawn to him. It was unforgettable.

Ninety kilometres (56mi) north of Puerto Plata in the Dominican Republic, Silver Bank is one of the best places in the world for swimming with humpbacks (my other favourite is Tonga, *see* p. 187)). This submerged bank, measuring approximately 32 x 16km (20 x 10mi), rises from the depths of the Atlantic Ocean to an average depth of 30m (98ft) below the surface. The limestone plateau is scattered with coral heads that have been responsible for sinking a few ships over the years. Recognised as one of the world's most important breeding and calving grounds for the North Atlantic humpback whale, the Dominican government has designated the Silver Bank as a Marine Mammal Sanctuary, allowing only 600 people to visit the seamount each season, to provide crucial protection for these whales and their habitat.

Each year, around 5000 to 7000 humpbacks visit this region as part of an extraordinary 2000km (12,402mi) migration southward from their chilly feeding grounds in the North Atlantic to the warm waters of the Antilles for breeding and calving. The season for whale watching and swimming is typically between December to mid-April. Upon approaching the Silver Bank, it's not uncommon to be greeted immediately by whales; their massive flukes (tail fins) slapping the water and huge, elongated pectorals pointing high in the sky. Or even a full body breach to get you excited, and to remind you of just how small you are (and how big they are!) It can be a wild time in the water for these whales. Some females are here to calve, while others are on heat and looking for a mate ... and the males know it. Testosterone levels are at an all-time high for the boys and often frisky whales will jostle to get close to a female.

It's believed that whales consider scuba divers' bubbles as signs of aggression, so The International Whaling Commission has banned scuba within this Marine Mammal Sanctuary. The aim here is to remain calm, observing through your snorkel from the surface and creating as little disturbance to the whales as possible. This is known as a 'passive in-water encounter' and, considering a humpback can grow to 16m (52ft) long and weigh up to 36t (39tn), it's vital that the whale is calm and comfortable with you around. This is when encounters become magical, when you're just a small speck on the surface and the approaching whale controls the interaction. Every whale encounter is unique, so it's all about finding the right whale and setting before entering the water, to allow for the longest possible encounter. This could be a docile female and her male escort, a mother and her new calf, or my personal favourite a 'male singer'.

The only way to experience the Silver Bank is with one of the few commercial operators that have been granted a licence for the season. My friend Tom Conlin has operated whale swims on the Silver Bank since 1991 and has been instramental in advocating for the protection of the region (imagine the actor Jeff Bridges as a pirate). He offers week-long charters which fill up quickly, so it's best to book a year in advance (aquaticadventures.com). Gene Flipse of Conscious Breath Adventures also provides a fantastic, responsible experience (consciousbreathadventures.com).

Opposite Diving with the humpbacks of the Silver Bank. It's strictly snorkelling only (no scuba) here *Below* A large humpback flukes its tail during a heat run for a female

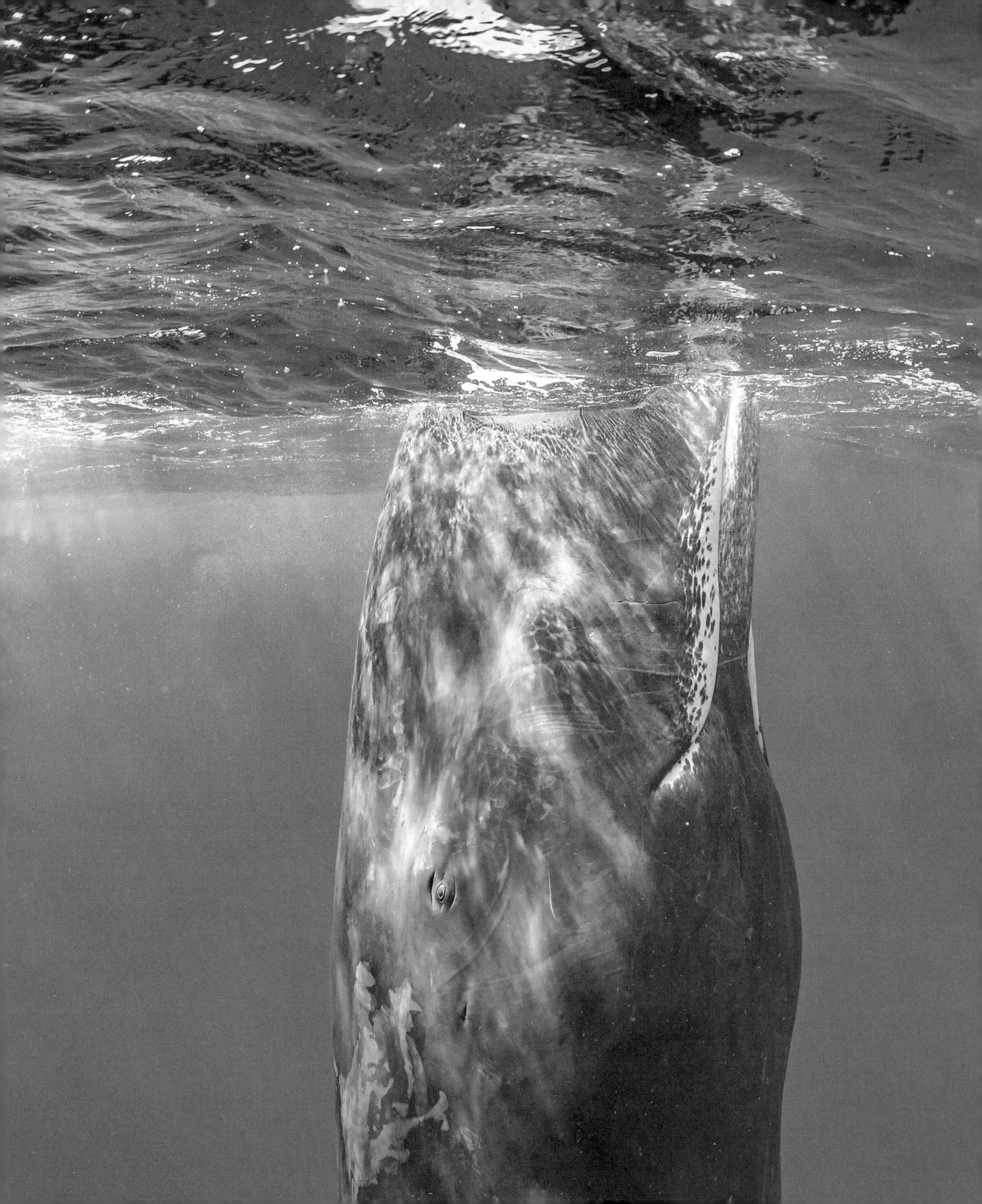

Dominica, The Caribbean
Freedive with Moby Dick in the world's first sperm whale sanctuary

Why it's special

In the heart of the Caribbean, Dominica is a beacon for marine conservation, being the first nation to declare a portion of its waters as a sanctuary for sperm whales. A permanent population of at least 200 of these gentle giants, the largest toothed predators in the world, are known to inhabit the deep offshore trenches on the western side of the island. With an emphasis on respectful and sustainable interactions, operators in Dominica offer a rare window into the lives of these creatures, under a government-issued permit. This is a unique chance to observe the nurturing bonds between mothers and calves, as well as the intricate 'coda' communications that define sperm whale pods, while gathering important data to help understand them better.

Best time to dive

Sperm whales can be spotted in Dominica year-round, but the best time is November to March when the sea is calmer, visibility is better and the whales' presence is more predictable. During this period, the nutrient-rich waters of Dominica are a hive of activity with whales breaching, socialising, and feeding. These months coincide with the migratory patterns of various marine species, enhancing the biodiversity experienced. August to the end of October is hurricane season, which can bring rough seas.

Gear
- As the sea temperature will be in the late 20s (°C) or low 80s (°F) and you're mainly on the surface with a snorkel, you'll only need a rashie or, at most, a 3mm wetsuit
- High quality mask, snorkel, and fins
- Reef smart sunscreen
- A windbreaker for those late afternoons on the water

Photography tip
- Wide is the only way to go! Stick with a 16-35, 11-24mm and a fisheye lens. Your strobes are staying home for this one

Sperm whales display many interesting behavioural patterns, so don't get lost behind the camera. Watch, observe and wait for the right moment to frame your shot.

Qualification
- While no specific diving certifications are required for swimming with sperm whales, comfort in open-water environments is essential. Participants should be able to remain calm in choppy, open ocean where the bottom is well and truly out of sight

Getting there
There are daily flights, 3.5-hour flights directly from Miami to Dominica with American Airlines. If you're coming from Europe, there are also flights that connect via various Caribbean airports with Silver Airways.

Opposite A vertical, hanging sperm whale spy hops in the Caribbean waters of Dominica

Dive in

If you've read Herman Melville's classic *Moby Dick* then you'll be familiar with the toothy silhouette of a sperm whale. The novel's real-life inspiration was a docile white whale nicknamed Mocha Dick. Originally spotted near Chile's Mocha Island, the albino whale was relentlessly targeted by whalers and, when attacked, would ram boats, causing some to sink. Mocha was eventually slain after coming to the aid of a cow (mother whale) whose calf was harpooned and killed. At 21m long, Mocha's body, pin-cushioned with 20 harpoons, produced 100 barrels of oil plus some ambergris, used for making perfume and more valuable than gold.

Historically, sperm whales have been heavily hunted and they are now designated as vulnerable on the IUCN Red List. Within their iconic, boxy forehead is the spermaceti organ containing a liquid wax that's been wanted by whalers since the 17th century, used in cosmetics, pharmaceuticals and textiles. Today, sperm whales' main threats are ship strikes, fishing gear ingestion or entanglement and land pollution (one more reason to pick up rubbish when we see it on the beach). Recently, in Dominica, their value has been recognised with the creation of an 800km² (308mi²) marine protected area; the world's first sperm whale sanctuary.

At 750km² (290mi²) in size, Dominica has been nicknamed 'nature island' because of its mountainous volcanic landscape. Imagine lush green rainforests, natural hot springs, hidden waterfalls and rainbows galore. But it's the leviathans lurking offshore that bring divers here. Within the deep, clear waters surrounding the island is a year-round population of at least 200 sperm whales, with some individuals believed to be over 60 years old. In Dominica's warm waters, these whales find shelter and an abundant supply of squid to feast on. Unlike baleen filter-feeding whales, sperm whales have teeth on their bottom jaw, which are useful for chomping fish and squid.

It's in these waters that you'll have the unique opportunity to freedive with them. With the largest known brain of any animal, sperm whale pods welcome divers with a curious intellect that can leave you wondering who is studying who. Female sperm whales glide through the water with a grace that belies their size, often accompanied by juvenile males who are yet to embark on their solitary journeys. Sperm whales are matrilineal, meaning the ladies stay together for life – grandmas, mums and daughters while the bulls (males) leave the pod in their early teens, perhaps never to return.

Witnessing sperm whales up close is nothing short of powerful and hearing their 'codas', equally so. Used mainly for echolocation, their unusual creaks and clicks are frequently studied and thought to be clan specific. Furthermore, sperm whales are the loudest animal in the world, with the ability to make 230 decibel sounds, loud enough to burst your eardrum (a jackhammer can reach 100 decibels). These codas are used by Dominican boat operators to locate sperm whales via a hydrophone that's dropped into the water. Once the clicks are heard, there's a 95% chance you'll find sperm whales close by and that's when it's 'go time'.

Under the guidance of seasoned professionals, snorkellers slip into the water for a passive encounter – allowing the whale to approach if they choose – so that the experience is on the whales' terms and their natural behaviour isn't disrupted. Encounters can be as short as a few seconds while a whale swims by, or up to 15 minutes (sometimes longer) if they choose to hang around. Known to be one of the longest and deepest diving whales, when the sperm whale dives down to feed, it will disappear for 45 minutes before reappearing, so patience is the name of the game here. On a full day's trip, you may only spend a total of half an hour in the water with a whale and, on some days, you might not see them at all (especially if orcas have recently been spotted in the area). Nevertheless, there's plenty of other marine life to see including pods of dolphins and other whale species like short-fin pilot whales, humpbacks and false killer whales. In fact, 22 of the 33 species of cetaceans known to be found in the Caribbean have been spotted within Dominica's waters.

Dominica's approach to whale watching is grounded in sustainability and respect, ensuring that each encounter is a step towards the greater understanding and preservation of these majestic creatures. A government-issued permit must be obtained prior to swimming with the whales, and then the interaction is strictly governed with rules in place to limit group sizes, noise levels and how close you can get to the whale. Learn more at thespermwhaleproject.org and divedominica.com

Opposite Within a sperm whale's forehead is the spermaceti organ, which contains a liquid wax

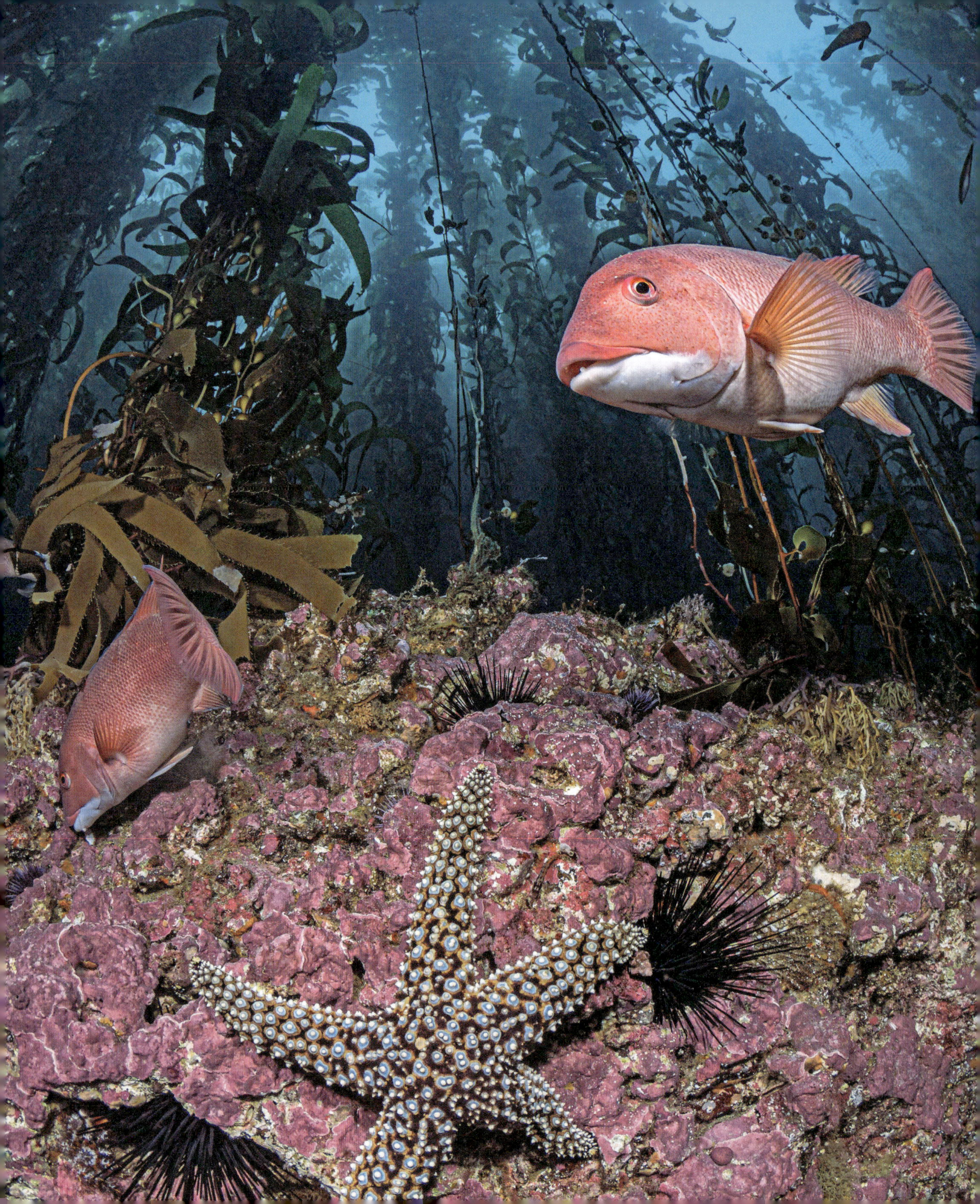

Santa Catalina Island, USA
Get by with a little kelp from my friends

Why it's special

California's state fish, the Garibaldi, usually prefers a solitary lifestyle, fiercely protecting its two feet of territory. But every once in a while, in behaviour labelled as a 'kelp social', they'll have a friendly get-together to check each other out and potentially choose mates. Once a popular aquarium fish, they're now protected in California, but you can find plenty of them living amongst the towers of kelp found here. Just an hour by fast ferry from Long Beach, this island is a quirky and fascinating destination above and below water. Owned by the Wrigley family (as in chewing gum), it has an interesting history. In Hollywood, it masqueraded as Amity Island in Jaws, and was used as a set for Spaghetti Westerns, and as a result, has a feral population of bison.

But the underwater environment is what lures thousands of divers each year. Here, kelp forests create a multi-tiered haven of life from the sea floor to the surface. Divers may spot friendly California sea lions, leopard sharks, lobsters, crabs, nudibranchs, or an elusive giant black sea bass. If you bring your own boat across, you'll have access to over 100 dive sites around the island. No boat? No worries; there are plenty of great shore diving experiencees including walking the famous stairs down into Casino Point's dive park and plunging straight into the action.

Best time to dive

The prime time to explore the kelp forests is from late summer to early autumn when the water is at its warmest and visibility is best. This season also coincides with the migratory patterns of several marine species. Mid-week–is best avoid weekends, if possible, and also the the weekend of the Catalina Wine Mixer, as featured in the movie *Step Brothers* (yep, it's a real thing). Preferably, visit between October and April, when there are fewer divers.

Gear
- A 7mm wetsuit or a drysuit
- Gloves
- A hood
- Boots
- Thick undergarments (if wearing a drysuit)
- A regulator that's suitable for cold water

A dive knife is a handy addition for entanglements in the kelp, but it's best to dive with care and not put yourself in such circumstances to start with.

Photography tip
A wide-angle lens and strobes are vital to illuminate the wide underwater kelp forest scene. My tip: shoot with a rectilinear lens and avoid shooting with a fish eye lens. You want your kelp to appear nice and vertical, opposed to being curved. Also, don't forget there are wonderful macro possibilities here.

Qualification
- Open Water Diver

Navigating the dense fronds and the potential for mild currents requires good buoyancy control and navigation skills. Therefore, diving in the kelp forests is best suited to intermediate divers. But, with that said, there are locations around the island for all levels of divers.

Getting there
From Los Angeles, there are daily ferry departures from Long Beach, San Pedro, Dana Point, and Newport Beach with the Catalina Express or the Catalina Flyer. These fast ferries take one hour.

Opposite California sheephead wrasse and a starfish in a kelp forest at Catalina Island

Dive in

Some years back, I had the opportunity to join two of my mentors on a trip to Catalina Island for a weekend of underwater cinematography. The island, so close to the hustle and bustle of LA, totally blew me away. Here in the Pacific Ocean, just 50km (31mi) south of Long Beach was this laid-back island, surrounded by a very special underwater environment. Forests of kelp create a vertical maze of biodiversity, providing a home to a wide range of species. The scene is reminiscent of goldfish tanks I've seen in my childhood, complete with long reeds of seaweed, bubbling treasure chests, and wind-up deep sea diver figurines, like diving inside a fish tank. But at Catalina Island, the goldfish are orange garibaldi, California's state marine fish and the reeds, a towering kelp forest. Maybe this was the inspiration for all of our childhood aquariums, I speculated.

Catalina's kelp forest is dynamic, with fronds growing almost before your eyes. Able to grow up to 60cm (24in) a day, they are the fastest growing plant in the sea. With an average water visibility of around 10–15m (32–49ft) – or up to 25m (82ft) on a really good day – divers can spot plenty of fish and other marine life amidst the towering marine flora. Schools of silvery jack mackerel dart between the kelp while curious harbour seals play peek-a-boo. It's not uncommon to come across the spiny California scorpionfish camouflaged against the seabed, or lobsters in the crevices of the rocky reef. Meanwhile, kelp bass, previously fished almost to extinction, can be found here using the kelp fronds to ambush prey, showcasing the kelp forest's role as both a nursery and a hunting ground.

One of the highlights of a dive in Catalina is spotting an iconic Garibaldi, aka the Catalina goldfish, named after the Italian general Giuseppe Garibaldi whose signature style was a bright red shirt. Growing up to 35cm (14in) long, Garibaldis like to eat sponges and algae, plus nudibranchs and tubeworms. Usually found on their own, these red-orange damselfish with heart-shaped tails create a striking contrast against the kelp. If you wear orange gloves, or have bright orange equipment, you might attract one of these fish to you, who may even be cheeky enough to nip you in an effort to ward you away from his territory.

For macro enthusiasts, the kelp forest is a treasure trove of biodiversity. Nudibranchs, with their flamboyant colours, decorate the kelp leaves, while crabs and snails navigate the sea floor with ease. A keen eye will spot intricately-patterned sea stars, bat stars and brittle stars colouring the ocean's floor, further adding to the aquarium vibes. This is also a vital habitat for juvenile fish, providing shelter and food as they grow. The juveniles of many open water species, such as opaleye and blacksmith, find sanctuary within the kelp, highlighting the importance of these forests for the life cycle of ocean fauna.

Santa Catalina itself is quite interesting and, over the past 7000 years, has attracted a wide variety of characters. From sun god worshipers to pirates, from prohibition bootleggers to missionaries, and then in 1919 it was added to the real estate portfolio of everyone's favourite chewing gum family; Wrigley. William Wrigley built the Catalina Casino in 1929, which, for divers, now serves as a landmark above the island's most popular dive site, the Casino Point Dive Park. Within this no-take marine park (one of nine on the island) you'll find smallwrecks and artificial reefs, plus, of course, plenty of kelp. While William has now passed away, his family continues to operate Catalina as a tourism destination and they have designated 170,000km² (65,600mi²) of the island to its non-profit organisation, the Catalina Island Conservancy, to ensure its future protection.

Opposite Garibaldis swim by some beautiful sea fans
Left An aerial view of Avalon Harbour

Santa Catalina Island, USA

Magdalena Bay, Mexico
Freedive alongside striped marlin with locals who've traded commercial fishing for ecotourism

Why it's special

In the small fishing village of San Carlos on Mexico's Baja California peninsula, local commercial fishermen are beginning to set aside their fishing gear in lieu of a new trade; ecotourism. Magdalena Bay (Bahia Magdalena) and the blue waters of the Pacific beyond the bay's barrier islands is where the action unfolds. As sardines form bait balls, sometimes in their thousands, striped marlin and Californian sea lions herd them to the surface before launching their attack. Striped marlin, which are usually hard to photograph due to their speed, will stick around a static bait ball until larger predators arrive, picking off sardines one by one. Freediving near the bait ball affords divers a rare opportunity to get close to these magnificent billfish.

Best time to dive

From late October to mid-December the water teems with sardines, attracting marlin and other pelagic species. The cooler water temperatures and nutrient upwellings create ideal conditions for the sardines, and consequently, for the marlins. If possible, avoid El Niño years when the waters are warmer.

Gear
- 5mm wetsuit for water temperatures in the mid 20s Celsius (high 70s Fahrenheit) Sun protective clothing for spending hours out on the open sea
- Reef safe sunscreen
- Waterproof windbreaker jacket
- Dry bag to keep your gear protected inside the panga

Photography tip
You'll want a lens that is not only wide, but has a zoom that allows different angles of photography. This is underwater action photography at its finest, so ensure your camera has a fast frame rate.

Due to the shallow depth of the bait balls and fast frame rates, no strobes are required.

Qualification
- Freediver (no dive qualification needed)

Divers should have experience with blue water freediving and be comfortable with open ocean conditions. The ability to manage strong currents and rapidly changing underwater scenarios is crucial, as is the strength and endurance needed for long days in the water, climbing in and out of the panga.

Getting there
Mag Bay can be reached via Loreto Airport, which connects to Los Angeles. It's then a 3-hour drive to Mag Bay. Alternatively, you can make the longer drive from La Paz or Cabo San Lucas.

Opposite Striped marlin can move at speeds of up to 80km/hr (50mi/hr)

Magdalena Bay, Mexico

Dive in

While the peninsula of Baja California Sur (South) is famous amongst divers for its incredible migration of mobula rays, there's another yearly event that swims under the radar (for now), Magdalena (Mag) Bay's sardine run.

Sports fishermen have long known about Mag Bay, but in recent years an ecotourism industry has begun to take off here with divers jumping into the water with elusive striped marlin as they hunt bait balls. Mag Bay, a spawning area for sardines, and the Pacific coastline beyond the boca (mouth) of the bay are a hotbed of marine activity attracting everything from seabirds to whales, dolphins, sharks, sea lions and even orcas. Each autumn, schools of sardines numbering into their thousands aggregate off the bay's coast, attracting striped marlin, a fish that's usually too quick to get anywhere near.

Marlins are a type of billfish, which have traditionally been a target for both recreational fishermen and commercial industries in Baja Sur, and marlin are currently worth a lot more on the hook than as part of a diving tour. So, this kind of ecotourism is fairly new to Mag Bay and regulations haven't yet been put in place for this emerging industry. As you board your panga (Baja motorised skiff/ fishing boat), you'll learn from your local captain and guide about their past life as commercial fishermen and how ecotourism is changing local communities. While this dive tourism is still only small in scale, and only operates for a limited part of the year, it's a welcome step toward conservation efforts for marlin, which are currently in decline and classified as 'near threatened' on the IUCN Red List.

Your adventure starts early in the morning as you depart Magdalena Bay. While it might take hours of bumping around the ocean before you see sardines, when you spot the frigatebirds congregating you know you'll soon be in the water with a bait ball, then it's go-time!

It all begins with the forming of the bait ball. First, the sardines get pushed to the top of the epipelagic zone (aka 'the sunlight zone') where they are corralled by the striped marlin. Meanwhile, frigatebirds and pelicans hover in the skies above, scouring the sea for schools of fish. Then, all of a sudden, a feeding frenzy ensues. Striped marlin dart through spiralling bait balls, peeling off individual sardines one by one, devouring as many as they can before bigger predators arrive, like a Brydes whale. For divers, it's thrilling to witness the coming and going of different predators, like sea lions, as the static bait ball slowly gets smaller (and visibility reduces) while the water goes cloudy with bubbles and sardine scales.

The marlin move with such precision that they have been dubbed 'the ballet dancers of the sea'. It's exhilarating to be in the open water with these fish as they hunt, though freediving near a static bait ball requires vigilance; the last thing you want is to get in the way of a billfish that can grow to over 200kg (440lb). And then there's the action from other angles as frigatebirds plummet into the bait balls from above, and whales appear from below, surprising divers who must quickly move away from their giant, gaping mouths.

For photographers and videographers, Mag Bay's clear waters provide exceptional visibility, sometimes up to 30m (98ft), enabling you to capture stunning scenes of these stripy, electric blue fish. One of the fastest fish in the sea, marlin can move at speeds of up to 80km/hr (50mi/hr, double the speed of Usain Bolt's fastest run), creating a real challenge when it comes to snapping that photograph! For this reason, freediving offers divers more agility in the water and helps in keeping pace with the fast-moving marlin. There are a few operators now offering this trip, including Dive Ninja Expeditions (diveninjaexpeditions.com) who donate a third of the profits from these trips to marlin conservation.

Apart from the Marlin, Mag Bay has plenty more to offer water lovers. If you're lucky, you may encounter a pod of transient orcas or even a flotilla of turtles numbering into the hundreds. And then there's the world's largest migration of mobula rays which happens twice-yearly on the Baja peninsula (June and July are the prime months to jump in the water with them). Whatever brings you to this part of Baja, be it marlin or mobulas, know that by participating in this kind of tourism, you're actively helping this industry to grow and, hopefully in years to come, to see the proper protections set up for these magnificent pelagic creatures.

Liveaboard options for Mag Bay include Mexico Liveaboards (mexicoliveaboards.com) and the Nautilus Fleet (nautilusliveaboards.com).

Opposite Striped marlin below a bait ball *Above* The late afternoon sun casts shadows across the sand dunes of Adolfo Lopez Mateos in Baja California

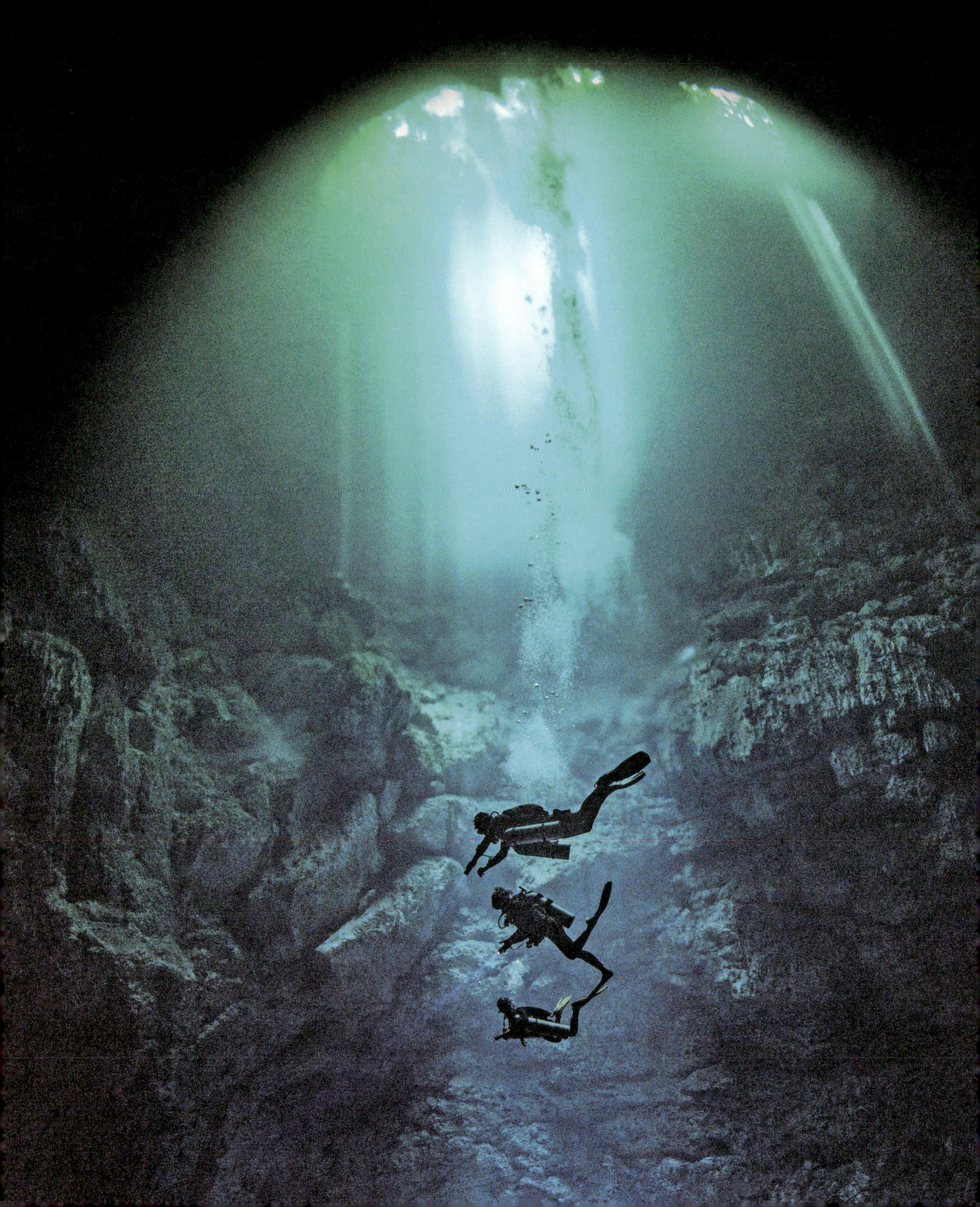

White Cave System (Sistema Sac Actun), Mexico

Dive into the world's largest submerged cave system, beneath the jungle's floor

Why it's special

Dotted along the Yucatán Peninsula, Mexico's cenotes are natural sinkholes that offer incredible freshwater diving. For the Mayan people, they are historically significant; in the absence of any other local source of fresh water, they relied on them for survival. Hidden amongst deep vegetation, these geological wonders were formed over millennia by the collapse of limestone bedrock, revealing a network of submerged caves and passages. In 2018, a connection was discovered between two large cave systems, Sac Actun and Dos Ojos. Together, they now constitute the world's largest submerged cave system. Acting as portals to the caves, each cenote has a unique character and mystery. From trees branching out of eerie hydrogen sulphide clouds, to ancient fossils, and sunbeams lighting up giant chasms, herein lies an unparalleled opportunity for divers to explore the hidden magic of the Yucatán Peninsula.

Best time to dive

The cenotes can be dived year-round, but the best conditions are typically from May to September, during which time the height and angle of the sun has the potential to create spectacular light beams in the water. Note that Mexico's hurricane season is July to October. Regardless of the season, water temperatures remain pretty consistent year-round at about 25°C (77°F). Filtered by the limestone earth, the crystal-clear waters offer excellent visibility, often exceeding 30m (98ft).

Opposite Incredible visibility at El Pit Cenote

Gear
- 5mm wetsuit for water temperatures of around 25°C (77°F)
- A reliable dive computer
- A dive light for navigating the caverns and highlighting their striking features

A buoyancy control device that's geared towards tech. diving and a line reel are recommended for safety and navigation in the more complex systems. Communicate with local divers and operators, prior to organising your trip.

Never enter a cave system without a professional team.

Photography tip

There are two ways to approach photography in the cenotes. The question is whether to take strobes or not. Both deliver incredible and striking results. With strobes and lights, you are choosing to illuminate the cave and the diver within.

Alternatively, without strobes, you are harnessing the natural light that penetrates the caverns, showcasing the sunbeams into the cenote. In all cases, shoot wide and don't be afraid to experiment.

Qualification
- Open Water Diver, for cenotes with no overhead restrictions

Good buoyancy control and comfort in confined spaces is crucial. Divers seeking to explore beyond the cavern zones should be certified in cave diving, as these environments require advanced specialist skills and knowledge for safe navigation.

Getting there

Tulum is a 1.5-hour drive from Cancun via shuttle or private transfer. Many dive centres along the Riviera Maya offer day trips to the cenotes.

Dive in

So, what makes the cenotes so special? Translated as 'cave with water', the cenotes of the Yucatán Peninsula hold significant cultural and spiritual importance to the Mayan people. For the ancient Maya, they were considered sacred gateways to the underworld, known as Xibalba, and were often used for spiritual ceremonies. For divers nowadays, sinking into the cenotes can feel like a mystical experience thanks to the stillness of the water, coupled with the ancient rock formations. As divers navigate through crystal-clear freshwater, exploring vast halls and narrow passageways, each turn offers a new perspective of this subterranean world. Though marine life is scarce, you might spot small freshwater fish darting amongst the rocks, or freshwater shrimp, perhaps even a turtle. In recent years, cave divers have found fossilised animals including mammoths, giant jaguars and sloths within the cenote Sac Actun. But perhaps the most momentous discovery was that of a teenage girl, nicknamed 'Naia' by researchers, whose 12,000-year-old bones represent the oldest and most intact skeleton ever found in Latin America.

In 2018, after a connection was made between the Sac Actun and Dos Ojos cave systems, the two were combined and collectively named Sistema Sac Actun, which is Spanish and Mayan for 'white cave system'. At 364km (226mi) long, this is the world's largest known flooded cave. For divers, there are plenty of cenotes to explore within the Sistema, with some great caverns for novices and complex labyrinths for cave divers. One of the more popular cenotes for divers (which, amazingly, is open only to divers) is located just 25km (15mi) north of Tulum in the Dos Ojos Natural Park. Here, the gigantic chamber of El Pit reveals layers of freshwater atop saltwater, creating haloclines that blur and bend the light in mesmerising ways. With a maximum dive depth of 40m (131ft), this one's suited to advanced divers. Like all cenotes, it's best to time your dive for the position of the sun to be overhead, and to arrive before other divers, so the haloclines haven't been disturbed.

Just 2.8km (1.7mi) from El Pit is the cenote Dos Ojos, Spanish for 'two eyes'. The 'eyes' are two sinkholes, connected by a 400m (1310ft) tunnel, which has a big, central cavern. With shallower depths (maximum 10m/32ft) this cenote is great for beginners and also for snorkelers. Also accessible via Cenotes Dos Ojos' entrance road is the cenote 'Pet Cemetery' (maximum depth six metres). Known as one of the region's most stunning caves, it's famous for its animal fossils, one of which is an extinct species of prehistoric camel. This is a popular spot for both snorkelers and divers.

The White Cave System really does have something for all divers, but a select niche of divers especially thrives here; cave divers. The world of technical cave diving is so different from your everyday recreational dive that most will find it downright terrifying. There's no swimming to the surface if things go wrong! You're deep in a cave with spaces so tight you'll need to take your tanks off to fit through. Your buoyancy control is paramount as one kick of your fins can stir up silt so fine it clouds up the cavern, blocking all visibility and lasting indefinitely. A fastened string guideline provides your only orientation of in and out; lose it and you're in a scary situation. Am I selling it to you yet? Cave diving is both exciting and terrifying. If this is your scene, then maybe it's time you visited Sistema Sac Actun.

Below Lighting up the darkness in Cenote Uku Cusam

Entering Sac Actun Cenote *Opposite* Sidemount diving in Cenote Dos Pisos

Cenote safety

Preparing for a Cenotes dive

While cenotes offer incredible diving experiences, they also present specific challenges due to their overhead environments, potential for tight spaces and varying water clarity which can lead to disorientation. There have been instances where divers have lost their lives in cenotes. Most accidents in cenotes and cave diving are attributed to a lack of proper training, insufficient experience, or failure to adhere to established safety protocols.

Lack of Proper Training: Diving in cenotes requires specialised training and certification in cavern or cave diving to learn specific techniques and safety measures needed to navigate these environments safely.

Inadequate Equipment: Using improper or malfunctioning equipment can be fatal. This includes failure to use a guideline, which is crucial for getting back to the entrance in low-visibility conditions.

Exceeding Personal Limits: Overconfidence in one's abilities in such challenging environments can be dangerous.

Poor Planning: Not adhering to dive plans, including depth and time limits, and not having a clear understanding of the cenote's layout can lead to accidents.

Air Supply Management: Mismanaging air supply in an overhead environment where direct ascent to the surface is not possible is particularly perilous. The good news is that the Yucatán has a long history of cenote exploration and here you'll find an established industry of safe and reputable dive operators.

Americas

Banco Chinchorro, Mexico
Smile at a crocodile in the clear waters of Banco Chinchorro

Why it's special

Banco Chinchorro is a coral atoll and UNESCO Biosphere Reserve with some of the Caribbean's best diving. Imagine colourful corals, all kinds of tropical fish, nurse sharks that follow divers like puppies, and, for those brave enough, snorkelling with crocs. While Australian saltwater crocodiles (salties) are formidable by reputation, the American crocodiles that inhabit the mangroves around the island of Cayo Centro display a surprisingly docile demeanour towards humans, owing to the unique relationship that they've developed with the fishermen who feed them. Here, amidst the largest population of these crocodiles in Mexico, snorkellers can stand in the shallows and observe them up-close. Beyond the clear waters of the atoll's lagoon, the barrier reef is also home to a 'graveyard' of over 200 ships, some dating back to the 16th century.

Best time to dive

While you can dive Banco Chinchorro year-round, the best time for crocodile encounters is between June and September when the weather is calmer, the visibility better and the crocodiles more active. Note that dive boats won't operate in rough seas (they don't want to add their vessel to the 200+ boats that are already wrecked there!)

Gear for croc snorkels
- Rash guard
- Mask and snorkel
- Booties, rather than fins, to stand in a depth of 1-1.5 metres (3-5ft)
- Raincoat or spray jacket for the boat trip out there
- Wetsuit for reef diving
- 2mm wetsuit in summer when the water is 30°C (86°F), or 3-5mm in winter when the water is 25°C (77°F)

Photography tip
For snapping crocs up-close, use a wide-angle lens that has a close focal distance. You'll want to be as close as permittable, to capture the amazing detail of the crocs.

Qualification
- Open Water for reef dives

Croc snorkels are best suited to those who have a lot of experience with large wildlife in the water. It's important to remain still, patient and relaxed within close proximity of large marine animals, whilst being prepared for the unexpected. Furthermore, divers must always adhere to strict safety advice and guidelines.

Getting there
From Cancun, Mahahual is a 4.5-hour drive (if you have a rental car). Plan your drive for the daytime, don't travel in the dark. If you're jumping on an ADO bus, it's 5.5 hours.

Opposite American saltwater crocodiles are much more docile than their Australian relatives

Dive in

About 30km (19mi) offshore from the port town of Mahahual on the Caribbean coast, you'll find the biggest coral atoll in the northern hemisphere; Banco Chinchorro. This 800km² (198,000ac) UNESCO Biosphere Reserve is a diver's dream with pristine reefs covered in corals and sponges, around 200 shipwrecks and a plethora of marine life including eagle rays, turtles (hawksbill, leatherback and green), lobsters, nurse sharks and whale sharks. Oh, and crocs.

Within the atoll's lagoon are three small islands. On the largest island, Cayo Centro (Central Cay), there's a population of about 400 American crocs that inhabit the mangroves. Although related to the formidable Australian saltwater/estuarine crocodile, the American crocodile has a less aggressive nature, and on Cayo Centro they coexist peacefully with the fishermen that set up here seasonally. The fishermen, who reside in huts built on stilts above the lagoon (palafitos), have an understanding with the crocs; at the sound of fish being prepared, the crocs, many of which have been given names by the fishermen, emerge from the mangroves to get their fish scraps. This is a waste disposal system that benefits both parties.

With this human/reptilian relationship cemented, divers have a unique opportunity to jump in the water with these crocs, accompanied by a local tour operator, with a permit from the Mexican government and following strict safety protocols. In-water snorkel encounters occur in shallow water near the palafitos, on sandy patches near seagrass beds, where guides use simple, wooden sticks to help maintain a safe distance between man and beast. Though, when you're standing on a weedy seabed, face-to-face with a prehistoric predator, a broomstick doesn't offer much reassurance.

Encounters with Chinchorro's crocs are conducted with a solid understanding of the reptiles' behaviour. The younger crocodiles can be skittish and unpredictable, while the older, larger ones (up to 4.5m/15ft) display a calmness that belies their fearsome appearance. The key is constant vigilance and respect for the animal's space, while your wrangler uses the wooden stick not as a weapon, but as a tool of communication and boundary. The clear water setting, which allows you to maintain eye contact with the croc, is also crucial. Groups of six rotate in and out of the water, with a limit of two snorkellers in the sea at a time, together with a wrangler and two 'spotters' standing close by to keep an eye on crocs coming in and out of the area. To date, there have been no recorded incidents of croc bites during these tours, but with that said, it is a relatively new tour offering.

If skindiving with dinosaurs isn't your thing, there's some fantastic reef diving around the atoll, with over 30 mapped sites in about 10–35m (32–115ft) of depth. These calm drift dives and wall dives are suitable for divers of all levels of experience. A favourite attraction for divers is the local population of nurse sharks, or 'Gatas' in Spanish. It's a nice feeling when one remains with you for your whole dive, which happens at a few of Banco's dive sites including the eponymously named site 'Gata'.

The corals and sponges on Banco Chinchorro are healthy and colourful and within them marine life abounds, thanks to the region being protected since 1996. Imagine giant brain corals and huge barrel sponges, black corals, elkhorns, sea fans and whips.

And then there's the 'ships graveyard' on the eastern part of the atoll, with shipwrecks that date back to the 16th century, now overgrown by corals.

Access to Banco Chinchorro is via a 1.5–2.5-hour boat ride (depending on sea conditions) from Mahahual, or from the small village of Xcalak, 12km (7mi) from the border with Belize. Dive trips don't go out every day; they are very much dependent on the weather and having a group of people. For croc diving, find out more at xtcdivecenter.com.

Opposite The wild sight of an American crocodile underwater
Below A cameraman gets up-close with an American crocodile

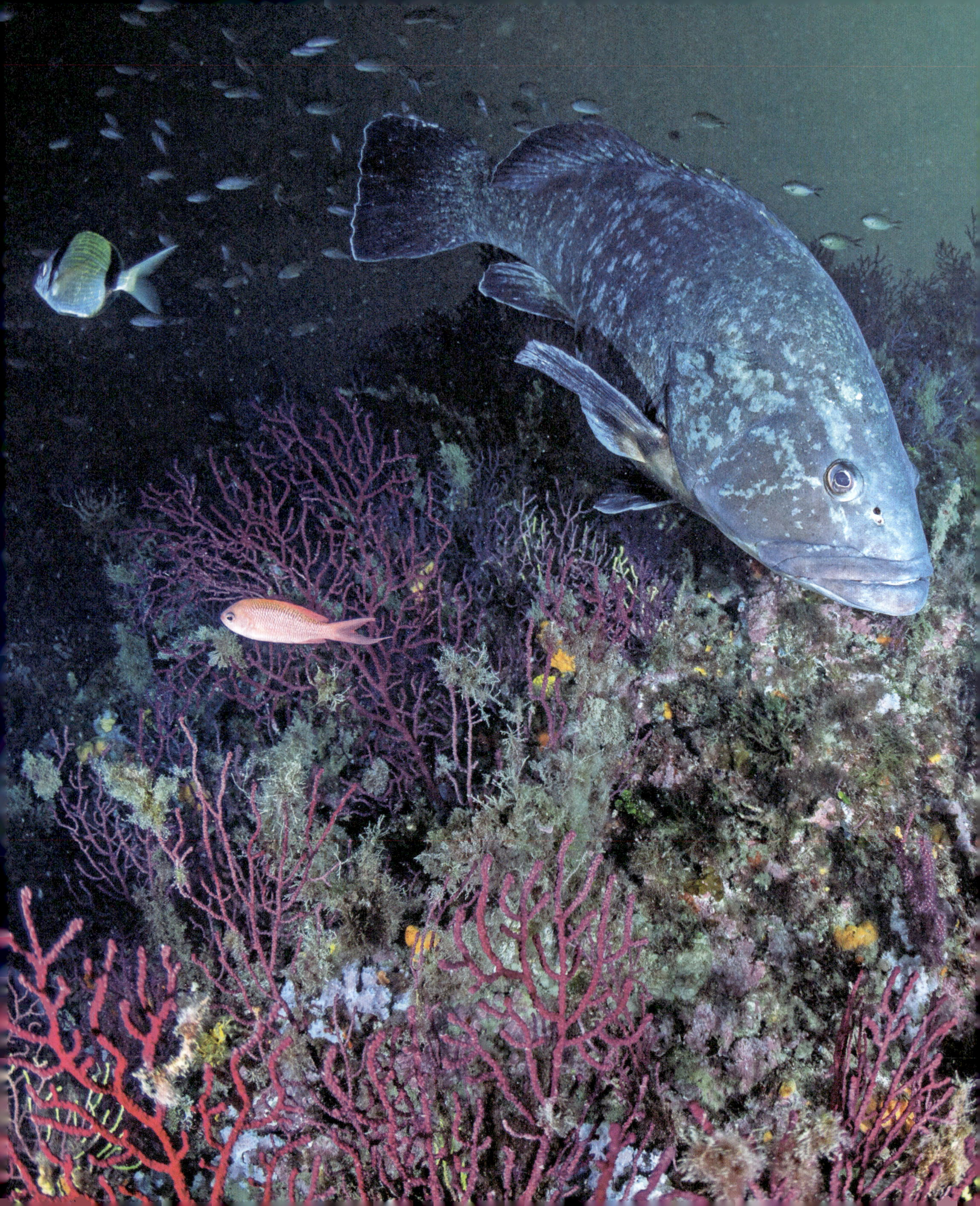

Europe and United Kingdom

1. Northern Norway (Arctic Circle) 104
2. The White Sea, Russia 111
3. Silfra Fissure, Iceland 115
4. Medes Islands, Spain 119
5. The Hebrides, Scotland 123
6. Scapa Flow, Scotland 127
7. Lundy, Devon, England 130

Northern Norway (Arctic Circle)
Freedive with orcas as they hunt for herring in the Arctic Circle

Why it's special

A close encounter with a pod of wild orcas is a dream for many divers. As the ocean's apex predator, orcas are equally as graceful as they are powerful. While efficient at hunting prey, their 'killer whale' misnomer has made them widely feared, yet there's never been a recorded attack on a human in the wild. Like their dolphin cousins, orcas travel in pods, but unlike dolphins, a male orca can weigh over six tonnes. Although globally distributed, orcas are rarely encountered; you could spend a lifetime underwater and never see one. One of the most reliable places for an encounter is the Arctic Circle, in northern Norway, during the herring run. If you can handle sub-zero temperatures and lots of breath holding to share a few fleeting moments with an orca, then you'll be rewarded with one of the greatest experiences of your life.

Best time to dive

From November to January, orcas can be found hunting the frigid waters of Tromsø, in northern Norway, for spring-spawning herring. Orcas follow the migrating herring into the fjords and, in a perfect scenario, they separate smaller patches of herring from the larger shoals and force them to the surface. November and mid-January are best, as there's still sunlight in northern Norway. In the last week of November, the Polar Night Season sets in until mid-January, and the days turn to 24 hours of darkness.

Opposite The incredible lights and tones of the Arctic Circle *Previous* Dusky grouper, Medes Islands, Spain

Gear
- 8mm wetsuit with a hood
- 8mm wetsuit gloves
- 8mm neoprene hood (if your wetsuit doesn't have one attached) with a neck and face seal
- Socks
- Freediving equipment; mask, fins and weight belt

Sub-zero winds are not pleasant after diving, so bring a heavy duty coat and gloves for your time on the tender.

Photography tip
Pack a wide-angle lens and a camera that operates well with minimal light

When diving in freezing temperatures, you'll need to adapt your equipment for operation with thick gloves and ensure your camera housing can handle the freezing temperatures. Personally, I wear thinner 5mm gloves which give me a better feel for my camera's settings, however, they leave me with frozen hands that don't work properly for days

Qualification
- Due to the sporadic and fast-paced nature of orca/herring feeding frenzies, freediving is best
- Previous cold water diving experience is recommended. Not only can the conditions be extremely hard on the body, but with the added neoprene and dive weights divers can overexert themselves rather quickly

Getting there
Tromsø is a great launching pad for your Arctic adventure and is a one-hour flight from Oslo. Look for a curated experience with an experienced operator that ticks all the boxes in terms of ethical practices.

Northern Norway (Arctic Circle)

Europe and United Kingdom

Dive in

For as long as I can remember, I've dreamed of diving with Orcas. So around ten years ago, when a good friend regaled his recent experience of diving with them, I excitedly interrogated him for more information; how, when and most importantly, where?

Northern Norway is not your typical diving destination and, until my friend told me about it, I'd never considered diving there. In this part of the world, you won't find any palm trees or coral cays, in fact, it's quite the opposite. This is a landscape carved by deep fjords and towering mountains, where Arctic blizzards can deposit metres of snow overnight and comfort levels are stretched. In the six times that I've returned to Norway for this experience, there have been many mornings where we've spent hours shovelling fresh snow out of our dive boat before we could even leave port. With that said, if you can handle the stinging winds and frigid waters of the Arctic Circle, then you may just come face-to-face with a pod of orcas. And if you're fast enough on the shutter, perhaps you'll even snap some photos as they race by, often in the blink of an eye, on their herring hunt.

Orcas can travel at speeds of up 45km/hr (28mi/hr), so there's no time to assemble clunky scuba gear. On this adventure, freediving is the name of the game, and it's ultimately the orcas that control the encounter. If they do draw close, your encounter will likely be brief. This is undoubtedly an experience for the dedicated diver, especially for those who (like myself) have had a lifelong interest in orcas.

To many non-divers, the term 'killer whale' is more familiar than orca, though it misleads. Many moons ago, they were nicknamed 'asesina ballenas' by Spanish sailors who saw them hunting whales. This translates to 'whale killer'. While some orcas do indeed hunt whales, their diets vary with seals, dolphins, fish, rays and even seabirds on the menu. For North Atlantic orcas, shoals of herring are an important staple of their diet. They've even developed an interesting hunting technique whereby they round up the herring into a ball and then slap their tails, stunning the fish. This is called carousel feeding.

Orcas are smart and their behaviour is fascinating to observe underwater. Each pod has a complex social order, with the oldest females running the show (female orcas can live to 90). These females control the hierarchy of the pod and the security of the young, who remain a part of their mother's pod for their entire lives. The large male (bull) orcas tend to work the pod's perimeters with an investigative nature while protecting the females. I vividly remember a time that I came face-to-face with a bull orca. Carefully sliding into the water, I'd hoped to observe a feeding pod from a distance. Immediately, the bull broke away from the pod and approached me head-on. He was about six metres (20ft) long with a dorsal fin towering at around 1.5m (5ft). His beauty and inquisitive nature had me mesmerised.

Underwater, sound travels four times faster than through air, and orcas rely heavily on sound, especially while hunting. Once you've held your breath and dived under, you'll know that orcas are nearby when you hear their clicks and whistles. It's likely that they'll know you're there well before you can see them. Like bats, orcas make high-pitched noises, and then wait for an echo in order to assess how close something is. Personally, the sound of orcas communicating underwater is one of the loveliest sounds I've ever heard (and felt).

While the excitement of diving with orcas, combined with the fairytale landscape of the Arctic sounds like a dream, the reality is that this experience is one best suited to seasoned divers. Picture this; sub-zero wind chill, freezing water, choppy seas, limited sunlight, and to top it off, the possibility that you won't see any orcas. But the challenge is worth it. Not only are orcas the apex of the ocean, but diving with them in the Arctic is, in many ways, the apex of all underwater experiences.

Opposite top Orcas work together and attack a bait ball of herring *Opposite bottom* Legendary freediver Didrik Hurum gets ready to dive into the orca action

Photography

'Capturing that killer shot'

Underwater photographers: this may just be your most challenging shoot yet. Around November in northern Norway, the sun begins its descent below the horizon for winter, heralding the start of the polar nights. The availability of light, or rather 'the absolute lack of light' means you'll be shooting in the dark or, at best, with a small window of sunlight. 'Freezing' and 'dark' are certainly not ideal conditions for an underwater photographer. Patience and perseverance are essential; I didn't see any orcas on my first visit to Norway, and it took six consecutive return trips to capture the photos that I wanted. Whether you see orcas or not, this part of the world is alluring and adding to that allure is the northern lights. From September to March, the green, red and violet 'aurora borealis' flicker and dance across the dark sky. After a big day on the water, it's a real treat to rug up with a hot drink and look skyward for one of the planet's most glorious natural wonders. So, grab that same wide-angle lens that you've used all day to photograph orcas, place it on your tripod, set a long shutter speed and, just like the orcas, patiently wait for the magic to happen.

A fleeting moment in time. Capturing this photo changed my life in ways I never could have imagined

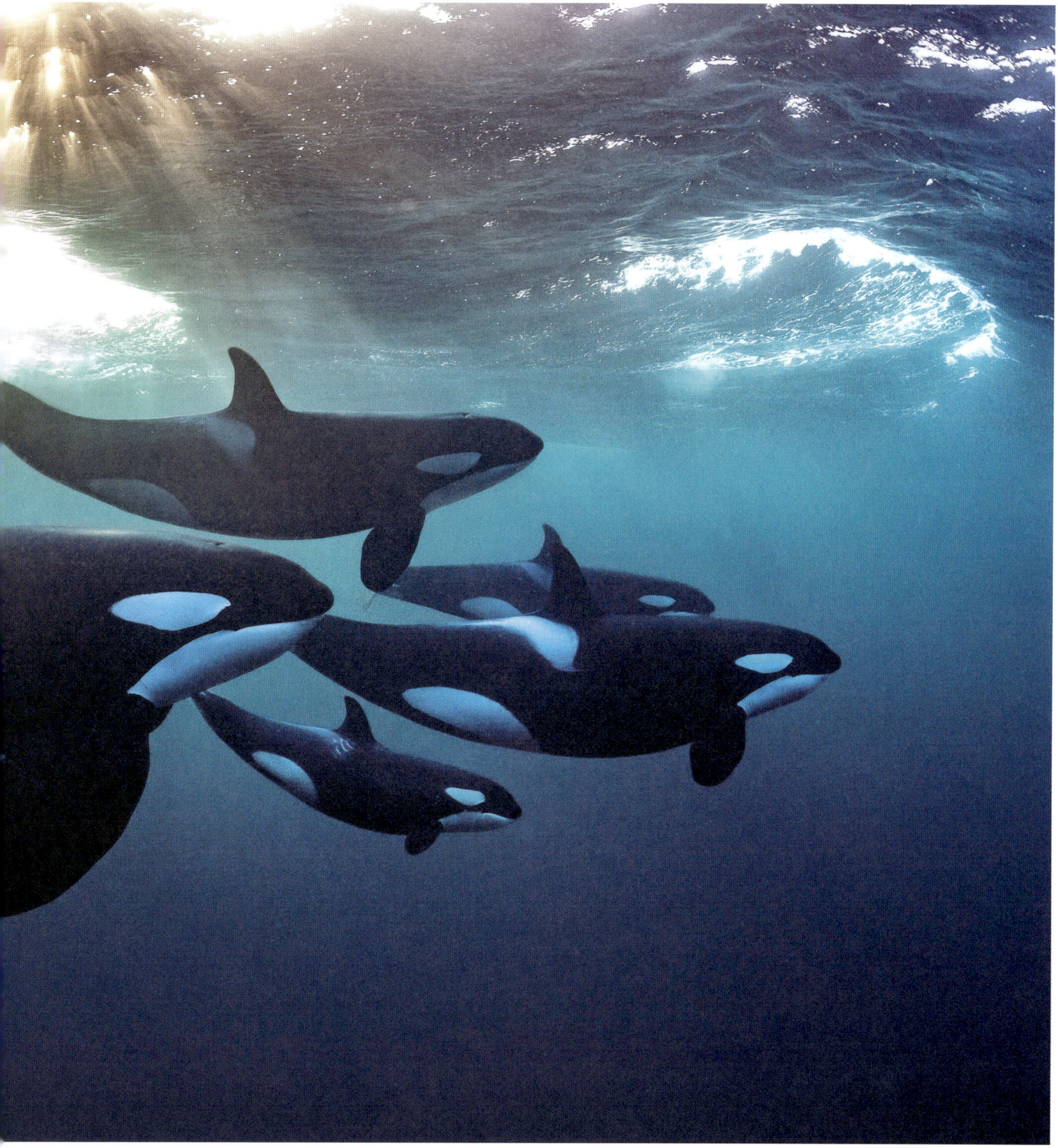

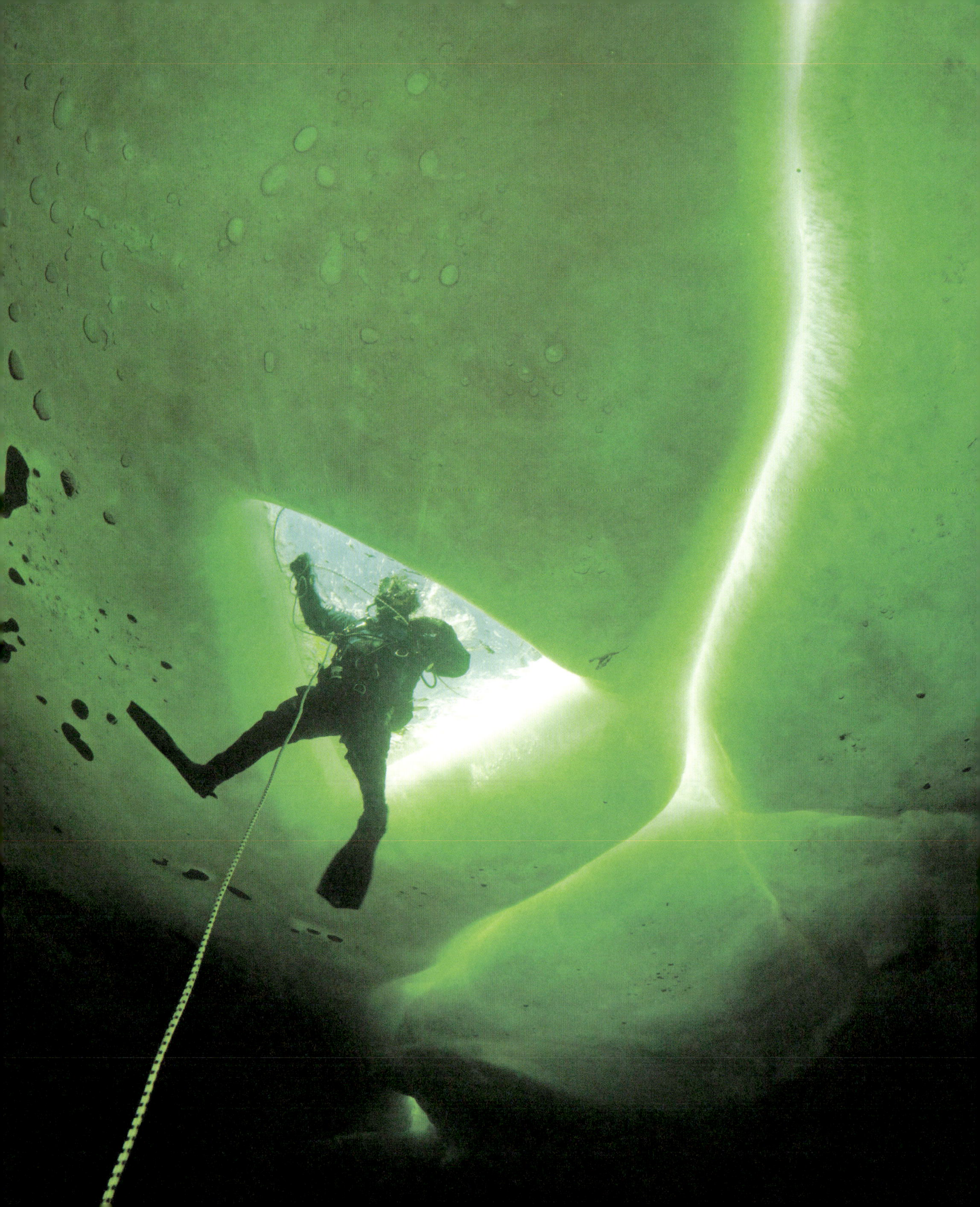

The White Sea, Russia
Float with angels and ghosts in the remote Russian wilderness

Why it's special
In the remote, north-western part of Russia, the White Sea is a world away from any tropical dive holiday you've ever taken. Forget palm trees and 30°C (86 °F), these waters are −2°C (28°F) and black, not blue. This expedition is as much about the topside experience as the world below, travelling overland through an icy wilderness, sweating inside sled-pulled saunas, sawing holes in the ice, and being mind-numbingly cold. Underwater, the dive environment is characterised by cold water sponges and anemones, intricate ice formations, and perhaps a chance encounter with a beluga or sea angel. Dive times are limited to how long your body can handle being underwater, which is usually about half an hour. This is one of the most mentally and physically challenging dives you'll ever do. For this reason, it'll also be one of the most memorable.

Best time to dive
The prime season for ice diving in the White Sea is during the middle of winter, typically from mid-February to mid-April. During this period, the ice is sufficiently thick and stable enough to get to the best dive sites. Earlier in the season (February) is colder and darker, whereas April brings more sunlight and slightly warmer (or, shall I say, less freezing) temperatures, but more challenges due to melting ice.

Gear
- A drysuit and accompanying woolly undergarments
- Specialised 7mm dive mittens
- 9mm neoprene hood, at least
- A regulator specifically designed for extremely cold temperatures
- A reliable dive computer that can handle the freezing elements
- A powerful underwater light to navigate the dark waters

Photography tip
Given the unique nature of these dives, cameras with low-light capabilities that can also handle freezing temperatures are essential.

Remember, make the most of the available ambient light and get close to your subject. Strobes are essential. With the high density of particles in the water, ensure you have your strobes positioned correctly to avoid backscatter. Lastly, keep an eye on your batteries, as their life will be significantly reduced in these freezing temperatures.

Qualification
- Advanced Open Water Diver
- Drysuit Certification
- Ice diving certification (this can be taken during your stay at the Arctic Dive Centre)

The ability and fitness to handle extreme cold and navigate under ice is crucial. Previous cold water diving experience is essential.

Divers should also be comfortable with the potential for limited visibility and the need for precise buoyancy control.

Getting there
The Arctic Circle Dive Center provides road transfers from Kuusamo or Murmansk airports and from Chupa railway station to their base at Nilmoguba Village.

Opposite Following a rope back up to the maina (sawed entry hole) in the White Sea, northern Russia

Dive in

In the city of Murmansk in north-western Russia, where sunlight disappears for six weeks each year and air temperatures can drop to –30°C (–22°F), members of the Walrus Club continue a long-held tradition of swimming year-round. Even in the middle of winter, when the water is sub-zero, the Walruses take the plunge for 'health, strength and self-respect'. As the old Russian proverb goes, 'Everyone is young in the winter cold.' With that in mind, this next dive offers both a challenge and an adventure, but above all, it'll leave you feeling years younger.

A six-hour drive south of Murmansk is the little village of Nilmoguba, on the mouth of the Nilmo River. This village serves as a gateway to Russia's White Sea. Located within the Arctic Basin, the White Sea is the only sea in Europe that freezes every year. In recent decades a small trickle of hardcore divers has started travelling here to experience what is arguably the world's best sea ice diving. In this remote and frozen land, there's absolutely no escaping the cold (ok, except for inside the little heated huts – more about that soon). So, to really enjoy this dive you need to embrace the cold and choose the right local guides, as your life is in their hands.

The adventure begins with your journey to Nilmoguba village, where the local train station is called 'Polar Circle'. After checking in to the Arctic Circle Dive Centre (ice-diving.com) you'll load everything shovels, saws, ropes and dive gear, onto sledges. Your guides will lead the way with snow mobiles towing small, hand-built cabins across the ice floe to your dive site. These heated wooden huts serve as a mobile dive camp, providing a warm place to prepare for dives and to thaw out afterward.

After choosing a dive site based on tides, currents and the strength of the ice platform, your dive master will cut a 'maina' into the ice. 'Maina' is one of nine Russian words for 'hole in the ice'. Tethered to your tender (dive guide), you'll enter the icy underworld, maintaining constant contact via a 20m-(66ft-) long rope. At first, the –2°C (28°F) water will hit you like a brick to the face. This is the coldest that saltwater can get before it turns to ice; expect that your fingers and face will go painfully numb. Unlike the bare-skinned Walrus Club members, you'll be wearing a drysuit which will keep your extremities warm, so long as there's no leaks in your suit!

Beneath the ice, the visibility can range from as little as four metres (13ft), up to several tens of metres. The marine life is surprising with about 720 species of flora and fauna: anemones, sponges, and algae existing alongside sea stars, sea urchins, and vivid colonies of soft corals. If you're lucky, you may even spot a sea angel; a tiny, mostly transparent slug with wing-like appendages. Growing no bigger than five centimetres (2in), these shell-less sea snails have a striking shape and are a macro photographers' dream subject. Though you're mostly diving in darkness, overhead it's ever changing as sunlight pierces through the ice's natural sculptures. The scene above is bathed in a surreal glow of emerald green, its hues shifting with the snow's blanket atop the ice. If you're lucky, you may even see a similar iridescent green in the sky later on if the auroras show up.

Another sight that you could be lucky enough to see is a beluga. With distinctive ghost-white skin and bulbous foreheads known as 'melons,' belugas are highly sociable and curious creatures, often approaching divers and sometimes mimicking divers' movements. Their communication involves varied vocalisations of chirps, whistles and clicks, earning them the nickname 'canaries of the sea.'

Emerging from the water, frozen to the core and burdened by the weight of excessive diving gear, your mind will wander to the thought of the banya (Russian sauna) and how fast you can get inside. Like ice swimming, banyas have been around for centuries and they're also credited to good health and wellbeing. There's no doubt that a dive trip to Russia's White Sea is about as wild as any dive adventure could be! So, the only question now is, 'are you brave enough to take the polar plunge?'

Opposite Belugas are highly sociable creatures

The White Sea, Russia 113

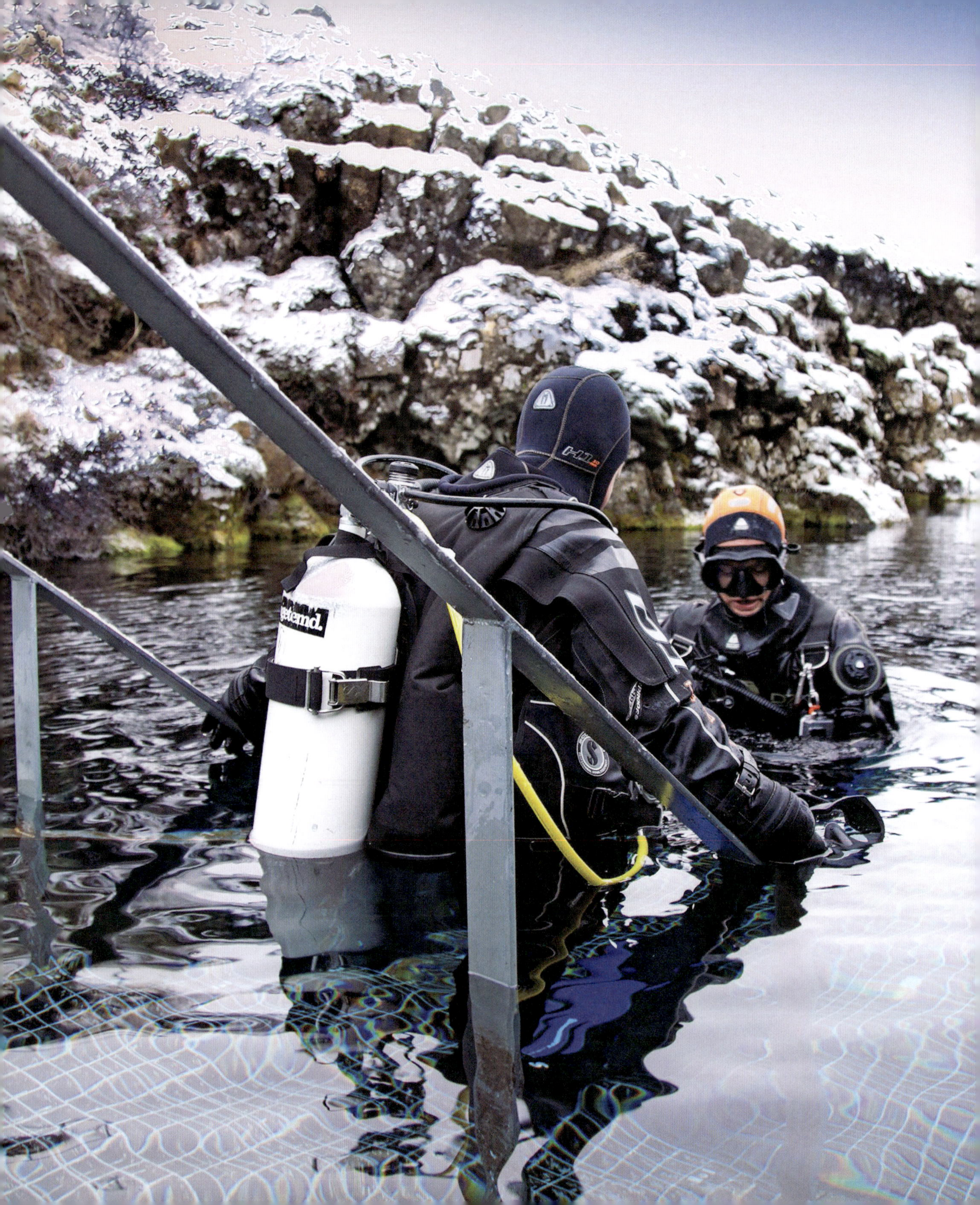

Silfra Fissure, Iceland
Feel the squeeze of two continents at once and chill in the clearest water you'll ever see.

Why it's special

Silfra Fissure lures divers with unparalleled visibility and the thrill of diving between continents – Iceland is the only place in the world where you can do so. Two tectonic plates slowly drifting apart, create a narrow chasm that gets spring fed with pristine glacial water. Here, a gentle current pushes divers and snorkellers through the narrow Silfra Crack, providing a sense of weightlessness. The breathtaking water (literally), comes from Langjökull glacier 60km (37mi) away, maintaining an icy temperature of 2°C to 4°C (35–39°F) year-round. The fissure's extraordinary visibility and geological landscape creates an overwhelming sensory experience for divers.

Best time to dive

Silfra Fissure is accessible year-round, offering a distinctly different experience in each season. Summer (June to August) sees longer daylight hours and milder temperatures, while winter (December to February) transforms the landscape into a winter wonderland with the possibility of witnessing the Northern Lights as the sun sets (days are much shorter in winter). Crowds thin out during winter, too. Diving during the shoulder seasons of spring and autumn offers favourable conditions without extreme weather challenges.

Gear
- A drysuit is essential to keep warm in the frigid waters
- 7mm drysuit gloves or, if possible, specialised dry gloves
- 7mm neoprene hood, at least

It's highly likely your Icelandic dive operator will have the best and warmest gear for you to hire for your Silfra dive. Check with them prior to travel.

Photography tip
With unlimited visibility, Silfra Fissure is incredibly grand in stature. Shoot wide, without strobes. Add a diver for scale without scale, there's no grandeur.

Qualification
- Open Water Diver
- Drysuit Certification or have proof of 10 logged drysuit dives

Due to extremely cold water temperatures, completing a drysuit certification is mandatory. Divers should have good buoyancy control and be well prepared both mentally and physically for the full force of the cold.

Getting there
After flying into Reykjavík, it's a one-hour drive along the Golden Circle driving route to Thingvellir National Park, home of Silfra Fissure.

Opposite There's a platform at the beginning of your dive, providing an easy entry and a final opportunity to check over your gear prior to submerging

Dive in

Is Silfra Fissure all that it's cracked up to be? Though you'll find it on many 'must do' dive lists, the truth is, the dive site itself is small and for those who love seeing marine animals, well, within this fissure fish are noticeably absent! So, why do so many divers submerge into this freezing crack each year? Quite simply, because Iceland is the only place on the planet where you can dive between two continents. And for underwater photographers, conditions don't get much better.

Silfra Fissure owes its existence to the diverging North American and Eurasian tectonic plates. The rift, constantly widening at an average rate of two centimetres (1in) per year, forms the Silfra Crack a mesmerizing underwater corridor filled with clear, glacial water. Silfra, meaning 'silvery', was formed in 1789 when a major earthquake opened the fissure and water from Langjökull glacier filled the gap, continuing to do so today. Apart from the novelty of diving between tectonic plates, Silfra's drawcard is its incredible visibility, reaching up to 100m (328ft), a photographer's dream (if your fingers aren't too numb to push the trigger). This visibility also makes Silfra a popular site for snorkelers. The water's clarity is thanks to natural filtration through porous volcanic rocks during its underground journey from Langjökull glacier. This process, which can take up to 100 years, creates what's believed to be the clearest water in the world.

Descending into Silfra, you're met with moss-covered lava fields, ancient algae formations (including the bright green 'troll hair' algae), and underwater flora in vivid hues, all combining to create a visually stunning landscape. Though fish are noticeably absent, if you're very lucky, you may just encounter the elusive Arctic char, a cold-water fish species adapted to Silfra's conditions.

The Silfra dive site is quite small – about 600 x 200m (1970 x 660ft) in total – but is divided into four distinct sections, beginning at Silfra Big Crack with a platform where you enter the water. Next, you move into the 200m (660ft) section that is Silfra Hall, where you'll navigate rocks and boulders before reaching the 100m-(328ft-) long Silfra Cathedral. Here, a gentle current guides you through a natural corridor, providing an intimate encounter with the geological forces shaping the Earth. Finally, you'll reach Silfra Lagoon where the visibility may allow you to see right across the 120m (394ft) lagoon to the exit point of your dive. Average depths are around 7–12m (23–39ft) with 18m (59ft) being the maximum that you're allowed to descend to.

Preserving the pristine conditions of Silfra Fissure is a collective responsibility and dive operators adhere to strict environmental guidelines to minimize impact. This includes a ban on the use of gloves to prevent potential damage to the delicate moss and algae covering the rocks. A requirement for this dive is to be drysuit certified. If you're not familiar with diving in a drysuit, it can be a unique feeling and challenging to get used to. Getting your buoyancy right is tricky. But don't stress, Silfra is an ideal and forgiving environment to learn drysuit diving.

Note that Silfra can be very busy mid-season; for a less crowded option, check out Nesgjá in northern Iceland. While it's a smaller (and shallower) dive site than Silfra, it offers the same experience of diving between tectonic plates in clear glacial water.

While the underwater wonders of Silfra are incredible, the surrounding topside landscape adds another layer of magic to the experience. Silfra Fissure is situated within the UNESCO World Heritage Thingvellir National Park and there are some amazing hikes to do including one that leads to the well-known Öxarárfoss Waterfall. Depending on the time of year, you might also see the Northern Lights dancing across the Arctic sky. The combination of the celestial display above and the subaquatic marvels below creates a truly transcendent experience.

Silfra is a fissure; part of the diverging tectonic boundary between the North American and Eurasian plates

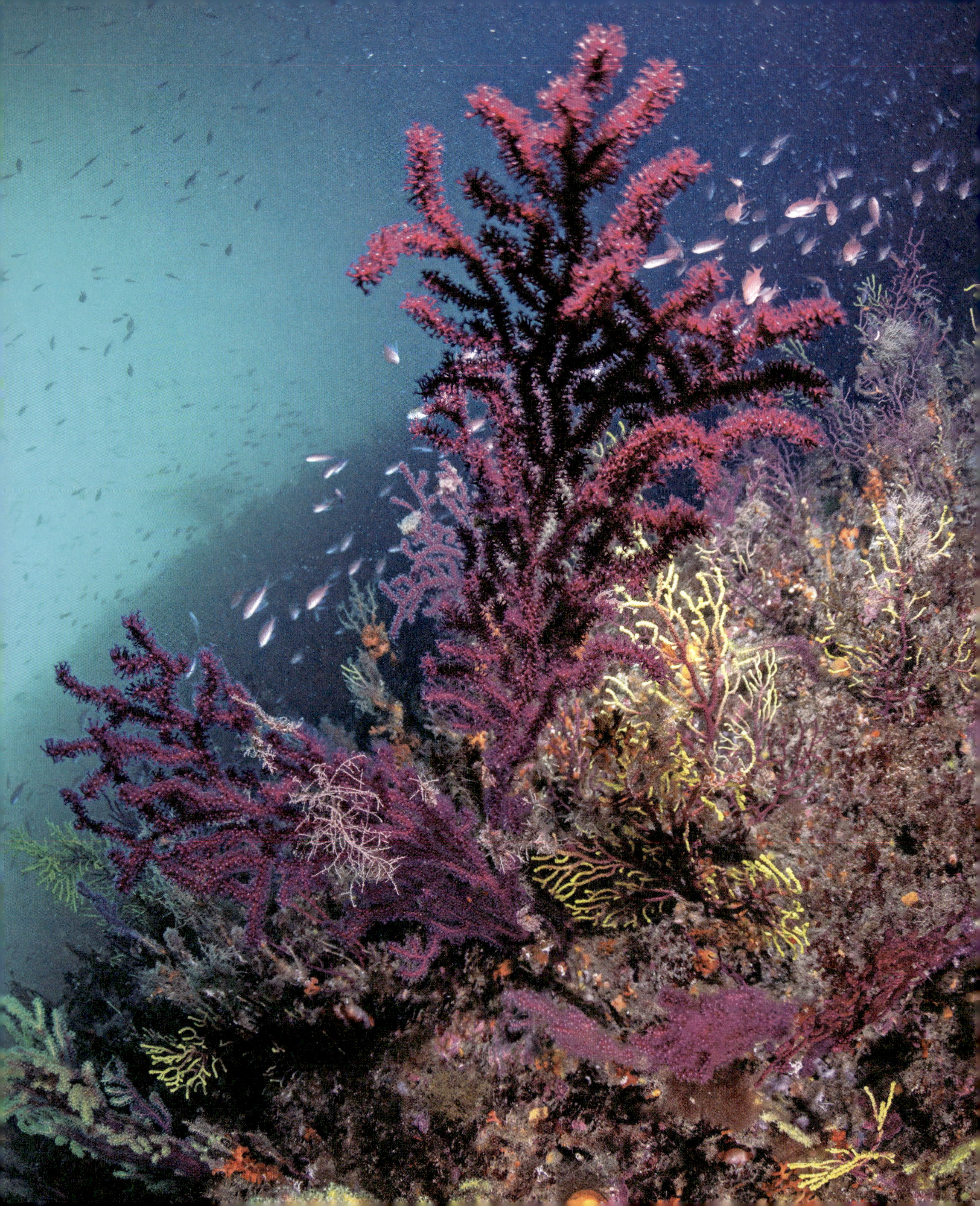

Medes Islands, Spain

This former pirates' playground is now one of the Mediterranean's most flourishing marine reserves

Why it's special

Protected as a marine reserve since 1983, the Medes Islands (Illes Medes in Catalan) are a conservation success and one of the best spots to dive in the Mediterranean. Less than two hours' drive from Barcelona, it's a favourite weekend getaway for Catalonians. Within the waters of this seven-island archipelago are vibrant corals and sponges in hues of purple, yellow and orange. The convergence of warm and cold currents at this geographical crossroad enriches the water with nutrients, creating a haven for marine life and fostering an underwater ecosystem that is both robust and delicate. This exceptional environment, from shallow gardens to deep caves, combined with the archipelago's varied dive sites makes the Medes Islands a premier destination for divers seeking a quintessential Mediterranean diving experience.

Best time to dive

While you can dive here year-round, the warmest conditions are from June to October, when water temperatures can rise to a pleasant 24°C (75°F). Visibility also peaks during these months, often reaching 30m (98ft). The cooler winter months bring the chance to see different species, though water temperatures drop to around 14°C (57°F). Diving outside the peak summer months means fewer boats and a better experience within the reserve.

Gear
- A 5mm wetsuit is a pretty safe bet, unless diving in the middle of winter when thicker neoprene is needed
- A dive light is a needed to illuminate the crevices and caves, and to see the true colours of the corals and sponges

Photography tip
A wide-angle zoom is perfect for framing the seascape of Islas Medes. Strobes are also essential.

Qualification
- Open Water

Islas Medes caters to all levels of divers, with shallower sites perfect for beginners and more complex cave and tunnel dives for more advanced divers.

Getting there
From Barcelona, drive two hours to the town of L'Estartit, where the Medes Islands lie just 1km (0.6mi) from the shores of the Costa Brava.

Opposite With a variety of dive sites, the Medes Islands are suitable for all levels of divers, including beginners

Dive in

Located just a kilometre off Spain's Catalonian coast in the world-renowned Costa Brava region, Illes Medes is a collection of seven small islands hosting a variety of dive sites, from shallow seagrass meadows to dramatic, plunging walls. Once ravaged by fishing, the waters of this marine reserve have rebounded, now teeming with life and drawing divers from around Europe.

The aquatic environment here is a testament to nature's resilience. Since becoming a marine reserve in 1983, the islands now serve as a crucial breeding ground for many Mediterranean species. Within the labyrinth of tunnels, caves, chimneys and arches exists a diverse array of marine flora and fauna including red coral (this is one of the only spots you'll find it in the Med), dusky groupers, octopuses, and moray eels. Above the rocky outcrops, dense schools of salema porgy create a living curtain, while barracuda spiral overhead in a silvery dance. The reserve's strict protection has allowed the ecosystem to flourish, with each dive offering encounters with denser shoals of fish, larger pelagic species, and lush meadows of posidonia herb (Posidonia oceanica) which are critical for marine biodiversity.

The islands are not just a refuge for sea life, but a crossroads for migratory paths. It's not uncommon to encounter eagle rays gliding gracefully through the water or to be startled by the sudden appearance of a sunfish (mola mola), its large, flat body an oddity amongst other sleeker-shaped fish.

With some great shallow water diving, this is a suitable spot for divers of all levels including beginners. Probably most well-known (and a favourite for photographers), the dive of El Dofi (Catalan for dolphin) on Meda Petita has a system of tunnels cutting 70m (230ft) through one side of the island to the other, with depths ranging from 5–27m (16–88ft). Famously marked with a dolphin statue at the entrance of the cave at 12m deep, common sights on this dive include groupers, gorgonians, red corals and bream. Another well-loved (aka busy) site is La Vaca on Mede Grande, where you're greeted by colourful gorgonians at the entrance of a light-filled cave and plenty of big groupers further in. There are various tunnels leading off the main cave, with walls and pillars to be explored, and depths ranging from 11–25m (36–82ft).

As you fin through the clear waters of the Medes Islands, the history of this archipelago as a base for pirates and privateers seems almost palpable. Between the 15th and 18th centuries, pirates conducted raids on the nearby coast, retreating back to the islands with their spoils. Once feared, today they are celebrated with a festival every September in the town of L'Estartit. These days, the islands themselves (which have remained uninhabited since 1934) are off limits and only accessible by boat. (I once swam to the islands in the region's annual ocean race, which was an amazing experience.)

Above the waves, the Medes reflect the charm of the Costa Brava, with rugged cliffs and hidden coves that have inspired artists and adventurers alike (Salvador Dali once resided in neighbouring Cadaqués). The local culture is deeply connected to the sea, with some fishing villages now turning to diving, yet still retaining their traditional character. Diving in the Medes Islands is as much about embracing the local way of life as it is about the underwater exploration—a dive here is a dive into the heart of Catalan maritime heritage. I dived the Medes for many years while I lived in Barcelona, as it was a convenient two hour-drive away. Not only is it some of the best temperate diving in the Mediterranean but diving in Catalonia is a lifestyle, where the act of diving with friends is followed by a very typical and very long Mediterranean lunch. After all, what's a great dive, if it can't be followed by a hearty meal with friends?

Opposite top Vibrant corals and sponges. *Opposite bottom* A Dusky grouper hides in the reef of Medes Island

Medes Islands, Spain

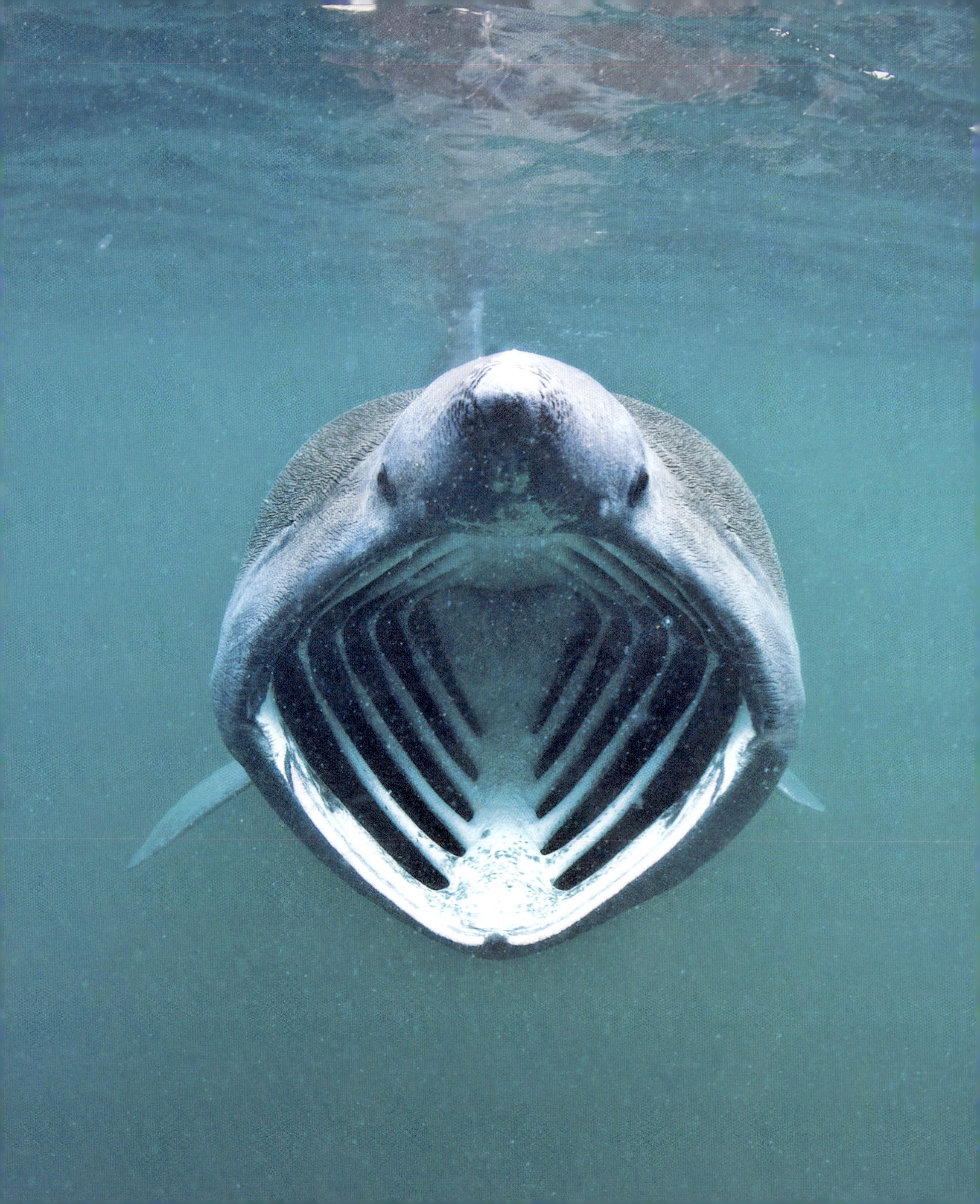

The Hebrides, Scotland
Dive with creatures so elusive and strange looking, they're almost mythical

Why it's special
Each spring in Scotland's remote Inner Hebrides, when the water warms and the plankton blooms, basking sharks arrive to feed and breed. Weather dependent, snorkelers can swim alongside this giant shark, which is rarely seen and widely misunderstood. Even the word 'basking' is misleading, since it spends most of its time deep underwater; perhaps its Italian name, 'squalo elefante' (elephant shark) is more fitting. With their elephant-like skin texture, triangular dorsal fin and gaping mouths, they are not the prettiest sharks in the sea, but they're certainly one of the most iconic. This is a unique opportunity to encounter an animal that most folks will never see, in the sea of the scenic Hebrides.

Best time to dive
From May to October (the northern hemisphere's summer) plankton concentrations peak, drawing basking sharks in search of a seasonal feast. The months of June and July offer the best opportunity, when the weather is most favourable, daylight hours longer and temperatures relatively mild.

Gear
- 7mm wetsuit
- Gloves
- A hood
- Boots
- Freediving equipment; mask, fins and weight belt

Photography tip
A wide-angle lens with a camera that performs well in low light.

Flash photography of basking sharks is not permitted.

Qualification
As most encounters take place on the surface while the sharks are surface feeding, snorkelling gear is best and there's no need for any dive certifications.

Getting there
The drive from Glasgow to Oban takes about three hours. It's worth taking the scenic route past the famous 'Rest and be thankful' viewpoint. You can also travel by train with ScotRail.

Opposite Basking sharks filter large volumes of water, extracting microscopic plankton

Dive in

Watching a giant shark swim towards you with its mouth open wouldn't normally seem an idylllic situation, but for divers visiting Scotland's Hebrides Islands, this is exactly what they've come to see. Well, also the seals, dolphins and whales. But the basking sharks are the headline act in this underwater show, so much so that Scotland has created a Marine Protected Area (MPA) for them here in the Sea of the Hebrides, the world's only sanctuary for basking sharks.

In a country that's famous for Kelpies and Selkies and the monster of Loch Ness, and whose national animal is the unicorn, the outrageous silhouette of the basking shark almost adds it into the realm of Scotland's mythical creatures. With its big, sharky form and a gaping mouth decorated with gill rakers, the ocean's second biggest fish is uniquely identifiable. This fantastic beast, which can grow up to 11m long and weigh over four tonnes, spends 90% of its time at depth, making surface sightings almost as rare as spotting Nessie. But each year, during spring and summer in the northern Atlantic, they can reliably be encountered in the remote Inner Hebridean isles, where they come to feed and breed.

Despite their size, basking sharks (or, as they're called in Scots Gaelic, cearbans) are gentle giants. Peacefully navigating the coastal currents with their mouths agape, they filter large volumes of water, extracting microscopic plankton that thrive in these temperate waters. They are one of only three shark species that eats plankton; whale sharks and megamouths are the other two. As is the case with many shark species, they've been overhunted and their slow rate of reproduction doesn't help their survival as a species. The oil from their liver, which keeps them buoyant and constitutes almost a third of their body weight, was once used as fuel for Victorian lamps and their huge fins have also made them a target for the shark fin soup trade. Nowadays, their biggest threats are ship strikes or getting caught in trawls or gillnets.

Despite their docile demeanour, basking sharks can swim pretty quickly and they can breach – as one did back in 1937, resulting in history's only recorded human/basking shark fatalities. A group were fishing on a small boat when a basking shark breached, capsizing the boat and drowning three passengers. Generally, they will steer away from big things in the water, so your best bet for a close encounter is to remain as still as possible when you spot one approaching.

Basking Shark Scotland offers daytrips and multiday trips, based from the wee town of Oban. Due to shark sightings being so close to the surface, snorkelling and freediving are offered instead of SCUBA, which is also the case with seal swims. Basking sharks can be hard to spot and on some days, you may luck out. On others, the seas may be too rough to head out onto the water. So, for your best chance of seeing one, book a multiday tour (baskingsharkscotland.co.uk).

Creatures of the imaginarium
The race to discover 100,000 sea creatures

To see basking sharks in such shallow waters is a real privilege. These deep-diving sharks can descend to depths of up to 2000m (6500ft), well beyond the sun's rays and into a realm of other-worldly creatures. We know so little about the ocean's occupants; to put a number on it, scientists believe we've only identified about 10% of all the creatures in the sea. There's layer upon layer of biodiversity existing in the darkness, and it's under increasing threats such as overfishing, global warming and deep-sea mining. At the heart of the issue is this – we can't save something if we don't know it exists. The ocean's health is vital to all life on Earth, from the air we breathe to the food we eat. This is where the Ocean Census comes in. In 2023, a group of global partners banded together with an ambitious mission to discover 100,000 new species in the sea. While new discoveries have averaged around 2000 a year since the 1800s, new technologies such as AI and digital imaging is facilitating a speedier approach to finding and describing species (oceancensus.org).

Opposite A basking shark gorging on plankton that's concentrated in surface waters

The Hebrides, Scotland

Europe and United Kingdom

Scapa Flow, Scotland
Vikings, selkies and shipwrecks in Scotland's northern isles

Why it's special

In the far north of Scotland, about 32km (20mi) from the mainland, lies the archipelago of Orkney. These wild, windswept isles are famous for Neolithic sites and abundant wildlife, including much-loved seabirds such as puffins. There's a rich history of Viking sagas and naval operations from the world wars. Of particular interest is Scapa Flow, a natural harbour that's seen its fair share of action over the years. On the radar of wreck divers are seven battle ships that were scuttled here during WWI, presenting an incredible underwater museum and artificial reef with an interesting story attached. Near the wrecks, on a skerry named the Barrel of Butter, there's a colony of seals that you can snorkel with between dives. So, grab your drysuit and pick up some peedie tatties (local cinnamon coated toffee treats), it's time to dive into the rich history of the Orkneys!

Best time to dive

Spring and summer (May to September) offer clearer visibility and relatively milder temperatures, averaging about 12°C (53°F) in the water. While in autumn and winter (October to April) water temperatures drop to about 7°C (44°F), diving is still possible with the appropriate thermal protection. There is very little winter diving with most dive boats not operating. Diving season is April to November.

Gear
- A drysuit is essential
- Gloves and hood
- Thick undergarments
- Warm clothing to wear on the surface between dives
- Torch and reliable dive computer

The boats all cater to both open circuit and technical dive gear setups, with both single and double tanks for hire as well as stage bottles although you need to take your own rigging for these. No other hire gear is available.

Photography tip
To capture great images of the haunting beauty of the wrecks, shoot wide and pack powerful strobes.

Qualification
- Advanced Open Water Diver
- Deep diver specialty
- Drysuit certification
- Wreck diver certification
- Solo Diver certification

Due to extremely cold water temperatures, completing a drysuit certification is mandatory.

Getting there
There are several options for reaching Stromness. Fly into Kirkwall and take a taxi to Stromness. Flights are available from Aberdeen, Glasgow, Inverness and Edinburgh. There is also Ferry from Scrabster to Stromness. For this option, fly to Inverness and hire a car to drive to Scrabster (two hours). Diving is usually done by 2pm so it's good to have a car to explore the islands attractions. There is also an overnight ferry from Aberdeen to Kirkwall.

Opposite A diver explores the eerie relics of Scapa flow

Dive in

At the end of WWI, with peace agreements underway, the German High Seas Fleet was chaperoned to Scapa Flow, a large, natural harbour in the Orkneys. While the fate of their 74 ships was being decided, the Rear Admiral Ludwig von Reuter begrudgingly pulled down the German flags, as instructed, and sent home 20,000 men, keeping just a caretaker crew. As discussions about what to do with the ships dragged on among the Allies, some wanting to keep a few ships for their own navies, the Rear Admiral decided to take matters into his own hands. His orders had been clear – if the fleet was ever seized by the Allies, he should scuttle the ships.

His chance arose on the morning of 21 June 1919 when the British left Scapa Flow for training exercises. The Rear Admiral and his men hastily swept around their ships, opening as many torpedo tubes, seacocks and portholes as they could so the water would rush in. And, in the process, he re-hoisted the German flags. This was to be a historical day, with the loss of 52 ships in five hours being the biggest shipping loss in a single day, and the final German military deaths of WWI. Nine German sailors died (and others were injured) during a brawl with the British after the Germans declined to help save the sinking ships.

After several salvage operations over the years, seven ships remain at Scapa Flow today, registered under the Ancient Monuments and Archaeological Areas Act of 1979. These four light cruisers and three giant battleships have become artificial reefs, decorated with marine life. With permits from the Island Harbour Authorities, divers can explore these underwater relics at depths ranging from 20–50m (66–164ft) and visibility ranging from two metres (7ft) to as high as 20m (66ft) on some days (if you're very lucky). The opportunity to explore a collection of large, historic wrecks in relatively shallow conditions makes the site at Scapa Flow one of Europe's best wreck diving destinations, if you can brave the freezing temperatures.

The name Scapa Flow comes from the Old Norse 'Skalpaflói', meaning 'bay of the long isthmus'. This isthmus has seen lots of activity throughout history, including during Viking times when longships would pull in for respite during their voyages. Its strategic location and vast harbour made it an important hub for maritime activities, travel, and trade. Out in the middle of Scapa Flow, a lighthouse sits atop a small rocky island with an intriguing name. Barrel of Butter was so-called for the historic practice of local seal-hunters paying the laird of the skerry one barrel of butter per annum for the right to hunt there. For Scotsmen that believe in local folklore, killing seals is considered bad luck, lest they kill a selkie – a magical, shapeshifting creature who could change between human and seal forms. With Barrel of Butter's proximity to the WWI German shipwrecks, it's a popular stopover for divers who want to snorkel with the seals. Or, should I say, selkies?

The diving is almost entirely by liveaboard, however the boats return to Stromness each night, so although you 'live aboard' you also have access to the town and its facilities. Diving in the UK is different to the organised diving experienced in Australia and other parts of the world and should be understood to prevent issues. The boat operators act as a taxi service to the wreck. They will give a site brief, but divers need to plan and execute their own dives. Dives are unguided and solo divers will not get any help finding a buddy as most divers are from clubs. As such it is a better destination for buddy pairs, groups or certified solo divers.

Scapa Flow diving needs to be booked well in advance and there are a few local operators, based in the small town of Stromness, many of which use converted trawlers, apart from the newer vessel Huskyan (huskyan.com). See orkney.com for more information.

Opposite A diver illuminates wreckage from WWI in the waters of Scapa Flow *Below* The Blockships at Scapa Flow

Lundy, Devon, England
Puffins and pinnipeds on a wild islet in the Bristol Channel

Why it's special
Lundy Island, a historic islet in the United Kingdom's Bristol Channel, is known for hiking and birdwatching, including puffins which outnumber humans 15 to 1 (though, to be fair, only a handful of people live on the island). Beneath the waves, Lundy is heralded as the premier destination for diving with Atlantic grey seals. Set within a marine conservation area, Lundy has clear waters, kelp forests and rugged underwater topography, creating an ideal setting for close encounters with these charismatic seals. Known for their inquisitive nature, often initiating interactions with divers. Diving in Lundy offers the rare opportunity to observe and better understand the behaviours of these seals in their natural habitat.

Best time to dive
While the seals are present year-round, the summer and early autumn months coincide with the seals' more active period. The prime season is during the warmer months from June to October when water temperatures range from 12°C (53°F) to 16°C (60°F) and visibility is typically at its British best, sometimes exceeding 10m (33ft). Seal pups are born during November and December, which is a nice time to observe them from a distance but not to dive with them as they are easily disturbed.

Gear
- A 7mm wetsuit or a drysuit
- Gloves
- A hood
- Thick undergarments (if wearing a drysuit)
- Seasickness tablets, for the ferry ride across

If you're not joining a guided tour, then BYO all dive equipment plus necessary spares, as there's no dive shop on Lundy. You can hire gear from Easy Divers in Devon (easydiversnorthdevon.co.uk).

Photography tip
A wide angle zoom lens will allow for seal portraits, as well as great action shots of many seals together. Avoid using flash photography as it may scare the seals.

Qualification
- Open Water Diver
- If diving with a drysuit, ensure you're both certified and experienced.

Comfort with cold water conditions is beneficial and good buoyancy is important to ensure both diver safety and minimal disturbance to the marine environment.

Getting there
In the summer months, Lundy is connected to North Devon via its supply ship, the MS Oldenburg, with 2-hour trips departing several times a week. Alternatively, there's the option of a quick chopper ride.

Opposite Face-to-face with a friendly grey seal

Lundy, Devon, England

Dive in

Twenty kilometres (12mi) off the coast of North Devon, two hours by an often-rough ferry ride, you'll find the granite outcrop that is Lundy (meaning 'puffin' in Old Norse) Island. Known for its medieval history and abundant birdlife, this tiny islet in the Bristol Channel is also the UK's first Marine Conservation Zone. Within its pristine waters there are some great dive sites including pinnacles, wrecks and drop-offs. On the edge of the Atlantic and influenced by the nutrient rich Gulf Stream, these waters are home to an abundance of marine life including anemones and all five kinds of Britain's cup coral. To the delight of divers and snorkellers, it's also home to a breeding population of friendly Atlantic grey seals.

Plunging into the chilly waters of Lundy, divers are met by undulating kelp forests and rugged rocky reefs, the perfect playground for seals. In the rocky shallows that fringe the island, in depths of around five metres (16ft), these curious creatures are often quick to make their presence known, approaching divers with a gentle and inquisitive demeanour. Their playful antics, from mirroring divers' movements to gently tugging at fins and dive gear, create a wonderful sense of connection between diver and pinniped (fin-footed mammal). Engaging with an incredibly cute and playful seal is unforgettable; it almost feels like an organised play date. Remember however, like any wild animal experience, it's best to let the seal guide the interaction while you remain still and calm, giving it space and allowing it to come closer as it chooses.

For photographers, Lundy's diving conditions are ideal for capturing the seals' charismatic personalities. The young seals are particularly curious, often coming close to see their reflections in your camera housing's dome port or to play in the bubbles from your regulator. Adult seals, larger and more composed, usually watch from a distance, their large eyes expressing a sense of wisdom. Lundy's clear water provides good visibility, sometimes around 10m (33ft, good by UK standards) allowing you to capture the intricate details of the seals' faces and their sleek, mottled fur.

Apart from seal diving, Lundy's marine reserve offers a rich and unique environment to be explored. The no-take zone around the island has allowed the marine ecosystem to thrive, providing a home for a variety of fish, crabs and lobsters, together with other marine species – an estimated 2500 per square metre of seabed. Kelp forests, swaying gently in the current, add to the island's enchanting atmosphere. Lundy has been leading the way in marine conservation in the UK for close to 40 years. With its coastal waters fiercely protected by locals, Lundy became the UK's first established Marine Nature Reserve in 1986 and then the first Marine Conservation Zone in 2010. The conservation efforts here are ongoing and the number of divers is strictly controlled.

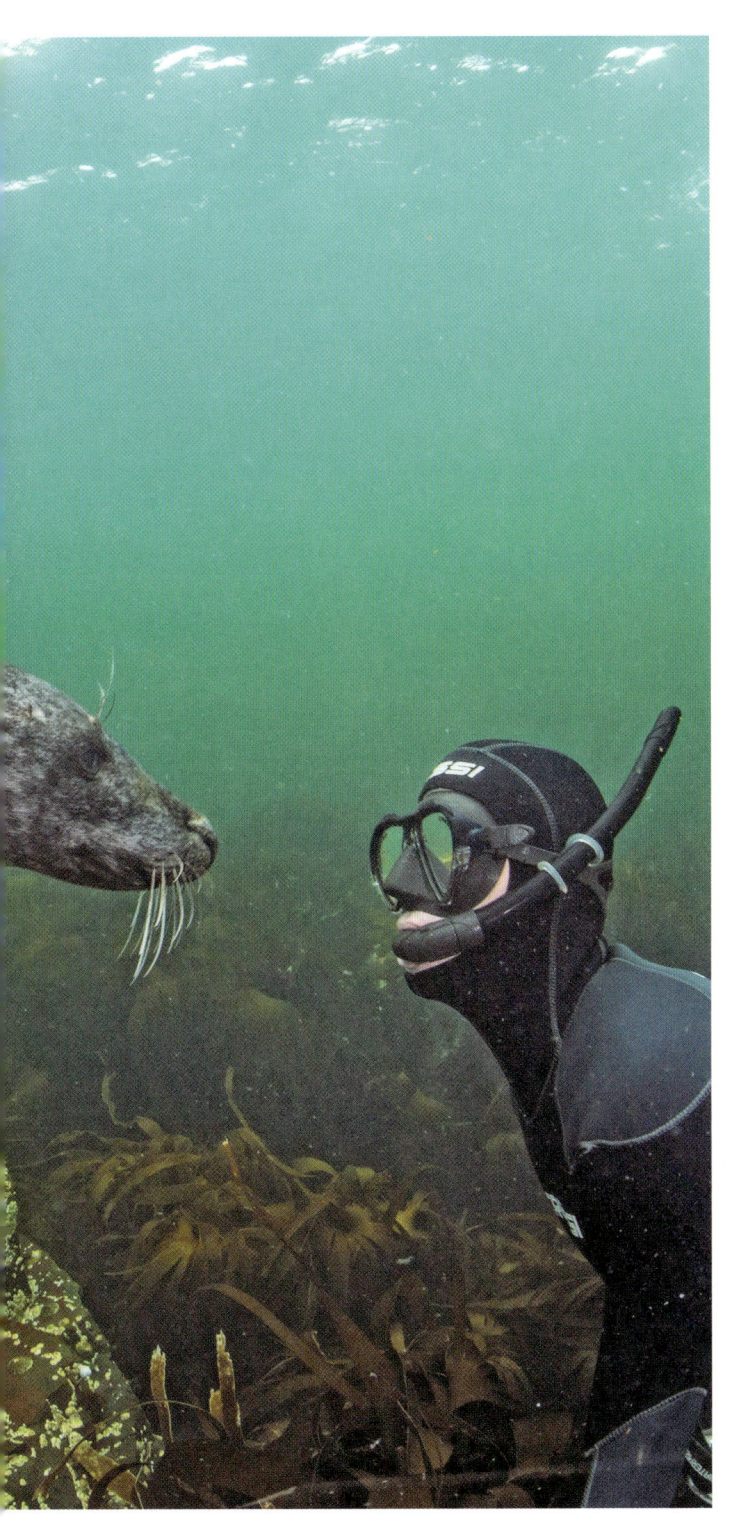

Thoughtfully catering to divers, a beach building has been built near the jetty with change rooms and an air compressor, plus a luggage transport service for divers who are coming across via a private boat. Before heading across to Lundy, check out landmarktrust.org.uk/lundyisland and fill out the Dive Facilities Booking Form, where you can request to use the island's air compressor for refills if you're travelling in a group.

Beyond the fantastic diving, Lundy island itself is worth spending a day or three, exploring. With no cars, no streetlights and very little pollution, there are wild spaces aplenty and a nostalgic feeling of yesteryear. The island has a fascinating history, including its use as a base for Vikings from the 8th Century and some archaeological evidence of people living here during the Bronze Age. There are over 200 shipwrecks, with ten of them being dive sites, and three lighthouses. To wind up your trip, be sure to head to the historic Marisco Tavern, the pub that never closes, a great spot for a hot meal and a game of Lundopoly after a day of diving.

Grey seals are known to be inquisitive *Above* Atlantic puffin

Lundy, Devon, England

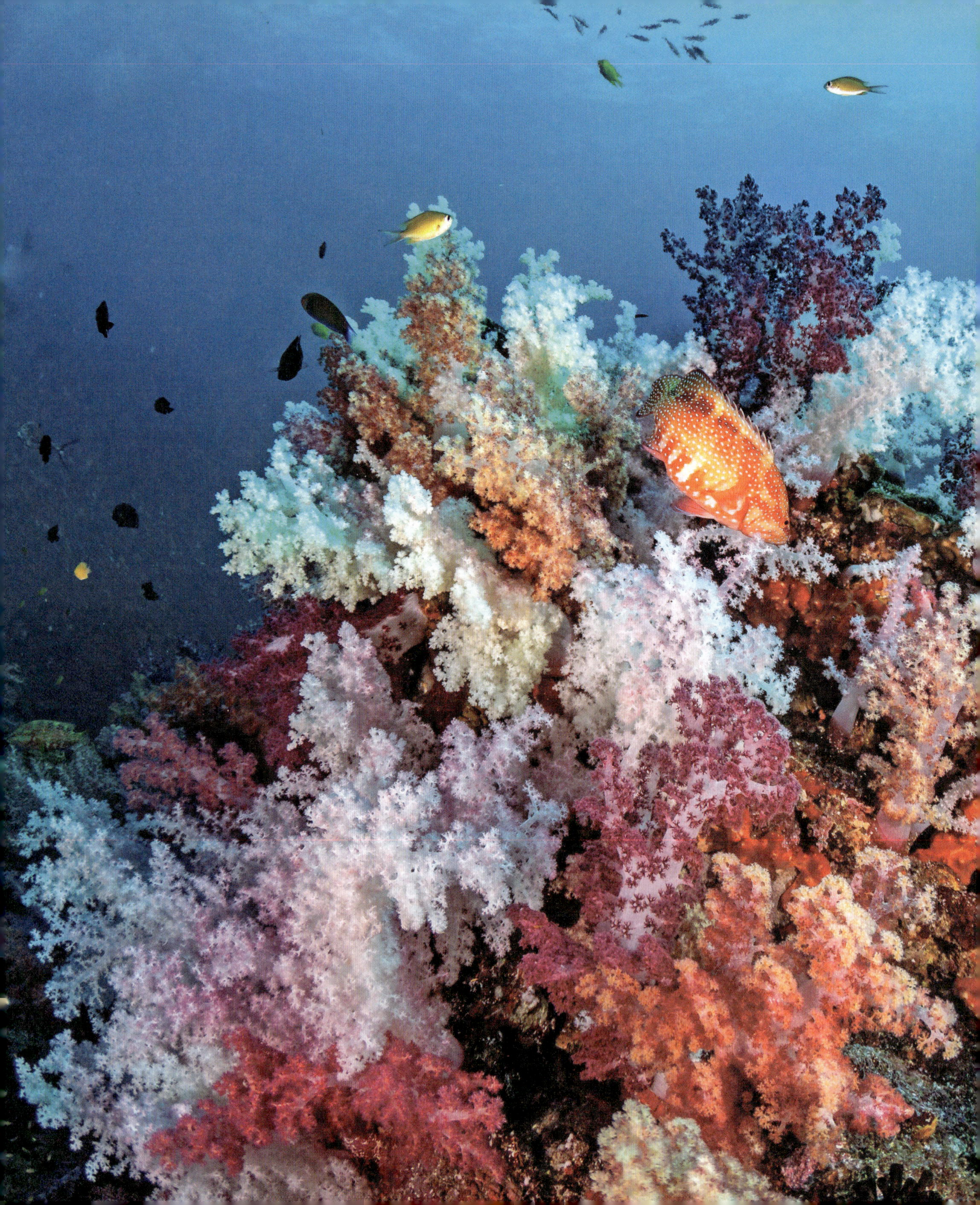

Asia

1. Similan Islands, Thailand 136
2. Mergui (Myeik) Archipelago, Myanmar. 143
3. Misool, Raja Ampat, Indonesia. 149
4. Waigeo, Raja Ampat, Indonesia. 153
5. Lembeh Strait, Indonesia 158
6. Sipadan Island, Malaysian Borneo. 165
7. Tubbataha, Philippines 169
8. Anilao, Philippines. 172

Similan Islands, Thailand

Great food, great diving, great people. What's not to love here?!

Why it's special

Known for their distinctive granite bouldered coastlines, stunning fringing reefs and pinnacles, the islands of the Similan and Surin Islands are known as 'the pearls of the Andaman' and have been protected as a national park since 1982. The islands' underwater topography is remarkable with large boulders, canyons and swim-throughs. Thailand's Andaman Sea dive sites are especially known for vibrant soft corals, and an array of tropical fish and pelagic species, including mantas and the odd whale shark. The pinnacle of pinnacles here is Richelieu Rock, a submerged bommie at the northern tip of the Surin Islands, widely regarded as one of the top five dive sites in the world.

Best time to dive

From November to April the waters are at their calmest and visibility is at its peak, reaching up to 40m (131ft). February and March offer the best conditions. During the monsoon season from May to October the islands are closed to visitors due to rough conditions.

Gear
- 3mm wetsuit for water temperatures around 27-29°C (80-84°F) from Nov-Apr
- Cold currents (aka 'the green monster') sweeping between islands can see temperatures drop suddenly
- Reef safe sunscreen
- Sun protective clothing for your time on the boat

Photography tip

The Similans has plenty to offer photographers. In my trips to the region, I've found the coral seascapes of fans, whips and sponges amongst large boulders mesmerising. For this reason, I like to shoot with a wide-angle zoom.

Qualification
- Open Water

While beginners can enjoy the shallow coral reefs and bays, advanced divers can challenge themselves with deeper drift dives. The Advanced Open Water Diver certification is recommended to experience everything this region has to offer.

Getting there

There are daily direct flights from Bangkok to Phuket. During the Similan Islands season, liveaboards depart from Khao Lak, 1.5 hours' drive north of Phuket, and during monsoon season, liveaboards divert to the southern Andaman Sea, to dive sites near Koh Lanta, departing Chalong Bay.

Opposite Green sea turtles are the only herbivorous marine turtle, feeding mainly on seagrass *Previous* Koh Bon Island, Thailand

Similan Islands, Thailand 137

Asia

Dive in

What's not to love about Thailand; the people are friendly, the food's packed with flavour and there's a thriving dive scene. Over the years I've dived hundreds of sites around Thailand and found that while the Gulf of Thailand might be infamous for its dive schools and late-night antics, the Similans, on the country's west coast, have some of the best diving in south-east Asia.

Formed by ancient volcanic activity, the island group has about 20 main dive sites, each with unique characteristics. From the gentle, sloping coral reefs at Island Four (Koh Miang) to the sheer walls and deep canyons of Elephant Head Rock, the variety is astounding. On the western and southern sides of the islands, big, granite boulders litter the underwater seascape. This side of the islands is better suited to more advanced divers, due to varying currents and greater depths. There are some fun diving opportunities through overhangs and canyons, festooned with soft corals housing a variety of colourful, tropical fish. When the visibility is good (it ranges between 20–40m/66–131ft), you can spot reef sharks, turtles, giant trevally, tuna and maybe even some mantas out in the blue. At Elephant Rock (Hin Pusar), a variety of shark species, including leopard, blacktip and whitetip reef sharks circle and glide past granite boulders, stacked one on top of another down to the ocean's bed. For less experienced divers, West of Eden offers shallower depths and milder currents, and plenty of soft and hard corals and gorgonians.

The eastern side of the Similans has a different vibe to the west, with sloping reefs and big coral gardens dropping down 30–40m (98–131ft) or so. Over the course of several dives, you'll become acquainted with the Similans' residents – clownfish peering from their anemone homes, parrotfish nibbling on hard corals, fusiliers above, turtles and ribbon eels below. Within the reef's crevices hide smaller lifeforms like ornate ghost pipefish, nudibranchs and shrimp. East of Eden is a well-known site; with its gentle current, this is a great spot for a relaxing drift dive. In the far north of the islands, Breakfast Bend is home to turtles, leopard sharks, Kuhl's stingrays and a variety of fish including triggerfish, groupers and napoleon wrasse.

The Similan Islands have some of the most beautiful sea fans on the planet

The best way to experience the Similans is on a liveaboard. Choose wisely as you'll get what you pay for; sometimes even just paying a few hundred more can mean the difference between too many divers onboard, bad service and poor dive practices versus the trip of a lifetime. All Similan liveaboard itineraries also incorporate dives in Koh Tachai, Koh Bon, and Richelieu Rock, just north of the Similan National Park. The best diving that I've done in Thailand has been at these locations, though there can be strong currents here.

Richelieu Rock is a crescent of steep sided boulders, with the highest point at the apex, which almost breaks the surface. It forms an enclosed 'bay' teeming with fish – in fact you'll struggle to see the reef itself through all the fish. The pinnacle is shrouded in thick schools of glass fish, with large schools of big eye and two spot snapper, fusiliers, squirrel and soldier fish. The steep sides of the boulders form vertical walls, and still there are plenty of swim throughs and gaps, within which you can find the small stuff, ornate ghost pipefish, seahorses, anemones, porcelain crabs and nudibranchs. It's one of those dive sites that appears to have been specifically 'designed' – rather than just a random act of nature.

It's worth mentioning that the Similans are very well-known and you won't be discovering any new sites with no one around (Mergui (Myeik) Archipelago will give you this, *see* p. 143).

With previous visitor numbers of over 7000 a day putting a strain on the islands and their reefs, in 2018 the national parks authority restricted visitor numbers, and these days only 3325 people a day are permitted within the park at one time. Divers must purchase and display a permit. The park is heavily patrolled, so expect to be boarded by rangers, there to check the number of divers matches the number of permits. Furthermore, liveaboards are no longer allowed to moor directly above the dive sites, so all diving is now done via tender while the larger vessels are moored a safe distance away.

Top tip: choose an itinerary that visits the more popular sites such as Richelieu Rock and Koh Tachai mid-week, to avoid the weekend crowds. And choose a small liveaboard to ensure you're diving with small groups of divers. Sea Bees Diving's MV Marco Polo (sea-bees.com) takes a maximum 12 divers, while the Junk and the Phinisi sleep 18, though many trips have just 12 divers on board (masterliveaboards.com).

Donald Duck Bay, located at the Northern end of Similan Island Eight *Opposite* Richelieu Rock is a horseshoe-shaped pinnacle which reaches the surface from a depth of 30m (66ft)

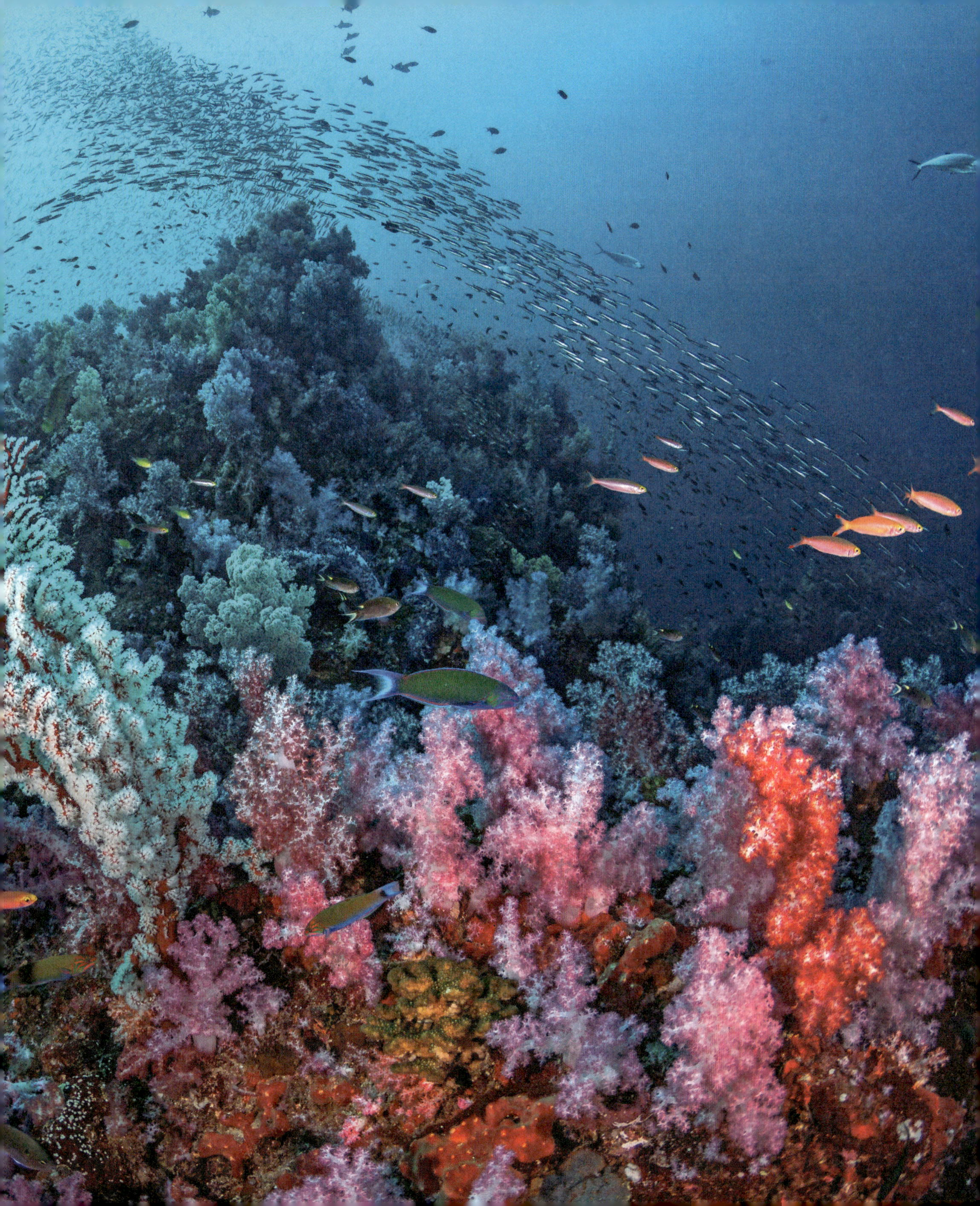

Asia

Mergui (Myeik) Archipelago, Myanmar

For decades sea gypsies have had this region all to themselves ... until now

Why it's special

Off limits since WWII, the Mergui (pronounced mer-gwee) Archipelago in southern Myanmar opened to liveaboard dive boats in 1997 and, since then, word-of-mouth about the region has started to spread through the diving world. Their relative isolation and history of being closed to tourists (due to Burma's military regime) has helped them maintain their pristine and undeveloped state. Just north of Thailand's Similan and Surin Islands (*see* p. 136) in the Andaman Sea, but nowhere near as busy, the Merguis host a great diversity of marine life. Imagine mesmerising pelagic schools and megafauna including mantas and whale sharks; thriving vibrant coral fan gardens and macro life; and hidden beaches and lagoons. And still, many sites remain unexplored, waiting to be discovered.

Best time to dive

From late October to mid-May there are calm seas and blue skies. Visibility is better and the water temperature is a steady 27°C (80°F). This period aligns with the migratory patterns of large pelagics including mantas and whale sharks (Feb–May is prime). Liveaboards do not operate during the monsoon season, from June to October, as there can be rough seas, rainstorms and strong onshore winds.

Gear
- 3mm wetsuit for water temperatures around 27°C (80°F) from late Oct to mid-May

Photography tip
Mergui has a bit of everything; megafauna that necessitates a wide-angle lens, coral garden seascapes that suit a wide angle zoom and incredible critters for your macro lens. If possible, pack it all, particularly your wide-angle lenses.

Qualification
- Advanced Open Water

The Mergui Archipelago has a mix of beginner-friendly sites and challenging dives that are best for experienced divers, given the strong currents at deeper sites. Most liveaboard itineraries are suited to divers with an Advanced Open Water Diver certification, to fully experience the intricate topography and dynamic marine life of the region.

Getting there
Liveaboards depart from Ranong on Thailand's Andaman coast. Air Asia flies daily from Bangkok to the small airport at Ranong, which takes just over one hour.

Opposite Horseshoe island, also known as Myin Khwar Island, is a highlight of the Mergui Archipelago

Dive in

In early 2020, I was invited on a dive expedition to the Mergui Archipelago to document and photograph a potentially large manta population. At the time, I only knew two things about this part of the world: one, that geographically the archipelago was situated just north of Thailand's incredible Similan Islands (*see* p. 136) and two, tourism in Myanmar is still relatively new, after decades of closure. With those factors in mind, I excitedly said yes.

Known to the outside world by their British colonial name of Mergui (the Burmese name is Myeik), these 800+ islands are scattered across 400km (248mi) of the Andaman Sea, down the coastline of Myanmar (formerly Burma). Perhaps the biggest allure here is the chance to explore a largely unknown region without seeing another dive boat for days, and diving sites that potentially have never been dived. Devoid of hotels and beachfront bars, these jungle-clad islands, some of them still unnamed, are inhabited only by a few thousand Moken 'sea gypsies', the indigenous people of the Mergui Archipelago. These semi-nomadic people have traditionally spent their days fishing or boatbuilding and are known for their incredible freediving abilities. For the Moken, the only tourists that they see are a small number of divers or adventure cruise ship passengers, passing through.

On our expedition, we set sail from Kawthaung (Myanmar's southern gateway to the archipelago), though commercial liveaboards also depart from Ranong across the Thai border. Most of our trip was based around several well-known sites, with the rest of our trip visiting unknown sites for exploratory dives.

Our captain's favourite dive was Black Rock, one of the Mergui's most westerly islands. Standing solitarily in the sea with a steep wall dropping down to over 100m (328ft), this pinnacle is a magnet for marine life, giant mantas, vast schools of barracuda, trevally, snapper and fusiliers clouding the waters. Underwater, this limestone rock is covered in soft corals and anemones; the reef's crannies and crevasses a haven for scorpionfish and other benthic critters. At night, the dive site transforms as colourful corals bloom and nocturnal creatures emerge to feed in the nutrient-rich waters.

Another favourite spot was Western Rocky. The island is known for its sharks including whitetips and blacktips, grey reef sharks and some large nurse sharks which can be spotted inside a tunnel dive that cuts through the island's core. Just north of Western Rocky, a dive site aptly named Shark Cave is also good for spotting nurse sharks, plus whip rays, blotched stingrays and the odd whale shark, and then there are smaller cuties like seahorses and anemonefish.

Perhaps the highlight of the trip, for me, were the huge gorgonian sea fans found in numerous locations, with a dive site named Fan Forest Pinnacle (also known as Rocky Peaks) being especially populous with gorgonians. To this day, I would say that the largest and most impressive gorgonian fans I've ever seen were in the Mergui Archipelago.

While the Mergui Archipelago has many amazing dive sites to explore, the visibility can be a bit all over the place. Cold water currents bringing nutrients (commonly called 'the green monster') can rush through dive sites unexpectedly. Some areas have been fished hard, while others have been decimated by dynamite fishing. Then, on some dive sites, ghost nets litter the reefs. While the archipelago is just beginning to find its feet as a world-class destination for divers, it's crucial that the government protects the region, not just for the future enjoyment of divers, but also for the Moken people who call it home and depend on these waters for their food, lifestyle and income.

The MV Smiling Seahorse has been running liveaboard dive trips to Mergui since 2012 and offers several scientific and exploratory itineraries. Trips on this small boat, which takes only 16 divers, depart from Ranong in Thailand (thesmilingseahorse.com).

Pharaoh cuttlefish *Opposite* Colourful corals and fans of the Mergui Archipelago

Mergui (Myeik) Archipelago, Myanmar 145

Ghost busters

Saving the sea from a web of debris

Maybe you've seen it; a colourful patch of coral covered in a web of discarded fishing gear. Ghost nets, as this kind of marine debris is called, are responsible for the death of millions of marine creatures each year, from smaller fish to turtles and megafauna like whales and dolphins. Sometimes the nets are small, other times they are kilometres long. Alarmingly, it's estimated that 640,000t (705,000tn) of ghost fishing gear enters the sea each year, made-up primarily of synthetic materials that don't biodegrade. Ghost nets continue to kill long after they've entered the ocean, entangling and drowning creature after creature. Unfortunately, even the most remote corners of the planet are not immune to marine debris, including the beautiful Mergui Archipelago, where a lack of marine regulation and management makes it all the more vulnerable. This is a problem that every diver can help with, by untangling reefs (or marine creatures that have become stuck) and bringing the debris back to the surface and into a bin ... or even better, recycling it. Healthy Seas is one organisation that's helping with this problem, by collecting ghost nets and upcycling them into a nylon thread called Econyl. Econyl is being taken up by the fashion and interior design industries for things such as swimwear, rugs and carpets. Check out healthyseas.org if you want to volunteer as a diver, but be mindful that the work can be intensive, tedious and, at times, downright dangerous as there's a risk of getting caught in the nets yourself.

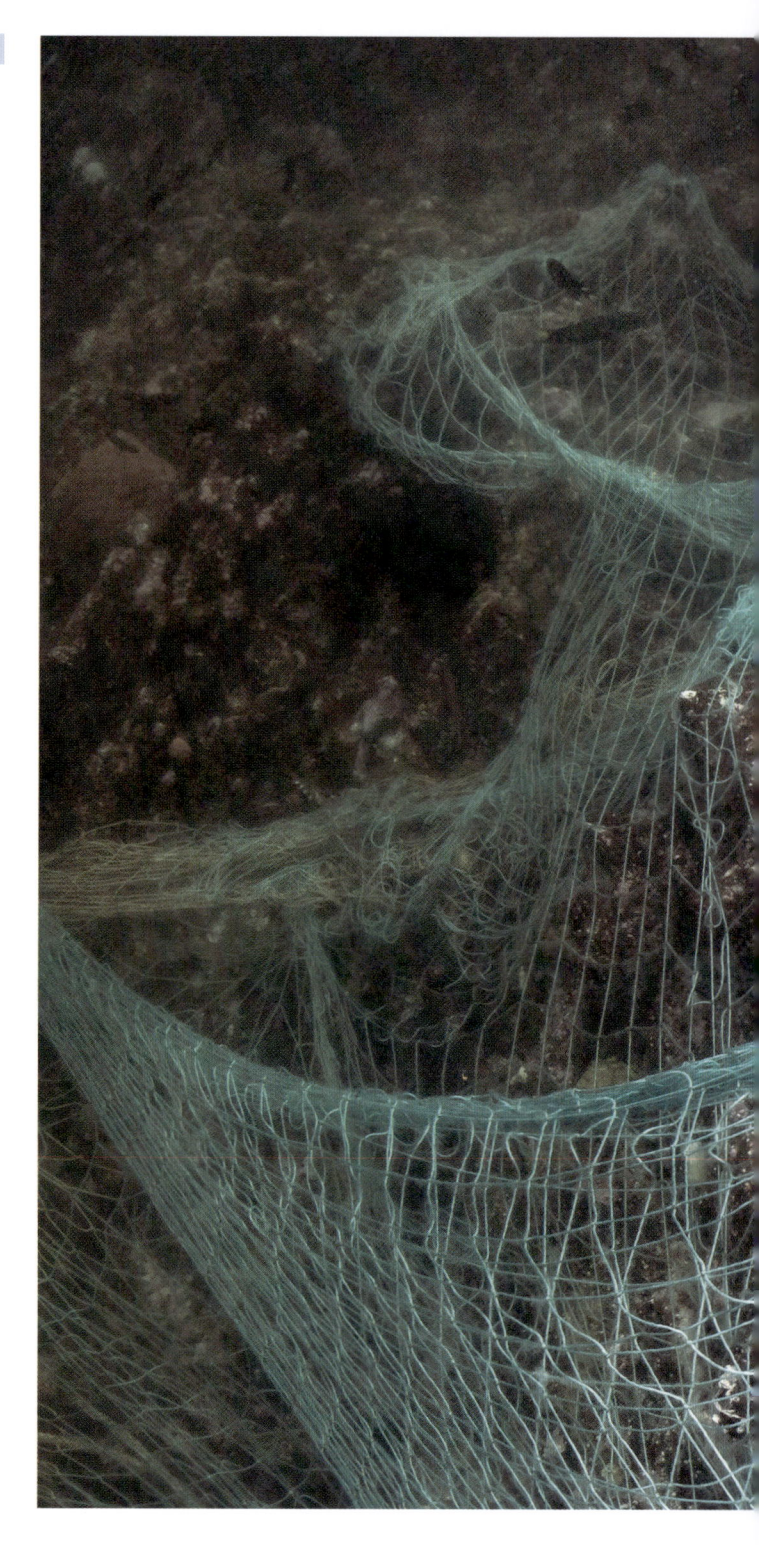

Asia

Ghost nets continue to kill long after they've entered the ocean

Mergui (Myeik) Archipelago, Myanmar

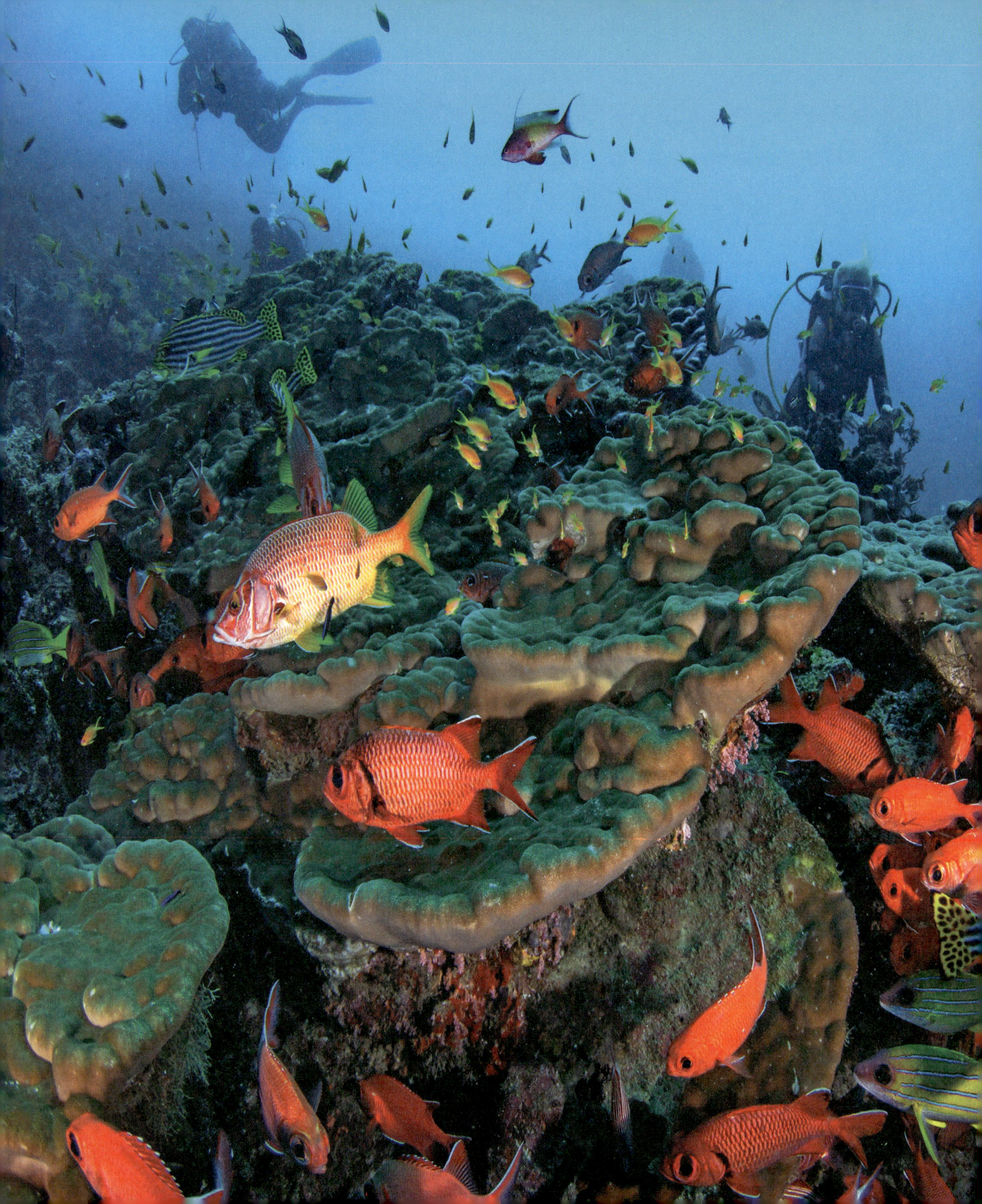

Misool, Raja Ampat, Indonesia

An ex-shark-finning camp that's now part of a protected marine reserve

Why it's special

You'd be forgiven for thinking you've travelled back to the Jurassic era in Misool; the landscape is untouched and, for the most part, there's no sign of people ... anywhere. Amidst this wild terrain, modern-day dinosaurs do still roam in the form of saltwater crocodiles, in the mangroves of western Misool. On the eastern side of the island, the villas at Misool Resort look out upon a turquoise lagoon on a small island that was once the site of a shark-finning camp. In a major win for ocean conservation, the resort's non-profit organisation employs locals as rangers to patrol these waters, ensuring that no fish are taken from the established 'no take zone'. With sharks aplenty, a manta cleaning station, colourful critters and a plethora of soft and hard corals, this is one of the best dive trips you'll ever do, if you have the time – and cash to splash – on such a remote destination.

Best time to dive

October to April is best due to calmer seas and milder weather. Mid-June to early September sees the South Monsoon hitting Misool with winds of up to 30–40 knots and choppy seas.

Gear
- 3mm wetsuit for 26-28°C (79-82°F) water temps.
- Reef smart sunscreen
- Sun protective clothing and polarised sunglasses
- A good torch for night diving
- Warm jacket for cool evenings

If you'd like to donate to the local kindy and primary school, bring some basic English books.

Photography tip
Misool really does have it all. The Coral Triangle boasts greater marine biodiversity than anywhere else in the world, so you're going to want to pack a few different lenses, both wide and macro. Strobes are a must.

Qualification
- Open Water

You can dive in Misool with an Open Water certification as there are many dive sites for varying abilities. To be able to comfortably dive more sites, I recommend having an advanced certification, and to have several dives under your belt already.

Getting there
You can fly directly to Sorong, West Papua from Jakarta, and indirectly from Bali. From there, it's a 150km (93mi) boat ride to Misool which takes about five hours depending on sea conditions.

Opposite Misool has some of the most biodiverse reefs on the planet

Dive in

Of the ampat (four) islands that make up Indonesia's Raja Ampat (four kings) region, the southernmost island of Misool is the most isolated and requires some effort to get to. Though most dive 'bucket lists' categorise the whole of Raja Ampat as one diving destination, the fact is, this region covers a whopping 40,000km² (10million ac) of land and sea, and there are some unique reasons to make the mission to Misool, even if it means doing the north on your first Raja trip (see p. 153) then coming here on a separate trip later on.

In 2017 Dr Mark Erdmann, vice president of Conservation International's Asia-Pacific marine programs, said that Misool is 'one of only a handful of places in the universe where biodiversity is improving rather than declining.' A big contributor to this is the hard work of some divers, the local clans they have collaborated with and an eco resort they built to fund it all. Back in 2005, Andrew and Marit Miners came to Misool for a unique, off-the-beaten-track dive holiday. Arriving at Batbitim island, they discovered the carcasses of dead baby sharks strewn across a beach, their fins removed for the commercial shark fin trade. Shocked by the finding, they established a conservation program which employed locals (some of whom were former shark-finners) and built a bespoke 40 guest resort on the site of the former shark finning camp.

These days, the Misool Marine Reserve is over 120,000ha (300,000ac) in size and employs 15 local rangers who patrol a designated no-take (no fishing) zone. There are reportedly now 25 times more sharks on Misool's reefs than there were a decade ago and the manta population has also increased. In terms of regular shark sightings, you can expect to see whitetip, blacktips, grey reef sharks and wobbegongs. If you're night diving, you may also be lucky enough to spot an endemic Raja Ampat epaulette (walking) shark.

If you search online 'diving Misool', you'll find that the five star Misool Resort is the only accommodation that comes up (misool.info) and, despite its high prices, it books up well in advance. Unless you're exploring the region as part of a dive liveaboard, or you have a local contact that can refer you to a homestay (check out the 'guides' page on stayrajaampat.com), there really aren't many options here. Densely forested and with steep mountain ridges, Misool has no roads or airports, and few residents. There's a once-weekly, nine-hour ferry from Sorong or, if you're staying at Misool Resort a five hour bumpy ride in their speedboat. The extra effort of getting here, and the expense, is the main reason that Misool gets far fewer visitors than the northern islands of Raja Ampat. But this is part of Misool's magic – the dive sites are pristine, and your group will likely have them to yourselves.

Of the 60+ dive sites around Misool, many of which are coral reefs, there's a variety of options for both beginner or advanced divers. Thanks to the island's location next to the nutrient-rich waters of the Ceram Trough and the Indonesian Throughflow, there's incredible biodiversity, from big pelagics like whale sharks and mantas right down to cute critters like the Raja Ampat pygmy seahorse (or Santa Claus pygmy). Dive site names like 'Magic Mountain' (famous for its year-round mantas) and 'Nudi Rock' hint at what you can expect.

From sea mounts to swim-throughs and walls covered in colourful soft and hard corals, whips and gorgonians, Misool's underwater topography is diverse. The top-side scenery is worth exploring, too, with pristine coves and even a lake full of stingless jellyfish, like the one in Palau (see p. 178). Many would consider Misool as a 'once in a lifetime' kind of trip, though, to be honest, it's likely that you'll be planning your return before you even get home.

The coral triangle

Can divers help save the global centre of marine diversity?

It would've been very easy to fill this entire book with locations only within the Coral Triangle. Just north of Australia, this so-called Triangle encompasses six countries (Malaysia, Indonesia, Papua New Guinea, Timor-Leste, the Solomon Islands and the Philippines) and harbours over 75% of the world's coral species. Here you'll find over 6000 species of fish and six of the world's seven sea turtle species. It's also a migration corridor for megafauna – in Raja Ampat alone, you'll find at least 16 species of dolphins and whales. Unfortunately, threats of unsustainable coastal development, shark-finning, overfishing and bad fishing practices (like cyanide fishing) are all taking their toll on this region. But with nature-based tourism bringing in $12 billion USD a year, dive travellers and ocean loving tourists have a unique opportunity to pressure governments into increased protection and creating more marine sanctuaries. One of the easiest ways to help safeguard the region is by choosing sustainable dive operations, even if it costs a few bucks more.

Opposite (clockwise) Raja Ampat pygmy seahorse; hermit crab; resting blenny; juvenile filefish

Misool, Raja Ampat, Indonesia 151

Asia

152

Waigeo, Raja Ampat, Indonesia
From whale sharks to wunderpuses, this is tropical diving heaven

Why it's special

Nestled in the heart of the Coral Triangle, the archipelago of Raja Ampat, comprising more than 1500 islands, cays and shoals is a mecca for adventurous divers seeking incredible underwater experiences. With its crystal-clear waters, vibrant coral gardens, and an array of marine life from mantas and whale sharks to macro wonders like the pint-sized pygmy seahorse, Raja Ampat lives up to its tourism tag of 'the last paradise'. The marine biodiversity here is staggering; there are more than 1400 species of fish and 537 species of coral – that's 75% of all known coral species. It really is a one-stop-shop, and the topside scenery is incredible, too.

Best time to dive

October to May is the best time for a liveaboard, and it's also the best time for mantas. December to March is known to have the best overall visibility. July to September is known for rain and strong winds, with most liveaboards relocating to Komodo and elsewhere in Indonesia, and some resorts closing for a month or two.

Gear
- 3mm wetsuit for 27-30°C (80-86°F) water temps
- Reef smart sunscreen
- Sun protective clothing and polarised sunnies
- A good torch for night diving
- Warm jacket for cool evenings

This is tropical diving at its finest, so there's no need for excessive gear.

Photography tip
See breakout section on page 157.

Qualification
- Open Water to advanced (there are many dive sites here to choose from)

Getting there
There are direct flights to Sorong, West Papua, from Jakarta and indirect flights from Denpasar (Bali). From there, you can jump onto a two-hour ferry to Waisai, in southern Waigeo which will be the gateway to many dive sites.

Opposite My wife, Melissa, enjoying the view over Wayag Lagoon

Dive in

Raja Ampat is a huge region that covers more than 40,000km² (10million ac) of land and sea. In recent years, it's become more popular with adventurous travellers, especially divers, and in recognition of its tourism value the Indonesian government has created a 46,000km² (11million ac) shark and manta sanctuary, where shark fishing and finning have been banned. Go Indo!

The name Raja Ampat means 'four kings', referring to the four main islands of Misool, Salawati, Batanta and Waigeo. The diving on Waigeo and its neighbouring islands is incredible. In this chapter, I've touched on just a few of the many wonderful dive sites that can be found in this northern part of Raja Ampat.

Waigeo itself is known for its excellent drift diving with walls of soft corals and sea fans, plus plenty of white and blacktip reef sharks and the odd green sea turtle. The island is also popular with macro enthusiasts seeking out cuties such as pygmy seahorses, ghost pipefish and colourful nudibranchs. In western Waigeo, Sel Pele Bay, a large bay with an island in the middle, has lovely sloping reefs and has gained a reputation for being the best spot to look for critters in Raja Ampat, such as the thumb-sized (and super cool) tiny bobtail squid and various other cephalopod species, like mimic octopus and the rather Austin Powers sounding wunderpus. When you're starting to feel waterlogged, you may want to check out one of the pearl farms to learn about the cultured pearl industry.

The northern part of Waigeo and further north into the uninhabited Wayag Islands are especially popular with liveaboards. Wayag Lagoon, with its towering limestone outcrops, has become the poster child for Raja Ampat tourism ads, despite it being near-impossible to get to (unless you're on a liveaboard). At Wayag's Ranger Station, you can stand knee-deep and be surrounded by blacktip reef sharks around the jetty. Wayag is also the site of a recent scientific discovery; in the calm waters of the lagoon there's a reef manta nursery, where juvenile rays feed and learn to swim away from the threat of larger predators. This is the world's first confirmed manta ray nursery; an exciting discovery for sure!

Venturing south of Waigeo you'll find the nutrient-rich waters of the Dampier Strait. The drift diving here is incredible and you're likely to see reef sharks, mantas, barracuda, dolphins and possibly whales. A couple of sites that you may have heard of here are Cape Kri (known for its large schools of big fish, such as barracuda) and Blue Magic, with its hard corals, mantas, wobbegongs and schooling fish. At the aptly named Manta Sandy and Manta Ridge, near Mansuar Island, you can reliably find groups of mantras that come here to be cleaned of their parasites by blacktip butterflyfish. You may be lucky enough to see them gliding together in trains – a truly spectacular sight.

These are just a few of the many dive sites that surround Waigeo in northern Raja Ampat, and on your own trip you'll find your favourite spots, which will most likely be ones that aren't written about in guidebooks or on the internet. Raja Ampat is the kind of place where it's still possible to find such spots if you're adventurous, talk to locals and have enough time to explore its nooks and crannies. It's also the kind of place that's still finding its feet in terms of protection and conservation, so each individual diver that comes here has a responsibility to aid in its caretaking, picking up rubbish, wearing reef safe sunscreen, etc so that 'the last paradise' doesn't become 'paradise lost'.

Beyond Waigeo's many dive sites and stunning beaches, the island's interior is also worth exploring with waterfalls and virgin jungle teeming with endemic birds and plants. In terms of accommodation, there are plenty of basic homestays on Waigeo, plus some great dive resorts as well as several liveaboards cruising the waters of Waigeo.

Opposite Raja Ampat's biodiversity is unparalleled, boasting some of the richest and most diverse marine ecosystems on the planet *Above left* A small red crab utilises the protection of staghorn coral *Above right* Wonderpus octopus

Waigeo, Raja Ampat, Indonesia   155

Asia

Photography

Petite portraits: Capturing a pygmy seahorse

Pygmy seahorses are the smallest of seahorse species, measuring only about 1–2.7cm (0.5–1in) in length (the size of your thumbnail). They are known for their remarkable camouflage abilities, often blending seamlessly with the vibrant corals they inhabit. To photograph one of these mini mares, you'll need patience, good buoyancy control and the right macro gear.

I've spent countless hours capturing pygmy portraits and here's what I've learned. First of all, it's important to prioritise the care of the seahorse and its gorgonian home, as both are extremely delicate and can easily be affected from factors such as being touched, air bubbles hitting them, or from light sources. The pygmy seahorse depends on the fan for survival, so if the fan dies, so also will the pygmy. I like to begin by spending time watching my subject and getting the position of my strobes correct before taking my first photo, then I try to keep flashes to a minimum (five flashes, at the most) as there's scientific evidence that repeated flashes can have an adverse effect on these delicate creatures. Limit the use of a constant light source. I use strobes on their weakest setting with a diffuser. My preferred camera will have a crop sensor, to help with extra zoom, coupled with a 100mm (4in) macro lens and a dioptre, if you have one.

One of my first and (still) one of my favourite photos of a pygmy seahorse

Waigeo, Raja Ampat, Indonesia

Lembeh Strait, Indonesia
Go crazy for critters in this muck diving mecca

Why it's special
Lembeh Strait, a slender ribbon of water between North Sulawesi's mainland and Lembeh Island, is renowned as the world's best muck diving destination. Distinguished by its black sand environment, Lembeh hosts an astonishing diversity of peculiar creatures. In this macro-photography haven, every grain of volcanic sand seems to conceal critters. Frogfish, mimic octopuses, flamboyant cuttlefish, and myriad species of nudibranchs are just the beginning of the catalogue that thrives within these nutrient-rich waters. Beyond the sand, the Strait's artificial reefs and wrecks have become flourishing ecosystems, offering a home to a variety of species and providing divers with an array of habitats to explore.

Best time to dive
Diving here is year-round, and each month brings its own unique set of marine life, but the best conditions are typically from March to December, with calmer seas and optimal visibility. The January to February wet Season can bring rains and reduced visibility, but it also often leads to increased sightings of rare critters.

Gear
- 3mm wetsuit for 26-29°C (79-84°F) water temps
- A good dive light for night dives
- Fins that remain stiff when you kick, to avoid displacement of the ocean floor environment

If you're Nitrox certified, I encourage you to dive with Nitrox to prolong your bottom times. More bottom time equals more time searching for Lembeh's critters.

Photography tip
See breakout section on page 162.

Qualification
- Open water

Lembeh Strait's gentle currents and shallow sites make it accessible to divers of all levels. However, neutral buoyancy is critical to avoid disturbing the delicate muck environment and its hidden occupants.

Getting there
You can fly directly to Manado Airport from Singapore, then it's a one-hour drive to Bitung. A 15-minute boat ride across the harbour will have you on the island of Lembeh.

Opposite I love photographing these little critters. I think they have the greatest name in the sea – the hairy squat lobster

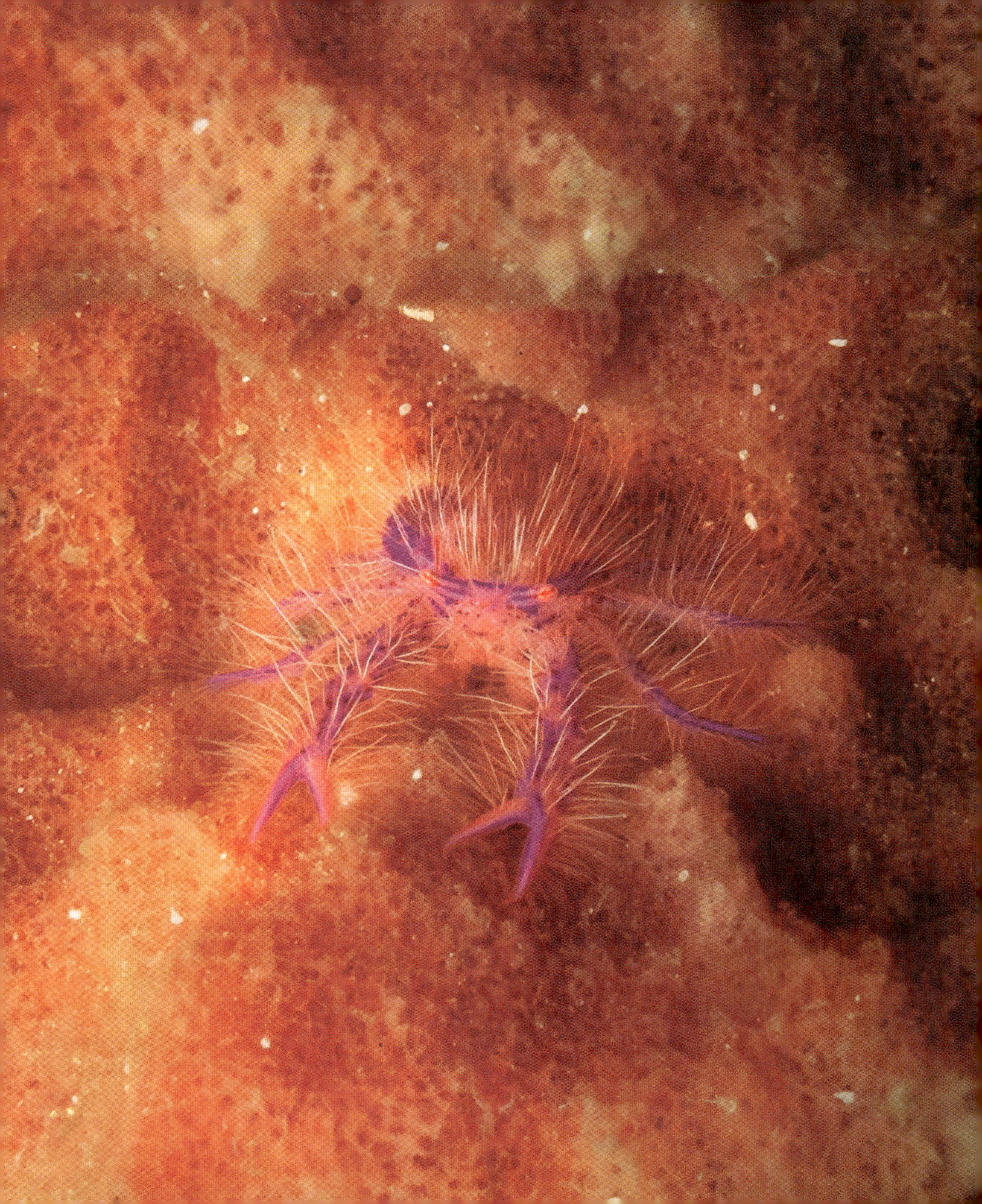

Asia

160

Dive in

Muck diving deserves to be in its own category; it really is nothing like your regular clear-water diving. In this scenario, it's less about finding pretty reefs. With limited visibility and light, you're not focussed on a big open scene, but rather on a tight corner or crevasse that some super bizarre, little critter has claimed as its home. Muck diving sites tend to have a lot of rubble, trash (such as old bottles and containers) and things that look out of place underwater. But don't let this turn you off; all of these foreign objects make excellent hiding places for a variety of exotic critters.

I fell in love with muck diving when we cruised through Lembeh Strait on a superyacht that I was working on. One of my strongest memories from the Strait is when we resurfaced from our night dives and waited for the zodiac to pick us up. Floating in the warm, equatorial waters, we'd rest our necks back into our inflated BCDs and look up at the star-filled sky. The vast expanse of the universe was a perfect contrast to the time we'd just spent on the sea floor, intensely searching for the tiniest of critters with our dive lights. Our itinerary had brought us from Raja Ampat to Lembeh Strait, where the two kinds of diving were completely different.

Entering the waters of the Lembeh Strait, you're immediately transported to an alien landscape. The dives are like a game of hide and seek, where the reward is the discovery of some of the ocean's most bizarre inhabitants, such as seahorses the size of a rice grain, nudibranchs with colours so vivid they seem unreal, and fish that walk rather than swim. Patience, buoyancy control and kicking slowly with raised fins are paramount, as the silty sand stirs easily if you brush against it. Nitrox is also preferable, as many critters are found in depths of around 20m (66ft) and the extra bottom time with Nitrox is welcomed. Other quirky characters to be found in these waters include pygmy cuttlefish, blue-ringed octopus, ghost pipefish, boxfish, mantis shrimp, frogfish, gobies, blennies and my favourite-named critter of all time, the hairy squat lobster. This motley crew are what macro dreams are made of.

Lembeh's black volcanic sand creates a dramatic backdrop for these extraordinary creatures to perform their daily (or nightly) rituals and the Strait's artificial reefs, like the famous Police Pier, demonstrate how human-made structures can be repurposed to support marine ecosystems. Over time, these sites have become encrusted with corals and sponges, creating the perfect habitat for a plethora of creatures. Night dives here are particularly enchanting, as nocturnal creatures emerge and the seascapes transform into bustling metropolises of marine activity.

The subculture of muck diving is a world unto itself and diving in the Lembeh Strait is as much about the culture as it is about the critters. Here, local dive guides have an encyclopaedic knowledge of the Strait's residents, often passed down through generations. They are the unsung heroes of Lembeh Strait's diving experience, spotting the tiniest of creatures for our delight and leaving a trail of satisfied divers.

I love muck diving; it attracts a rather tragic crowd of die-hard enthusiasts. It's not unusual to find muck divers who dedicate all of their dives to this exclusive pursuit. They're not interested in wide angled lenses, clear blue water or megafauna. Give these divers a jetty, some black sand and an unusual little critter that most of the world has never heard of and they're stoked. For me, it's another dimension in the wonderful world of ocean exploration. I love variety and the challenges that come with stepping into the micro world of macro. Slowing down and focussing on the smaller things brings the realisation that even in the ocean's unassuming corners, life thrives in extraordinary ways.

There are several dive resorts on Lembeh Island to suit most budgets, from Bastianos Froggies Resort (bastianos.com) and Thalassa Lembeh (thalassamanado.com) to NAD Lembeh Resort (nad-lembeh.com) and the luxurious Lembeh Resort (lembehresort.com). All these resorts offer photographic support and tuition, expert guides (spotters) and have excellent camera facilities.

Opposite (clockwise) Nudibranch dianas chromodoris; broadclub cuttlefish; honeycomb cowfish; hermit crab

Photography

Creating macro magic in the muck

Muck diving is a whole new world of underwater photography. It's all about little critters and macro lenses. Here are a few pointers that might help you make a start.

- Familiarise yourself with the local wildlife and the ecosystem in which you're diving. Compile a critter checklist of species you would love to see.
- Seek out an experienced, local dive guide. This will increase your chances of discovering new wildlife tenfold.
- Equip yourself with a reliable dive light and a focus light. Ensure your strobes are always set to a low level of brightness and use diffusers.
- Embrace the excitement of rainy or cloudy weather – it often brings forth more intriguing critters.
- A 100mm (4in) lens is a great foundation for this type of photography. If you want to go to the next level, try experimenting with super macro by using a wet dioptre (basically, an attached magnifying glass to your housing) for greater macro reach.
- Be patient and aim for capturing behavioural moments in your photographs.
- Uphold ethical diving practices, refrain from disturbing creatures for personal gain.

A pair of harlequin shrimp feeding on a starfish

Lembeh Strait, Indonesia

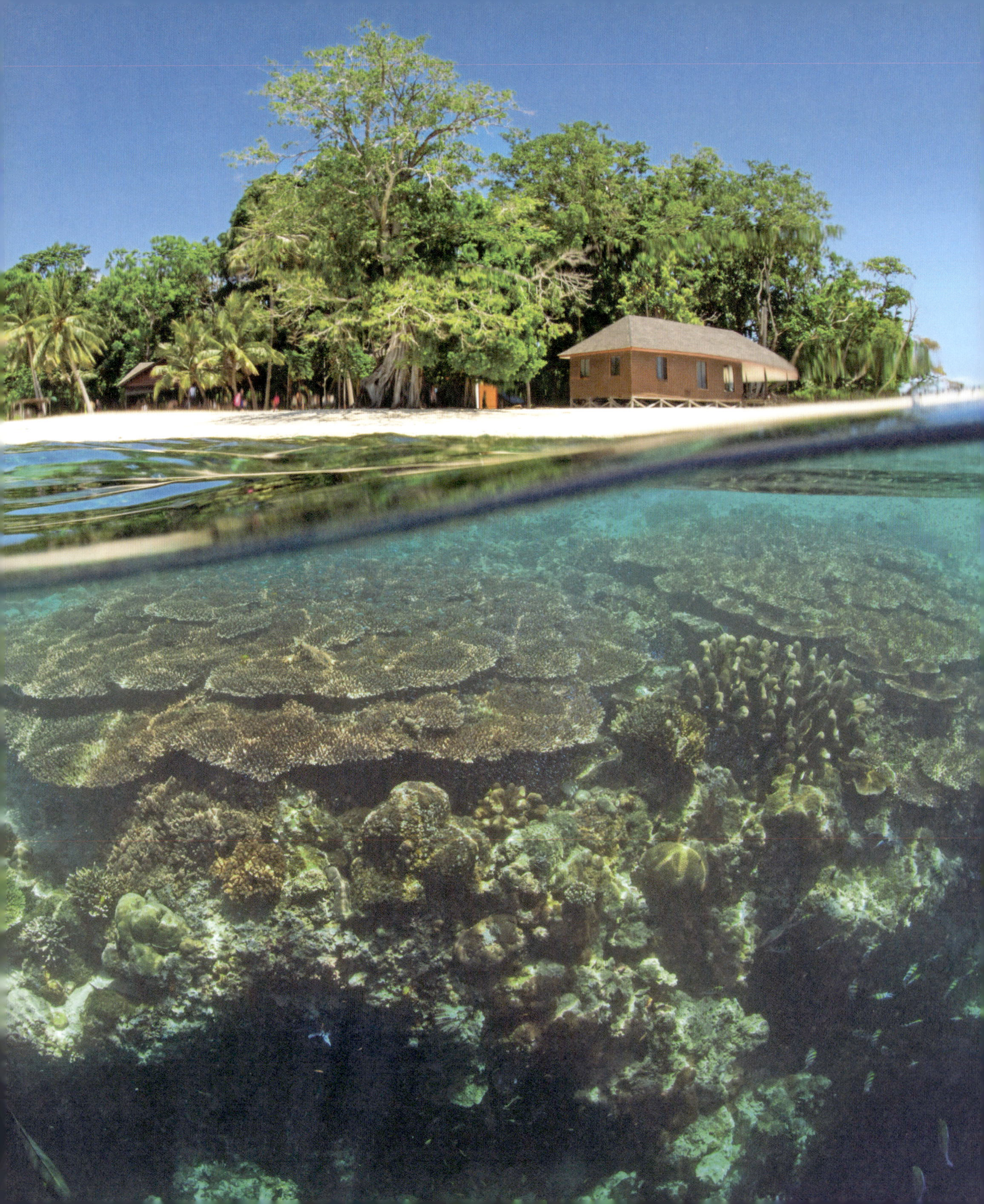

Sipadan Island, Malaysian Borneo

This giant seamount is Asia's ultimate oceanic island for divers.

Why it's special

Five degrees north of the equator and in the heart of the Indo-Pacific basin, Pulau Sipadan is Malaysia's only oceanic island. The island's unique position atop a steep underwater pinnacle provides a habitat for a variety of marine life. Just 12ha (30ac) in size, this tiny, mushroom-shaped island is surrounded by vertical drop-offs and nutrient-rich waters, which are a magnet for a wide range of pelagics including schooling barracuda, big-eye trevally, numerous shark species, including scalloped hammerheads. Vibrant coral gardens teeming with colourful reef fish such as snapper, sweetlips and unicorn fish add to the visual spectacle. But what's made this island famous is its abundance of turtles, with thousands of green and hawksbill turtles coming here to nest, mate and to fill their bellies with corals, sponges and algae.

Best time to dive

Between the dry season months of April and December the sea is usually calm and visibility ranges from 15–30m (49–98ft). The water temperature is around 26–30°C (79–86°F), and this time period also sees a higher concentration of pelagic species. If possible, avoid the high season between June and August, Easter and Chinese New Year, or make your bookings well in advance. Note that the island is now closed each December for recuperation of coral and marine life.

Opposite Sipidan Island as seen from a dive site called the Drop Off

Gear
- 3mm wetsuit for 26-30°C (79-86°F) water temps. or just a rash vest on shallow, shorter dives
- Reef smart sunscreen

Due to Sipadan's vertical walls and clear visibility, it can be easy to lose track of your depth. A good dive computer with a reliable maximum depth alert is recommended. A dive torch can be useful for exploring the nooks and crannies of the coral walls.

Photography tip
I like to photograph wide angle shots (like barracuda tornadoes) and also portraits of species (eg; turtles and rays) in Sipadan. A wide-angle zoom will cover both of these aspects.

Qualification
- Advanced Open Water

Due to strong currents and deep wall dives (and Government legislation enacted in 2022), Advanced Open Water Diver certification is required. Divers should be comfortable with drift diving and not being able to see the ocean floor as a reference.

Getting there
To get to Mabul or Kapalai, the islands with the closest accommodations to Sipadan, take a 45-minute boat ride from Semporna jetty. This jetty is a 1.5-2-hour drive from Tawau Airport, which has flights that connect with Kota Kinabalu and Kuala Lumpur.

Dive in

Located off the east coast of Malaysian Borneo, the tiny island of Pulau Sipadan (Malay for 'border island') is an isolated, oceanic seamount rising from the depths of the Celebes Sea. Perched atop an extinct volcano, this wall-diving wonderland sits 600m (1970ft) directly above the sea floor and has steep walls decorated in coral. Incredibly, part of the island drops away vertically only 10m (33ft) from the beach, offering an immediate descent into the abyss (this dive site is simply named 'Drop Off'). On my first visit to Sipadan, when there were still resorts on the island, you could walk straight out of your hotel and be diving this drop-off within minutes. With the government now implementing strict conservation guidelines for the island, that's no longer the case. More about that later.

In 1989, Jacques Cousteau's film *Borneo: The Ghost of the Sea Turtle* brought international attention to Sipadan. Cousteau proclaimed 'I have seen other places like Sipadan, 45 years ago, but now no more. Now we have found an untouched piece of art.' For divers, a visit to Sipadan is a journey into one of the most extraordinary marine environments on the planet. Entering the water, you're instantly struck by the clarity and warmth of the sea. Visibility is fantastic, averaging around 30m (98ft), offering panoramic views of walls decorated in vibrant soft corals, sea fans and sponges. Sipadan's location in the heart of the Coral Triangle means that it's home to over 3000 species of fish and hundreds of coral types. Diving here, you are likely to encounter everything from small colourful reef fish like anemonefish and damselfish to pelagics like schools of jacks and reef sharks. For many, the highlight of diving in Sipadan is the famous 'Barracuda Point', where immense schools (they really are humungous) of blacktail or chevron barracuda gather, creating a mesmerising whirlpool effect.

The island is also one of the world's most important nesting sites for green and hawksbill turtles, which you'll see as they rest and feed on the coral walls or glide effortlessly past. These heroes in a half-shell are especially abundant in the dive sites of Hanging Gardens and the aptly named Turtle Patch. For experienced cave divers accompanied by a local guide, Turtle Tomb offers an eerie tunnel dive into the final resting place of numerous turtles.

Being an oceanic island with vertical walls, currents can be strong here, as I experienced on my first visit when our group was swept out to sea. Despite this scary experience, the incredible diving drew me back, though the second time around it was a very different scene.

By the early 2000s, Sipadan had become very well-known, and the marine environment was being impacted by the increased number of visitors. Jacques Cousteau's earlier description of it being 'untouched' certainly no longer applied. His film and that famous statement put Sipadan onto divers' radars, ironically contributing to it becoming overrun – no longer the piece of art he described. In 2004, the Malaysian Government got serious about protecting Sipadan, removing all the island's resorts and establishing the Sipadan Island Marine Park. The closest accommodations are now on the islands of Mabul or Kapalai, about 15km (9mi) away.

These days, you'll need a permit to visit Sipadan, with an enforced limit of 176 permits given out for a total of two dives per person, per day. For the best chance of getting your hands on one, book your accommodation early, avoid the peak season and spend at least a week at your resort. Most resorts guarantee one day at Sipadan if you book three dive days, two if you book five, so the longer you stay, the more dive days at Sipadan. Since 2022, divers are now also required to have a minimum of an Advanced Open Water certification. Perhaps with these strict measures, the island may just return to the pristine state it was when Cousteau filmed here back in the '80s.

Surviving when things go wrong

Swept away at Sipadan

When I was a teenager, our family went on a holiday to Borneo, staying with my dad's mate, Wasli. At 16 and freshly qualified as Dive Master, I was keen to explore as many underwater environments as possible and I'd heard that Sipadan was amongst the top ten dives of the world. Wasli was eager to show us around his homeland of Malaysian Borneo, and even though it had been years since his last dive, he was determined to take me diving in Sipadan.

We set out early morning with a local dive guide on a small tender to a site on the edge of reef running alongside the island. The dive was routine for Sipadan; jump in and drift with the current, following the reef's edge for 60 minutes, then be met by the tender that's following the same current. Easy. Well, on this particular morning, when we surfaced after 60 minutes there was no boat, and to make matters worse, the surface current was tearing us out to sea. The island of Sipadan quickly disappeared.

The hours that followed felt like something out of a bad movie. We were incredibly remote and, since Borneo is equatorial, it wouldn't take long for us to be badly sunburnt and dehydrated. Most alarmingly, there was no air and sea search and rescue in this part of the world. Our young dive guide was stricken with fear, making him a massive liability. Any experienced diver will tell you that a panicked diver is the most dangerous of all divers; in the face of panic, one can quite literally climb on top of others to save themselves. I remember him taking off his fins, putting them on his hands and waving vigorously to no one for help. Trembling with panic, the current took him away faster, splitting the group. I was then left with the awful task of leaving Wasli (as he was too exhausted to join me) to go and collect our panicked guide, risking losing Wasli in the process. Ultimately, I was able to make the distance and reunite the group, clipping us all together. We then ditched our weights but hung onto our belts thinking they would make good tourniquets if we had a shark incident.

My saving grace was the role that I was thrown into, managing the situation while keeping the others calm. This responsibility occupied my mind, keeping panic at bay. With that said, I remember the feeling of dread as the sun began to set and I prepared myself mentally for a night of floating in the darkness out at sea.

At dusk, our rescuers magically appeared from nowhere in the form of two locals inside a dugout canoe with outriggers. In the early hours of the night, other local villagers also came to assist. We discovered that our dive tender had drifted in the opposite direction to our planned drift and figured we, too, would drift that way. When we didn't resurface, he searched for an hour or so before returning to shore. Apparently, no further search was undertaken because of the grand search area and the unlikelihood of our discovery. Thankfully, local fishermen took it on as an opportunity to earn some reward money and came searching for us.

Above A juvenile anemonefish within its anemone

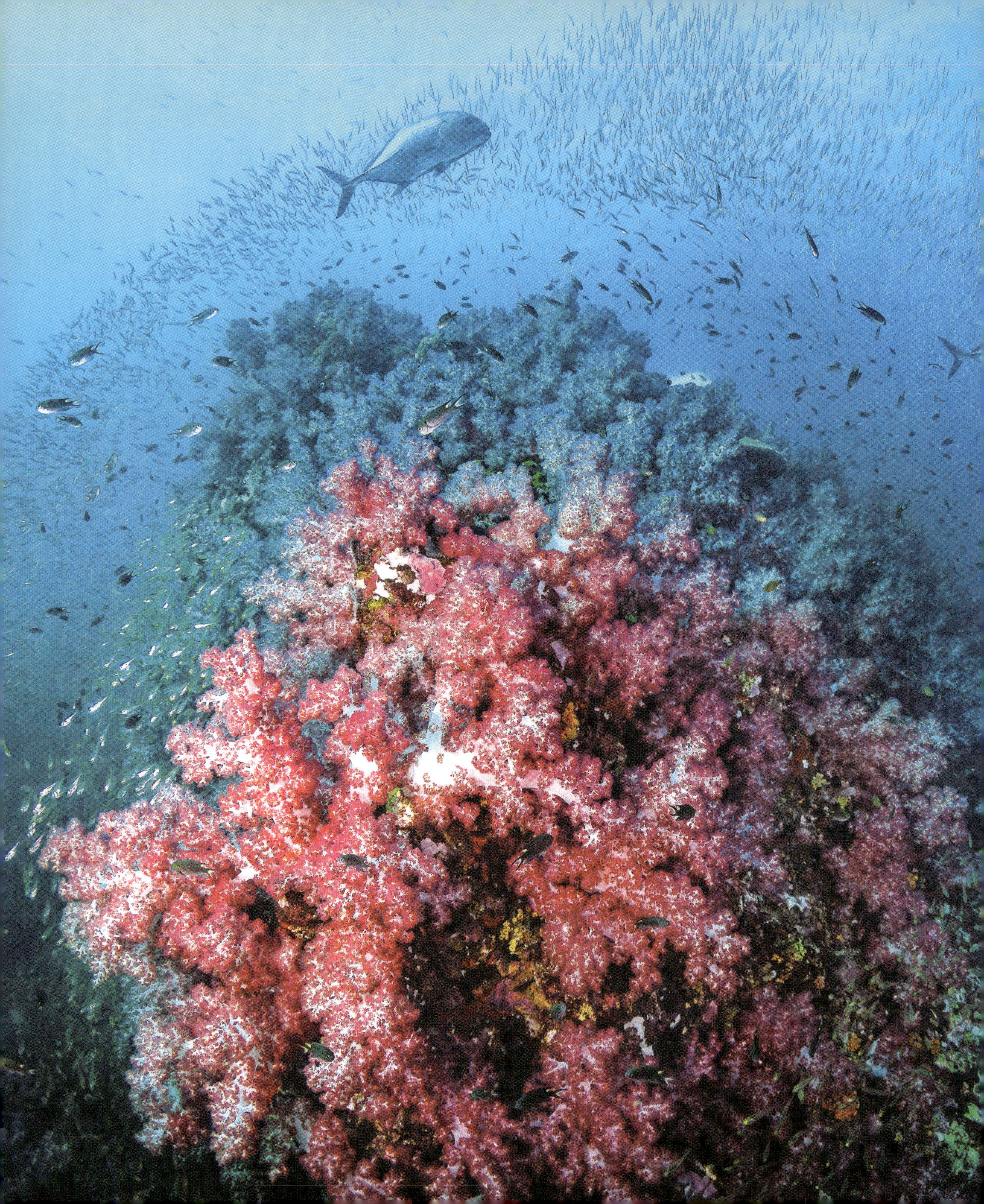

Tubbataha, Philippines
The pride of the Philippines, this marine mecca is as remote as it is colourful

Why it's special

The star attraction of the Philippines' dive scene is World Heritage-listed Tubbataha Reef, which offers the country's best diving in terms of species diversity, variety of dive sites and pristine conditions. Its remote location, a ten-hour steam from Puerto Princesa, limits the number of divers, as it's accessible only by liveaboard, and only during a very short dry season. Unfortunately, its remote location has also made it a target for illegal fishing and poaching, a problem that the government has tackled head-on with fantastic marine park management that's funded by the tourists that visit it. Expect the unexpected at Tubbataha while you're searching for nudibranchs and other macro marvels, you may be surprised by the sudden appearance of something not so small... like a whale shark!

Best time to dive

Dive liveaboards only offer trips to Tubbataha within a very small window; the dry season months of mid-March until mid-June. During this time skies are blue, seas are calm and visibility can reach over 30m (98ft).

Gear
- 3mm wetsuit for 26-29°C (79-84°F) water temps
- Reef smart sunscreen
- Sun protective clothing and polarised sunnies
- Good torch for night diving
- Reef hook
- Signal float for diving in strong currents and Personal Signalling Device

Photography tip
Both macro and wide have their place at Tubbataha, so pack both. Just be mindful that anything can arrive at any time; you don't want to have the macro lens on when the whale shark arrives!

Qualification
- Open Water

Some sites are more suited to Advanced Divers due to strong currents.

Getting there
Liveaboards to Tubbataha commence from Puerto Princesa, the bustling capital of Palawan. Various Philippine carriers provide frequent flights from Manila to Puerto Princesa, typically spanning an hour in duration.

Opposite As an atoll reef with a very high density of marine species, UNESCO has declared Tubbataha Reef a World Heritage-listed Site

Dive in

As I type this, the Philippines has just been awarded as Asia's Leading Dive Destination at the World Travel Awards ... again. Whether you're a novice diver or, like myself, have logged thousands of dives over the years, this archipelago, located on the northern tip of the Coral Triangle, has something to offer every underwater enthusiast. There are plenty of great dive sites scattered through the Philippines 7600+ islands, but one location stands out from the rest for its vibrant reefs and biodiversity; Tubbataha (pronounced too-bah-ta-hah).

Tubbataha Reefs Natural Park is a UNESCO World Heritage Site in the Sulu Sea, 160km (99mi) south-east of Puerto Princesa on the island of Palawan, in the far west of the Philippines. Accessible by liveaboard for only eight weeks each year in March and June, outside of typhoon and monsoon seasons, its reefs and atolls are in absolutely pristine condition, mainly owing to its remote location and also due to the active role that the Philippine government has taken in its protection. The country takes great pride in Tubbataha, even featuring a map of the park on the back of the 1000-peso banknote.

Located on Cagayan Ridge, a series of extinct underwater volcanoes, Tubbataha is comprised of two huge coral atolls, North Atoll and South Atoll, plus the smaller 1.6km (1mi) long Jessie Beazley Reef, which was unfortunately named after a ship's captain who crashed into it (it's a shame they didn't name it after another ship that famously ran aground here in 2005 – Greenpeace's Rainbow Warrior). On North Atoll is the Ranger Station, where military and civilians work together to protect the park from illegal fishing. The Philippine government created the Tubbataha Reefs Natural Park Act back in 2009. Every tourist that enters the park contributes to its management with an entrance fee. Now that's one fee I'm happy to pay!

Liveaboard trips are usually around a week long, with boats departing from Palawan in the afternoon, so the ten hour steam to the park is done while you're eating dinner and sleeping. There's definitely an excitement to waking up in paradise, then diving straight into the action. So, what can you expect to see in the tropical waters of this 97,000ha (240,000ac) park? Expect huge schools of predatory fish, such as barracuda and snapper; over 360 coral species (about half of all of the world's coral species) including gorgonian fans and whip corals; hawkesbill and green sea turtles, mantas; dolphins; and a healthy population of sharks, including tigers and grey reef sharks. Then there's the little guys, like pygmy seahorses and nudibranchs.

You may also be lucky to come across megafauna like whale sharks and potentially whales. My brother, Toby, had a surprise encounter with a whale shark during his last trip, while he was deep in the zone seeking out macro critters on a wall dive. He recounts that his dive buddy frantically signalled for him to turn around. He spun around to find a whale shark, or 'butanding' as they're locally known, cruising past him very close by. Toby still counts this surprise encounter as one of his favourite diving experiences.

Tubbataha has a range of dives from vertical walls that stretch down to over 100m (328ft), to shallow lagoons and colourful reef flats. In South Atoll there's the wreck of the Delsan a small ship whose anchor marks the start of a dive where you can see big fish, like dogtooth tuna and great barracuda, and grey reef sharks hunting inside a crack in the reef wall known as The Cut. In North Atoll, another small shipwreck called the Malayan is known for its wall diving and for large schools of hammerheads in the blue water just beyond the wreck. For more sharky action, Shark Airport is a cleaning station that attracts schooling sharks like grey reef, silky and guitar sharks. Just north of Shark Airport is Washing Machine, where you can find fish such as giant trevally, triggerfish and sweetlips and perhaps even some eagle rays and mantas. But beware it's named after its intense and sudden currents that can leave divers feeling disoriented.

As a generalisation, currents can get strong at Tubbataha, so the diving is better suited to those who've already got quite a few dives under their belt, and are physically fit enough for the sometimes-challenging conditions.

Opposite You may be lucky enough to spot a 'butanding' at Tubbataha *Below left* Thriving coral diversity *Below right* Ranger Station for the Park Rangers of Tubbataha Reef National Marine Park

Anilao, Philippines
Float amidst a galaxy of bizarre planktonic creatures from the deep

Why it's special

Blackwater diving, an exhilarating form of night diving, involves plunging into open ocean to encounter rarely seen often other-worldly creatures that emerge from the deep, attracted by lights that mimic the moon. Attached to a drop line from the dive boat, divers are suspended at around 20m (66ft) in the infinite darkness of the sea, while powerful lights attract a captivating array of tiny marine organisms.

Anilao, a coastal barangay (village) three hours' drive south from Manila (that's if you make ever it out of Manila's traffic), has gained a reputation as a premier destination for this unique diving and photography technique. Anilao's waters, renowned for incredible biodiversity, offer divers the chance to see and maybe photograph the ocean's most elusive nocturnal characters, from bioluminescent jellyfish to neon flying squid and transparent larval fish, in an underwater experience that feels decidedly galactic.

Best time to dive

The dry season is best for blackwater diving in Anilao, from November to May. These months offer calmer seas and clearer waters, essential for a successful blackwater dive. The absence of strong winds and currents during this period ensures a safer and more enjoyable dive, plus the diversity of marine life visible during these months is at its peak. The busiest months of the dry season are April and May, the quietest from January to March.

Gear
- 3/5mm wetsuit and a hood, due to the cooler temperatures at night and potential stings or irritations from microscopic organisms
- A reliable dive light (preferably with a narrow beam) is essential, not just for visibility but also to attract marine life
- A backup light
- A dive computer that can be easily illuminated
- A safety sausage (SMB)

Photography tip
With a dark background, transparent creatures and constant movement, blackwater photography is definitely challenging. Most photographers will have a custom-built blackwater set up. This may include, a macro lens (60-100mm/2-4in is a good start), a focus light to capture unique creatures, and two underwater strobes.

Qualification
- Advanced Open Water, night diving experience

Blackwater diving is unlike any other style of diving. Divers have limited to no visual references and are suspended in open water; vertigo is a common sensation. Divers will need to be familiar with night diving and have good buoyancy control.

Getting there
Anilao is about three hours' drive from Manila, depending on traffic. Dive resorts may offer an airport pickup, otherwise you can catch a bus to Batangas City and then jump in a Jeepney to Anilao from there.

Opposite **Larval wunderpus**

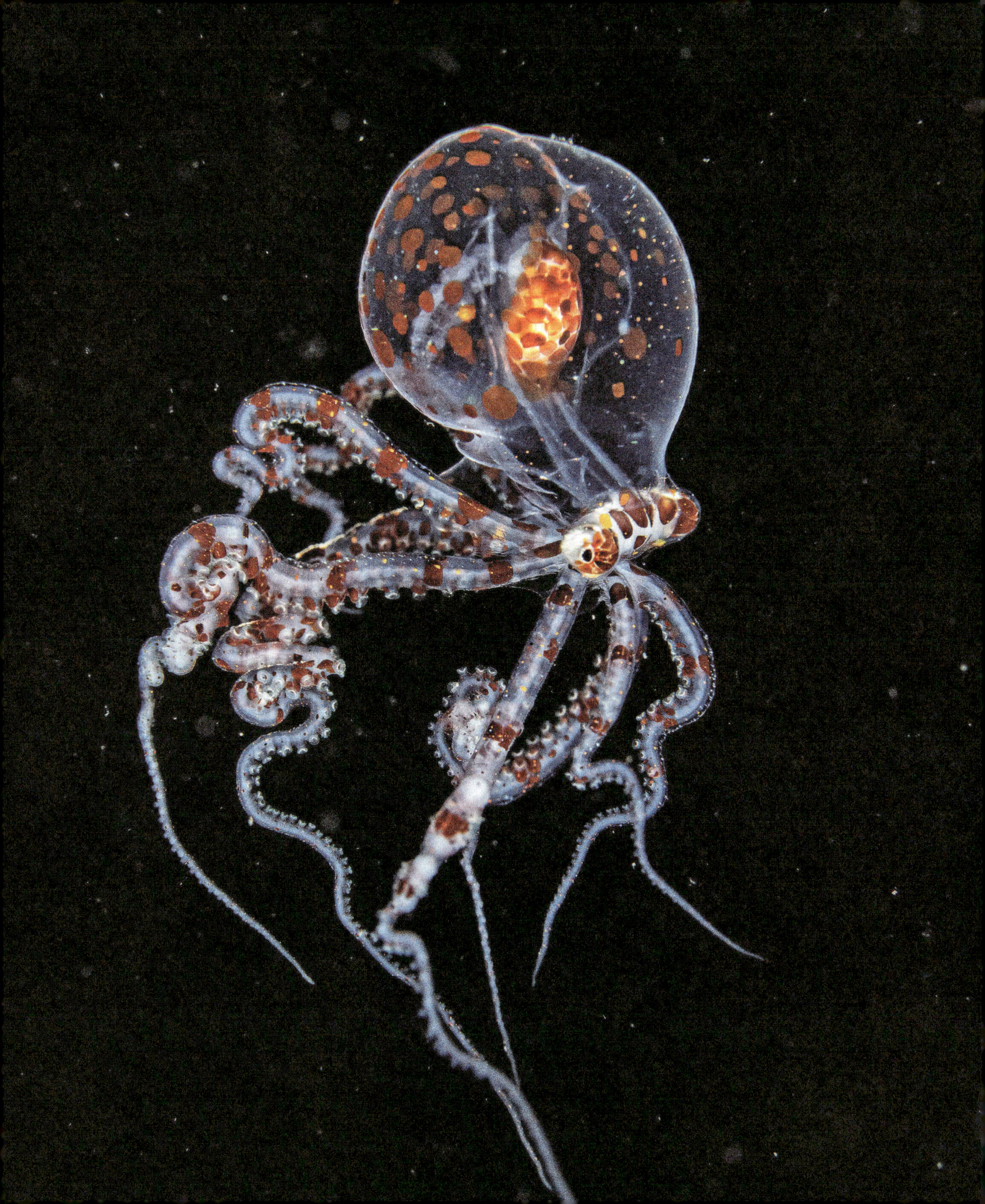

Asia

Dive in

Nestled in the touristy Batangas province, Anilao attracts underwater photographers and macro enthusiasts like a moth to a flame. The Philippines' first dive centre was established here in the mid '60s and it remains the most well-known and closest dive destination to capital city, Manila, 130km (81mi) away. Famous for its colourful reefs and incredible muck diving, Anilao is known amongst divers as 'the nudibranch capital of the world', and recently it's the extension from macro to blackwater diving that lures underwater photographers.

Located on a small peninsula, Anilao's deep channel provides a pathway for the upwelling of nutrient-rich water which attracts a range of deep-sea organisms. This, coupled with the area's minimal light pollution and the expertise of local dive guides, increases your chances of encountering rare and unusual species.

Your blackwater diving experience begins when you venture into the open sea at night, far from the comfort of coastal reefs (for this reason, it's best to do a few coastal night dives prior to trying blackwater diving, to get comfortable with diving in the dark). Unlike a standard night dive where you have physical reference points like a reef, blackwater diving allows you to spot organisms that might not be seen on the reef at night, as they habituate deeper waters, sometimes coming up from depths of over a thousand metres.

While preparing for your dive, your guides will lower lights into the dark waters beneath. These lights, attached to a weighted line, serve as beacons that attract a mesmerising array of planktonic creatures from the deep. This is when the scene turns galactic. Tiny organisms, many of which are in their larval stages, flicker and glow with bioluminescence, creating a living light show in the pitch-black water. It's a rare opportunity to observe the first stages of life for many marine species, including some that will eventually settle on the reefs.

After gearing up and listening to your dive briefing, you'll jump into the water. Your BCD will be attached to a drop line so that you can descend and zone in to this new sensory experience, without the worry of floating away from the boat in the darkness. There are times when blackwater diving provides zero reference points and in such a dark, cold and alien environment, it's easy to get disorientated; the trick is to remain calm and relaxed and to dial into observing the weird and wonderful world that has ascended from the depths. When you're done, you can ascend the line, grab a hot beverage, then flick through some of the most surreal and sci-fi themed photos you'll ever take underwater.

Apart from diving in the dark, the real thrill of blackwater diving lies in the unpredictability of species sightings, some of them as small as your thumbnail. You might witness the dance of a juvenile octopus with translucent skin, the erratic swimming of a larval fish with its developing features, or the eerie glow of a jellyfish as it pulsates through the water. The parade of creatures is diverse and everchanging, ranging from beautiful to downright bizarre.

Blackwater diving isn't for everyone and if you'd like to dive with strange critters in the dark, without heading out into the open ocean, you could try bonfire diving in Anilao. The concept is the same wherein you are floating near a powerful light, however, instead of dangling in the open sea, lights are placed on the sea floor at around 10–20m (33–66ft) deep, pointing up toward the night sky. As bonfire diving is done at a shallower depth, it is suitable for beginners.

For such a specialised style of diving, finding the right operator is crucial. Be sure to travel with a local company that regularly conducts blackwater dives, not just night dives. In Anilao, I recommend Crystal Blue (divecbr.com). Others include Solitude Acacia Resort (solitude.world/solitude-acacia-resort) and Buceo Anilao Beach & Dive Resort (buceoanilao.com).

Opposite A few very interesting characters lured up from the deep

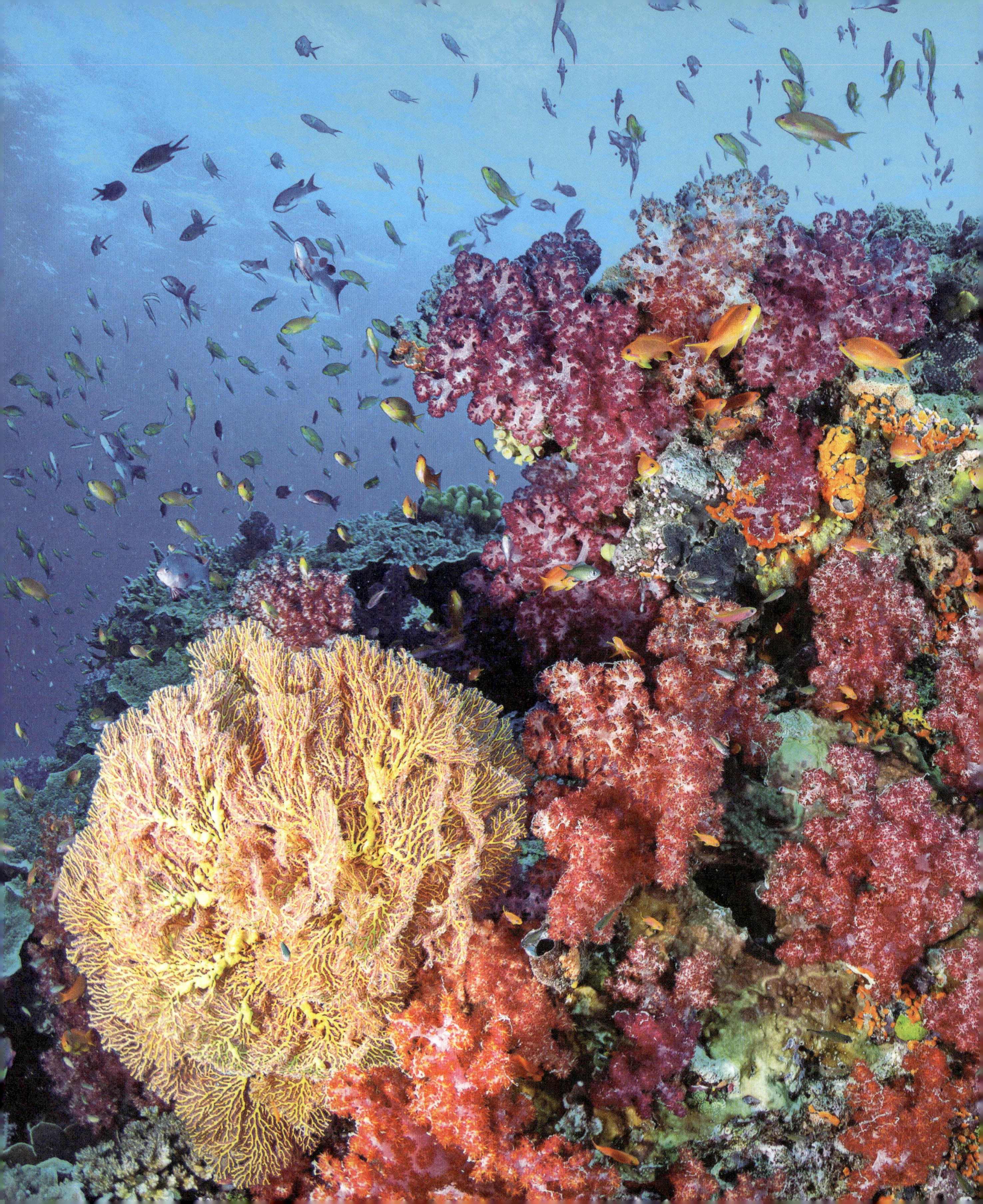

Pacific

1. Rock Islands, Palau 178
2. The Tuamotus, French Polynesia 182
3. Vava'u, Tonga 187
4. The Coolidge, Santo (Vanuatu) 190
5. Vatu-i-Ra, Fiji 194
6. Beqa Lagoon, Fiji 199
7. Wolf and Darwin Islands, Galápagos 202
8. Tufi, Papua New Guinea 208

Rock Islands, Palau
Take the pledge and dive into one of the world's most protected bodies of water

Why it's special

Hundreds of tiny, mushroom-shaped islands create a stunning backdrop to some incredible diving in the Rock Islands. From reef sharks and giant Napoleon wrasse to manta trains, gentle sloping reefs to dramatic walls, blue holes and caves to WWII wrecks, the crystal-clear waters of Palau offer something for ocean lovers of all sorts. Koror, Palau's biggest city, is the gateway to the action with speedboat tours heading south into the Rock Islands and reef wall beyond, each day. Alternatively, the resort town of Peleliu, just south of the Rock Islands, offers a quieter, off-the-beaten-path dive base. If you have cash to splash on a liveaboard, there's a handful of one-to-two-week options departing regularly from Koror, with 'spawning cruises' being my pick of the itineraries. These trips coincide with a number of marine life spawning events, the most frequent of which are the bumphead parrotfish and red snapper events, which occur at different moon phases most months of the year. Other, less frequent spawning events include Moorish idols, sea bream, sailfin snapper and orange-spine unicorn fish. During these events you'll find yourself diving amongst hundreds, even thousands of aggregating fish.

Best time to dive

During the dry season months from October to May, water temperatures are generally a balmy 27–30°C (80–86°F). Visibility is at its best and the season is in full swing.

Gear
- 3mm wetsuit for 27-30°C (80-86°F) water temps
- Reef smart sunscreen
- Sun protective clothing and polarised sunglasses
- Torch for night diving
- Reef hook
- Signal float for diving in strong currents

Photography tip
Palau has it all macro, zoom, wide, fisheye! Pack for them all, if possible.

Qualification
- Advanced Open Water and Nitrox

Palau has a variety of dive sites. Some are deep, many have strong currents and there's also some good wreck diving. Advanced certification is recommended to make the most of these varied conditions, and most divers here use Nitrox to maximise bottom time.

Getting there
You can fly directly into Koror from Brisbane, Singapore, Manila and San Francisco.

Opposite Nothing could prepare me for the first time I saw Palau's Rock Islands from the air *Previous* An explosion of colour in Vatu-i-Ra, Fiji, the soft coral capital of the world

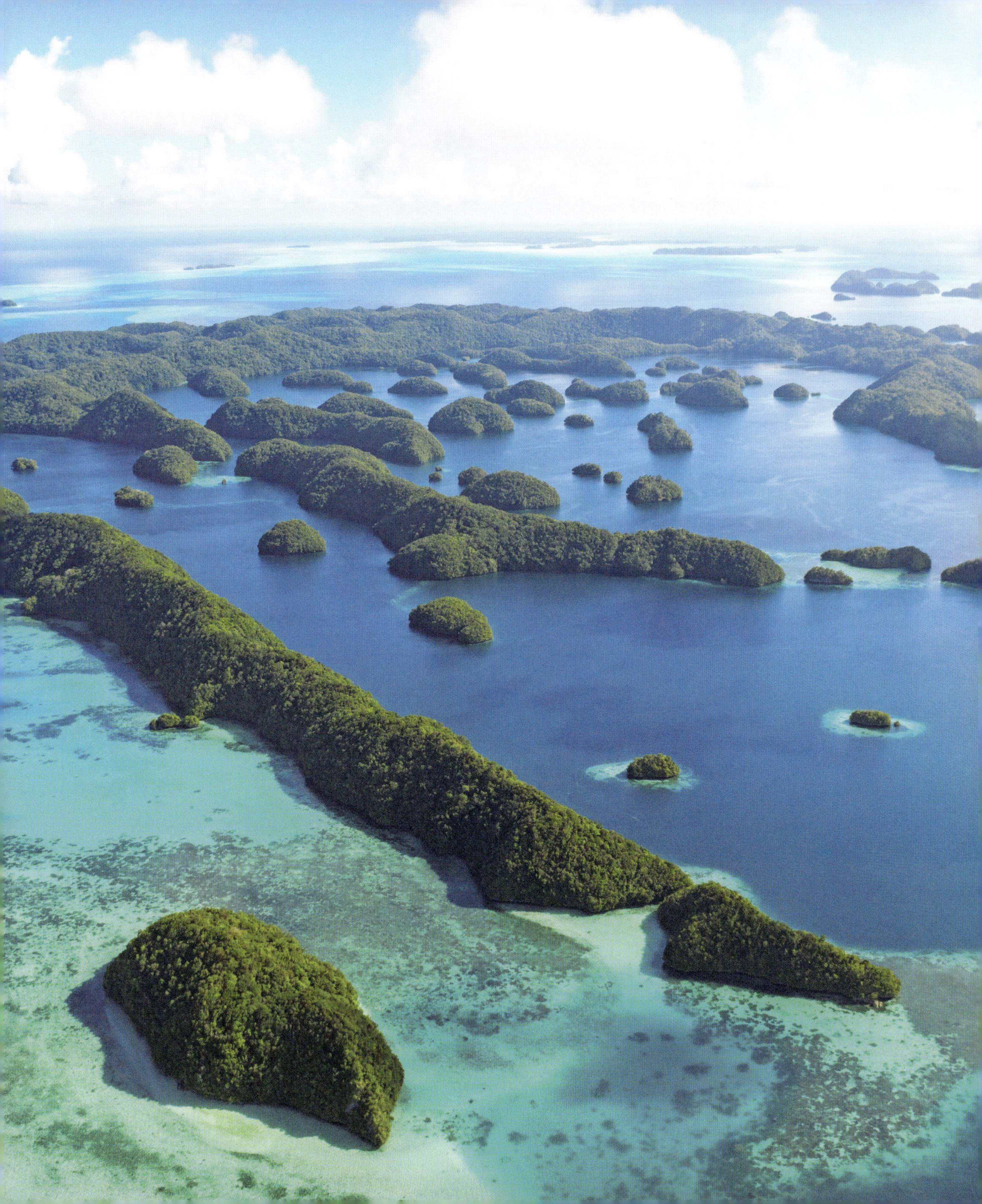

Pacific

Dive in

'Children of Palau, I take this pledge, as your guest, to preserve and protect your beautiful and unique island home. I vow to tread lightly, act kindly and explore mindfully ...' When entering The Republic of Palau, every visitor must sign The Palau Pledge. Palau is the first country in the world to incorporate such a clause of environmental protection into its immigration laws. They've also banned toxic sunscreens; created the world's first shark sanctuary back in 2009; and turned 80% of their waters into a non-commercial fishing zone. With over 1400 species of fish and over 500 species of coral, Palau is a diver's heaven, and thanks to the actions of its people it will continue to be for generations to come.

My introduction to Palau was when we cruised into the Rock Islands on a yacht and boy, did she offer a great first impression. Small forested islands scattered through turquoise waters, hemmed by drop-offs into the deep blue. I couldn't wait to jump into our Zodiac and go exploring. Fortunately, that was my job; choose a dive site and steer the ship's captain toward it, jump in the water with my camera, then present a highlights reel to my boss/the yacht's owner so he could decide if he also wanted to dive it. Then, we'd motor to the next anchorage and do it all again.

All of Palau is stunning, but the World Heritage-listed Rock Islands in Palau's Southern Lagoon, also known as Chelbacheb, offer an array of incredible dive sites around the 250+ islands, with many sites less than an hour's ride by speedboat from Palau's biggest city, Koror.

The drift dive at Blue Corner is a good place to start your Palaun dive adventure, being just 46km (28mi) (about 50–70 minutes by speedboat) from Koror. Imagine a shallow table and vertical wall drop-offs with giant gorgonian fans, hard and soft corals, cabbage corals and large schools of fish. Then there's reef sharks, dolphins, hawksbill and green turtles, eagle rays, and even the odd migrating whale or whale shark, together with visibility of up to 30m (98ft) and depths ranging between 8–30m (26–98ft). With fast-flowing currents that can change within seconds, this one's best suited to experienced divers. Bring your reef hook so you can hook into the plateau and relax between drifting and watch the underwater cabaret pass you by. The Blue Corner dive marries together nicely with a dive at the nearby Blue Holes. If you time it right with the currents, you can fin across to the Blue Corner straight after your Blue Holes dive. Blue Holes is a unique dive where you'll descend into a giant chamber with chimneys and tunnels leading off in different directions, with visibility of 20–50m (66–164ft).

The lesser known Siaes Tunnel and Siaes Point offer a similar experience to Blue Corner and Blue Holes, with plenty of action on the reef wall, and a stunning submerged cavern adorned with enormous gorgonian sea fans.

A great spot for newbie divers is Ngedebus Coral Garden (also known as Matthew's Place), 45km (28mi) south-west of Koror, with calm conditions and shallow depths of under 23m (75ft). There are plenty of lovely hard corals, amongst the best you'll find in the Pacific, plus rays and some unique fish including crocodile fish, lionfish and scorpionfish.

At the man-made German Channel, 37km (23mi) south-west of Koror (about 50 minutes by speedboat) you'll find rich, plankton-filled currents and cleaning stations full of busy butterflyfish and cleaner wrasse, luring mantas year-round (though December to March is prime). You may also spot leaf fish, crocodile fish, octopuses and nudibranchs inside the coral gardens on the sides, plus schooling sharks, jacks, barracudas and tropical fish aplenty. Visibility-wise, expect 20–40m (66–131ft), with the best visibility being on an incoming tide.

Ulong Channel is another favourite for divers, where, on an incoming tide, you can fly through the channel at high speed over enormous patches of cabbage corals, spying groupers, reef sharks and leopard sharks along the way.

These sites are just a few of the highlights, however there are many more including some great WWII wreck diving. And then there's the whole cave diving scene with incredible spots like Chandelier Cave, a convenient 1.6km (1mi) from Koror, sure to satisfy with its stalagmite and stalactite-filled chambers.

When you want some time topside, you can explore the Rock Islands by kayak, SUP (stand-up paddleboard) or on foot and find drawings of up to 4000-years-old in caves, plus some marine lakes. At Jellyfish Lake on Eil Malk island, you'll get lost in clouds of stingless jellyfish hypnotically pulsing through the water, following the sun. There's no diving allowed here, though, as the bubbles can harm the jellies. Note that Jellyfish Lake has been closed a few times in previous years, as high water temperatures have decimated the population from millions down to almost none.

There are a handful of dive liveaboards to choose from and several dive centres including dive industry pioneers Fish 'n Fins (fishnfins.com) and Sam's Tours (samstours.com).

Opposite (clockwise) Mating mandarin fish; reef manta; Jellyfish Lake on Eil Malk Island, Palau

The Tuamotus, French Polynesia
Go with the flow on a remote Polynesian atoll

Why it's special

Pink beaches, dolphin pods, walls of sharks and thousands of groupers; the Tuamotus are alive and thriving! Translated as 'remote' (tua) 'islands' (motus), this faraway string of atolls has incredible diving and a warm local culture, with just 16,000 inhabitants enjoying a simple, salty lifestyle. While fishing, pearling and copra (coconut flesh) have traditionally been the source of income for the Tuamotuans, in recent years tourism has steadily increased. Two of the biggest motus, Rangiroa and Fakarava, have unbelievable diving, with dives scheduled around the daily ebb and flow of the tide into central lagoons. With different creatures swimming in and out of the atolls' lagoons on each turn of the tide, no two dives are the same, so you can literally dive the same pass every day and enjoy new experiences.

Best time to dive

Both Rangiroa and Fakarava offer year-round diving, though there can be rain during the December to March wet season months. In Rangiroa, mantas and humpbacks can be seen from August to mid-October, while hammerheads and eagle rays are most abundant from January to March. In Fakarava, the grouper spawns during the full moon in either June or July, coinciding with the European summer, making this the busiest time of year to visit (book early).

Gear
- A 3mm wetsuit for 26-28°C (79-82°F) water temps
- Reef safe sunscreen
- On the grouper/shark dive you'll be partaking in some very long dives, and potentially diving in the low light of dawn and dusk, so I would recommend a 5mm wetsuit
- A good dive light for diving at night or the early hours of the morning
- Reef hook for strong currents
- Surface marker buoy

Photography tip

The visibility is incredible, and the wildlife is big, so go wide.

On some dives in the passes, the current can be very strong, so taking bulky camera gear is almost pointless (you won't be stopping or slowing down to focus or frame a shot). Try a GoPro for these strong current days.

Qualification
- Open Water (for inside the lagoon)
- All other dives, apart from inside the lagoon, are best suited to Advanced Divers due to strong currents and the presence of numerous predators. Excellent buoyancy control and comfort in dynamic underwater environments are crucial for safely experiencing this location.

Getting there

There are regular flights to Papeete with Air Tahiti Nui. You can then fly domestically with Air Moana and Air Tahiti to Rangiroa and Fakarava. There are no shuttles at Fakarava Airport, so arrange your transfer with your accommodation hosts prior to arrival.

Opposite Observing a playful bottlenose dolphin in Rangiroa

The Tuamotus, French Polynesia

Dive in

The Tuamotus in French Polynesia are the world's largest chain of atolls, and one of the prettiest places you'll ever visit. These 77 ring-shaped motus (islands) are the remnants of ancient volcanoes, their cores now sunken into the ocean, replaced by shallow, turquoise lagoons. Each of the atolls has a 'pass', where the water flows in and out from the central lagoon to the open ocean on every turn of the tide. Being propelled through the pass on an incoming tide, speeding by walls of coral, turtles, dolphins and sharks is pure joy. Opening your arms wide and gliding through the channel may be the closest feeling you'll have to flying, unless you're a skydiver.

I got to experience the wondrous Tuamotus when we sailed into one of the more remote atolls during a round-the-world voyage. This particular motu had no airport or inter-island ferry, so the only tourists to ever come here were private yachties. We dived the passes of a few atolls and explored their empty beaches before cruising across to the two biggest atolls, Rangiroa and Fakarava. An hour's flight from Tahiti, these atolls are the busiest of the Tuamotus. They each have an airport, restaurants, dive shops and boutique hotels or family-run pensions to accommodate tourists, who are mostly divers and snorkelers.

I have a strong memory of diving Tiputa Pass in the northeast of Rangiroa atoll. Knowing that the current would dictate my dive and that I'd need to keep my hands free (plus, I was looking after my boss underwater), I left my camera on the yacht. As often seems to be the way, it was during this cameraless dive that I had the best dolphin encounter of my life as a huge pod of bottlenose dolphins swam alongside me for what felt like forever. Bottlenoses are a common sighting in Tiputa Pass and there's a good chance that you'll see them, too. Other regulars include turtles, rays, barracuda and sharks including blacktips, grey reefs and the occasional tiger and hammerhead. At the pass's entrance, in the wet season months of January to March, great hammerheads are known to aggregate as they feed on squadrons of eagle rays, the perfect excuse for a return visit.

A 45-minute flight south-east of Rangiroa, the quieter atoll of Fakarava is a UNESCO Biosphere Reserve with some unique dive offerings. In the north of the atoll, The Garuae Pass is Polynesia's widest navigable pass (over 800m/2620ft wide) and the diving here is outstanding, with plenty of dolphins, rays, mantas and several species of sharks, the most populus being grey reef sharks. For the local people, who consider sharks to be totem animals or 'tāura', the sharks' presence is a good sign. In the more isolated, southern part of Fakarava's atoll, Tumakohua Pass is home to the famous 'wall of sharks' – a natural aggregation of grey reef sharks, numbering up to 700, that can be found here year-round, each morning on the incoming tide. The best time to encounter them is during the grouper spawn, when you are likely to see greater numbers.

The annual mass spawning of marbled groupers in Fakarava is a natural phenomenon that occurs during the full moon in either June or July, for less than an hour, just once a year. In the days leading up to the spawning, grouper numbers swell in the narrow pass (up to 18,000 have been recorded at one time), attracting hundreds of hungry grey reef sharks. There are a few things to see here: first there's the onset of thousands of marbled groupers (a usually solitary fish) filling the pass in the lead-up to the full moon. Next is the spawning, as thousands of groupers release their eggs and sperm into the water column to be whisked away by the outgoing current. And amidst it all, there's hundreds of sharks gorging on groupers.

Whichever motu you go to, you're guaranteed to fall in love with this remote part of French Polynesia. Whether you're learning to dive in one of the lagoons, drift diving a pass or exploring a pink sand beach, your tropical dive dreams will be satiated in the Tuamotus. Don't limit your time here; check out a couple of the motus and, to gain the most from the experience, it's worthwhile staying in a family-run pension to absorb as much of the local culture as possible.

Opposite Rangiroa *Below* Marbled groupers congregate to spawn

The Tuamotus, French Polynesia

Pacific

Vava'u, Tonga
Swim with frisky humpbacks in this tiny, island kingdom

Why it's special

In the far northern archipelago of Vava'u in the kingdom of Tonga, you can have an up-close encounter with one of the ocean's largest residents. On these volcanic isles, with their lush forests and deep blue seas, the pace of life is dictated by the tides, the seasons and the annual return of humpback whales. The experience of freediving with humpbacks in Tonga is both exhilarating and meditative; getting close to a mumma humpback and her calf is humbling. The calves, often curious and unencumbered by fear, are known to venture close. And then there's the 'heat runs', when several males jostle for the attention of a female, hoping to be the lucky one that gets belly to belly. While the cetacean action may lure you here, it's the islander hospitality that will leave its imprint on you long after you leave.

Best time to dive

Tonga's humpback season runs from late July to mid-October, with each month offering a different aspect of whale activity. July marks the beginning, when numbers are smaller. Robust males and early arriving mothers will showcase spectacular heat run behaviour and breaches. August sees an increase in numbers, including playful juveniles. By September, the waters are rich with socialising whales, making it the peak month for divers, particularly with mothers and calves. In October, the whales prepare for their journey south, but there are still opportunities for interactions.

Gear
- A 3mm wetsuit for 24-26°C (75-79°F) water temps. and long days on the water
- Freediving gear snorkel, mask, fins and weights
- Reef smart sunscreen
- Sun protective clothing for spending hours out on the open sea
- Dry bag to keep your gear protected
- Warm clothes for after your swim

Photography tip
Shoot with your favourite wide-angle lens. This is blue water photography, so no strobes needed.

Underwater photography has grown exponentially in recent years and Tonga is good proof of this. It's important to be conscious of other divers and most importantly to give the whales their space. Being up close with an unpredictable, wild animal that can weigh up to 36t (40tn) isn't the best setting to capture a new profile picture.

Qualification
- Freediver (no dive qualification needed)

While freediving with humpbacks doesn't require dive certification, comfort in open water and good swimming abilities are necessary. A good knowledge of cetacean behaviour and local regulations are imperative to ensure a responsible and respectful experience with the whales.

Getting there
Fiji Airways offers a direct flight to Vava'u from Nadi, Fiji on selected days. Alternatively, there are daily domestic flights from Tonga's main island, Tongatapu, which connects through to Nadi (Fiji), and on to Sydney/Warrang (Australia) and Auckland (Aotearoa New Zealand).

Opposite A mother humpback and her calf, under the watchful eye of an escort

Dive in

Each year, between 500–1500 Oceania humpback whales travel 3000km (1860mi) from their feeding grounds of the Southern Ocean to the warm, sheltered waters of Tonga to breed or nurse their young. A ban on commercial whaling in 1978 by Tonga's late King Tāufa'āhau Tupou IV (when the migrating humpbacks appeared close to extinction), coupled together with the 1986 ban on whaling around Antarctica and the Southern Ocean has seen humpback populations gradually replenished, and means Tonga now reaps the benefits of tourists coming to swim with these colossal marine mammals. For a country whose GDP mainly consists of fishing, agriculture and cash sent home by Tongans living overseas, whale tourism has become a vital contributor to the economy since the first whale swims in 1993.

The whales' journey to Tonga is one of nature's great migrations. In July they arrive, fatigued, but finding respite in Vava'uan waters (note that throughout the season they can also be found in smaller numbers in other parts of Tonga, like Ha'api and 'Eua, where water visibility may not be as good, but fewer operators make for a more intimate experience. Check out Kiko's Swim with Whales Tours (kikoswhaleswim.com). Once in Tonga, the mothers nurture their young and the males jostle with each other for available females.

As the season progresses, the behaviour of the whales evolves. The early competitive groups of males vying for the attention of females gives way to tender scenes of mothers teaching their young to breach and navigate. By season's end, these young whales are stronger, more adept and ready for their journey back south. Vava'u is largely focussed on whale tourism during the season (July to October) and there are numerous local operators who incorporate both lodging and whale swims from their small boats. There are also a few international operators and private expedition leaders, like Scott Portelli's Swimming With Gentle Giants, which has been bringing groups to Tonga for 20 years (swimmingwithgentlegiants.com).

The magic of Tonga's 170 islands can be found both in-water and on-land. Independent since 1970, Tonga is Polynesia's last monarchy and Christian values dictate society here today. Sunday is a day of rest – businesses close (including whale watching boats) and flights don't operate – by order of the king. The scent of umu-cooked feasts fills the air and the sounds of church choirs echo through village streets. Tongan culture, steeped in tradition and respect for the ocean, provides an ideal backdrop for your humpback encounter. Villagers' lives are intertwined with the sea, their daily routines marked by fishing, weaving, and the maintenance of their ancestral lands.

On every part of your adventure to Tonga, from the guesthouse you stay at, to the guides driving your boat, you're sure to experience the legendary laid-back hospitality of the Tongan people.

The increasing number of humpbacks in Vava'u is a positive sign that conservation efforts can and do result in recovery. It's a privilege to witness these intelligent beings as they reclaim ancient migratory routes once fraught with danger from commercial whaling. But still, it's important to do your research before going to Tonga and to only support operators who are acting in a sustainable manner, including adhering to industry rules, employing local guides and taking smaller groups of people. While the industry has regulations, such as swimmers getting no closer than five metres (16ft) to a whale and boat operators dropping swimmers into the water no closer than ten metres (33ft) (or 50m/164ft from whales with calves), in recent years these regulations have been ignored by some operators, meanwhile the number of licenses handed out to commercial operators has increased. For the future of this industry and to ensure that the whales are not affected by the tourism, your choices make all the difference.

Gazing into the eye of a humpback *Top right* Vava'u Tonga, paradise in the Pacific

The Coolidge, Santo (Vanuatu)

Dive deep in an underwater museum of WWII relics mixed with 1940s opulence

Why it's special

Whether you're a newbie to deep diving or a seasoned deep-sea adventurer, the SS *President Coolidge* on Vanuatu's stunning Espiritu Santo Island offers a fantastic wreck diving experience. Starting life as a luxury cruise liner before housing thousands of troops during WWII (and then eventually meeting its demise when it struck two 'friendly' land mines in shallow water), the ship is now an underwater playground filled with relics of a bygone era. With tropical water temperatures and a choice of diving to different depths depending on your experience level, plus the islander hospitality of the Ni-Van people, diving here is fun and about as relaxed as you can get for deep technical diving. Walking straight from shore to access the wreck, the Coolidge is, arguably, one of the best and most convenient wreck dives in the world.

Best time to dive

Though the Coolidge can be dived year-round, during the dry season (May to October) you can expect calmer seas, clearer visibility, and more favourable diving conditions overall. Water temperatures around the Coolidge generally range from 24–28°C (75°F–84°F). Vanuatu experiences its hottest and most humid weather over the months of January and March. It can get muggy and rather uncomfortable over these months. Additionally, over summer there's the increased risk of tropical cyclones, which can potentially disrupt diving plans and, well, everything and everyone.

Opposite My dive buddy exiting one of the Coolidge's cargo holds

Gear
- A 3mm wetsuit over summer and 5 mm over the winter months

Local operator Pacific Dive can provide all rental scuba equipment (BCD, regulators, mask and fins and computers) and can also provide technical diving equipment.

Photography tip

The main question is 'how can I capture this 200m (656ft) behemoth to its full potential?' Pack your favourite wide-angle lens and ensure that you stay in Santo long enough to dive the Coolidge several times, increasing your chances of getting good enough visibility to capture the bow and length of the ship when shooting her from outside. Inside is a different story. Here, strobes are turned on and you will be focussing on one of the many different chambers and artefacts within.

Qualification
- Advanced Open Water with a deep specialty is a great start.

Chances are, you'll be diving much deeper than you ever have before and the effects of nitrogen narcosis will be more present than ever. Always dive within your limits.

Getting there

The island of Espiritu Santo is a one-hour flight from Port Vila (Bauerfield) International Airport. Periodically there are direct flights from Brisbane/Meanjin to Santo.

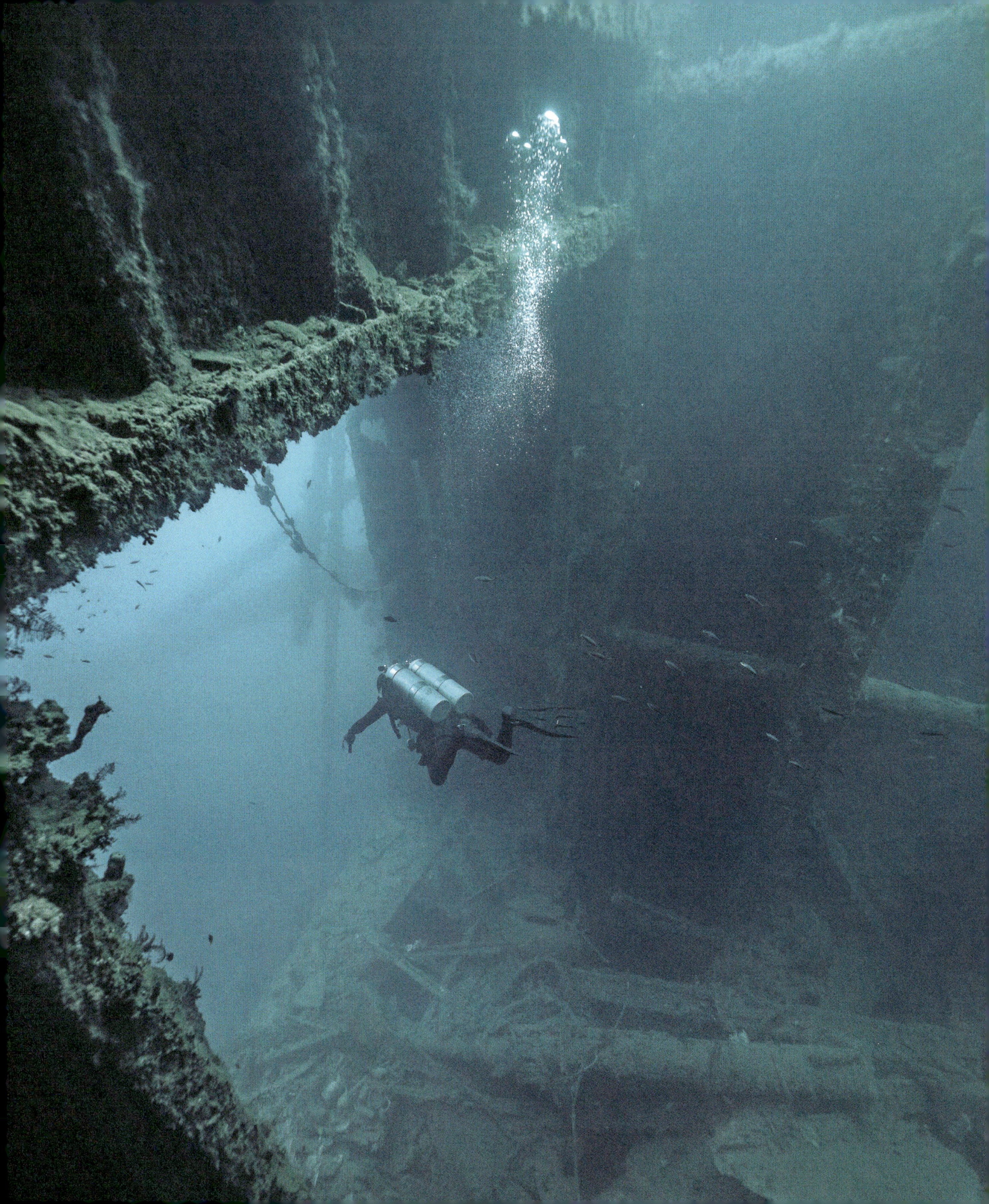

Pacific

Dive in

Vanuatu was the first place that I really sank my teeth into technical diving. At age 21, I moved to this South Pacific island nation and worked as a dive master. On the island of Espiritu Santo, Vanuatu's most northern and largest island, I learnt what it meant to dive deep, exceeding my no decompression limits and amounting long decompression stops. Suddenly, I wasn't diving 20m-(66ft-)deep reefs for 30 minutes; the new normal became more than 50m (164ft) every day, with dive times going well over an hour. This was deep diving at its best, on the SS President Coolidge.

The Coolidge isn't just any shipwreck; at 198m (650ft) long and roughly 22,000t (24,000tn), it's arguably one of the best wreck dives in the world, and, amazingly, you can walk straight off the beach to access it. Once a luxury passenger liner with rooms for over 1000 people, it was transformed into a troop carrier during World War II when 40,000 troops descended upon Espiritu Santo, making it the second largest American base in the Pacific. It was here, on a fateful day in 1942 while entering Santo's harbour that the Coolidge collided with its own U.S. mines. The ship's sailing orders had omitted vital information about safe entry into the harbour, and with fears of Japanese submarines looming large, the captain attempted to navigate through the most obvious of channels. A mine struck her in the engine room, followed by another near her stern.

Over the next 90 minutes, 5340 men from the ship got safely ashore, with only two lives lost. However, the Captain's attempts to beach and save the ship were short-lived. The Coolidge listed heavily on her port side, sank stern first, and slid down the slope into the channel. Today her stern sits in 72m (236ft) of water and her bow in 20m (66ft), creating a sanctuary for deep wreck diving and one of the most unbelievable shore dives imaginable. Gearing up on the beach, divers take a short walk to the tide line, and after swimming only 40-odd metres (131ft) the bow comes into view, marking the beginning of the colossal structure that is the Coolidge.

Diving the Coolidge is like entering a time capsule. Back in 1980, when Vanuatu gained independence from its French and British colonisers, it was declared that no artefacts would be allowed to be salvaged from the wreck. So today, with the ship still largely intact, divers can swim through its holds and decks, encountering an array of relics from guns, cannons and jeeps to helmets and personal supplies left behind by the troops. Then, there's relics like 'The Lady' (a porcelain bas-relief and divers' favourite), chandeliers, a mosaic tile fountain, elegant baths and grand staircases, which all add to the charm.

While the Coolidge is a labyrinth of corridors, rooms, and cargo holds, this shouldn't deter new divers. To truly appreciate the ship's magnitude and majesty, I recommend at least ten to 15 dives. After all, she stretches almost 200m (650ft) in length. But even with just a few dives you can get a taste of her grandeur.

For me, a return to Santo 20 years after I lived here allowed me to see how the wreck has fared over the years (particularly since Vanuatu gets its fair share of cyclones and earthquakes). While a few structures had collapsed (the promenade deck, mainly, and the swimming pool which popped out and fell to the ocean's floor), overall, the wreck hadn't changed much. It's still solid and safe to explore, with the right guides.

Diving in Luganville was pioneered by the legendary Allan Power back in the '80s. Allan operated a dive centre here right up to his death in 2018. He had made over 15,000 dives on the Coolidge and had taken over 20,000 divers to the Lady alone. His legacy is carried forward by Pacific Dive, situated within Luganville's Espiritu Hotel, run daily dives, and their local Ni-Van staff take great pride in the Coolidge. They are incredible guides, accruing tens of thousands of dives between them on the wreck over the years (pacificdive.net).

Opposite top The Lady, located at a depth of 30m (98ft) *Opposite bottom* An archival shot of the Coolidge on that fateful day of sinking in 1942

Vatu-i-Ra, Fiji
Dive into soft coral heaven between Fiji's two largest islands

Pacific

Why it's special

The strong currents that rush between Fiji's two largest islands create a highway of nutrient-rich water and, with it, a large diversity of marine life, from the little guys such as nudibranchs, pygmy seahorses, and ghost pipefish, to megafauna such as humpback and pilot whales. Known as the soft coral capital of the world, the waters of the Vatu-i-Ra Conservation Park have plenty of bommies, drift dives, and walls stacked with colourful corals that'll have you returning year after year. And after the sun goes down, you can soak up Fijian culture, sharing kava with the locals or enjoying a traditional 'meke' (performance) and 'lovo' (feast).

Best time to dive

While diving is available year-round, during the wet season months of December to April visibility can be reduced and there's a chance of experiencing a tropical cyclone. During the dry season months from May to November, it's less rainy and humid, but sea temperatures drop to as low as 24°C (75°F), with July to October being the coldest in the water.

Gear
- Wet season (Dec-Apr) water temperatures are around 30°C (86°F), and in the dry season (May-Nov) they can drop to 24°C (75°F), so I recommend a 3-5mm wetsuit if visiting during the Dry
- Reef safe sunscreen
- Lightweight, sun protective clothing

Photography tip
Fiji is classic South Pacific diving at its finest, with vibrant soft corals. Pack a nice sharp wide-angle zoom (24mm feels nice) and strobes to fully illuminate the coral gardens. For a stronger focal point, add your dive buddy into the shot in the background with their dive torch in hand.

Qualification
- Open Water certification

Getting there
Viti Levu's Suncoast is the jump-off point for Bligh Water and Vatu-i-Ra, a 2.5-hour drive from Nadi Airport.

Opposite Spotted eagle ray

Vatu-i-Ra, Fiji

Dive in

I love the South Pacific and especially Fiji; it has a kind of 'home away from home' feeling. The local greeting, 'bula', extends beyond a simple 'hello' to also mean 'life' and 'good health', and Fijians are known for sharing their positive outlook to all who can relax enough to embrace it. The locals aren't the only ones in good health; beyond the forested mountains and palm-fringed coastlines, there's a vibrant marine ecosystem brimming with life and colour. Many divers consider Fiji to be the soft coral capital of the world. But one region stands out for its soft coral biodiversity; the Vatu-i-Ra seascape, within the Bligh Water stretch of sea.

Located between Fiji's two big islands of Viti Levu and Vanua Levu, the Bligh Water was named after Captain William Bligh who passed through in 1789 in his seven-metre-long (23ft-long) launch boat, after escaping the infamous mutiny on the Bounty. On my own trips to Fiji over the years, we've also arrived by boat, but unlike Captain Bligh our interest was discovering what lay beneath the waves. Working on private yachts, my job is to design itineraries that take us to the world's best diving locations, and Fiji's diverse underwater ecosystem has always guaranteed a good time (dive sites with names like Heaven's Door and Black Magic hint to this). With its intricate shapes and textures, kaleidoscopic colours from brilliant pinks and purples to vivid oranges and reds Fiji's reefs are a true living canvas.

Vatu-i-Ra island (also known as Bird Island) is a small, volcanic island located within the 100km² (247,000ac) Vatu-i-Ra Conservation Park, about 80% of which is a 'no take' zone, meaning marine life here is abundant. Apart from over 100 fish species you may also encounter migrating humpbacks, long fin pilot whales, various species of reef sharks, dolphins and turtles, including Fiji's largest population of nesting hawksbill turtles. There are at least 50 dive sites to explore, plus the wreck of the Papuan Explorer, lying in 20m (66ft) of water.

For me, it's the walls of soft corals pulsating with clouds of anthias and other colourful reef fish that are most alluring.

The region hosts an abundance of dendronephthya, known for its intricate and branching structures that create a somewhat ethereal soft coral forest. Alcyonium, recognised for its unique colonial morphology, and sinularia, with its elegant fronds, all contribute to the soft coral diversity that defines the region.

There are a few favourable environmental factors that cause Vatu-i-Ra to be the soft coral magnet that it is. The region's warm tropical waters, ranging between 25–30°C (77–86 °F), provide an ideal habitat for soft corals, known for their sensitivity to temperature fluctuations. Furthermore, the complex network of ocean currents, including the South Equatorial Current and the North Equatorial Counter Current, ensure a nutrient-rich environment crucial for the sustenance of soft coral communities. It's on reefs like these that you really get a feeling for how the reef ticks; corals and gorgonian sea fans sift the nutrient-rich currents; small reef fish like butterfly, angel and surgeonfish hover about the corals, feeding on algae; and larger predatory fish like groupers or trevally patrol the reef above. Diving a healthy coral reef like those found in Vatu-i-Ra offers a wonderful opportunity to slow down and admire the intricate building blocks that help create these elaborate and fragile ecosystems.

At time of writing, the only land-based diving option is Ra Divers at Volivoli Beach Resort (volivoli.com) on the Suncoast. Captain Cook Cruises' Caledonian Sky offers diving in Bligh Water on its Remote North Discovery trips (captaincookfiji.com). If you want to squeeze maximum dive time in, then a liveaboard is your best option. NAI'A is a solid 40m (131ft) expedition ship that I joined on a previous trip (naia.com.fj). NAI'A has been leading dive trips in this region for decades and travels with a Fijian crew; a perfect blend of Fijian hospitality and good diving. Bula!

Opposite The world famous soft corals of Vatu-i-ra *Below* A pod of pilot whales in the clear open waters of Vatu-i-ra

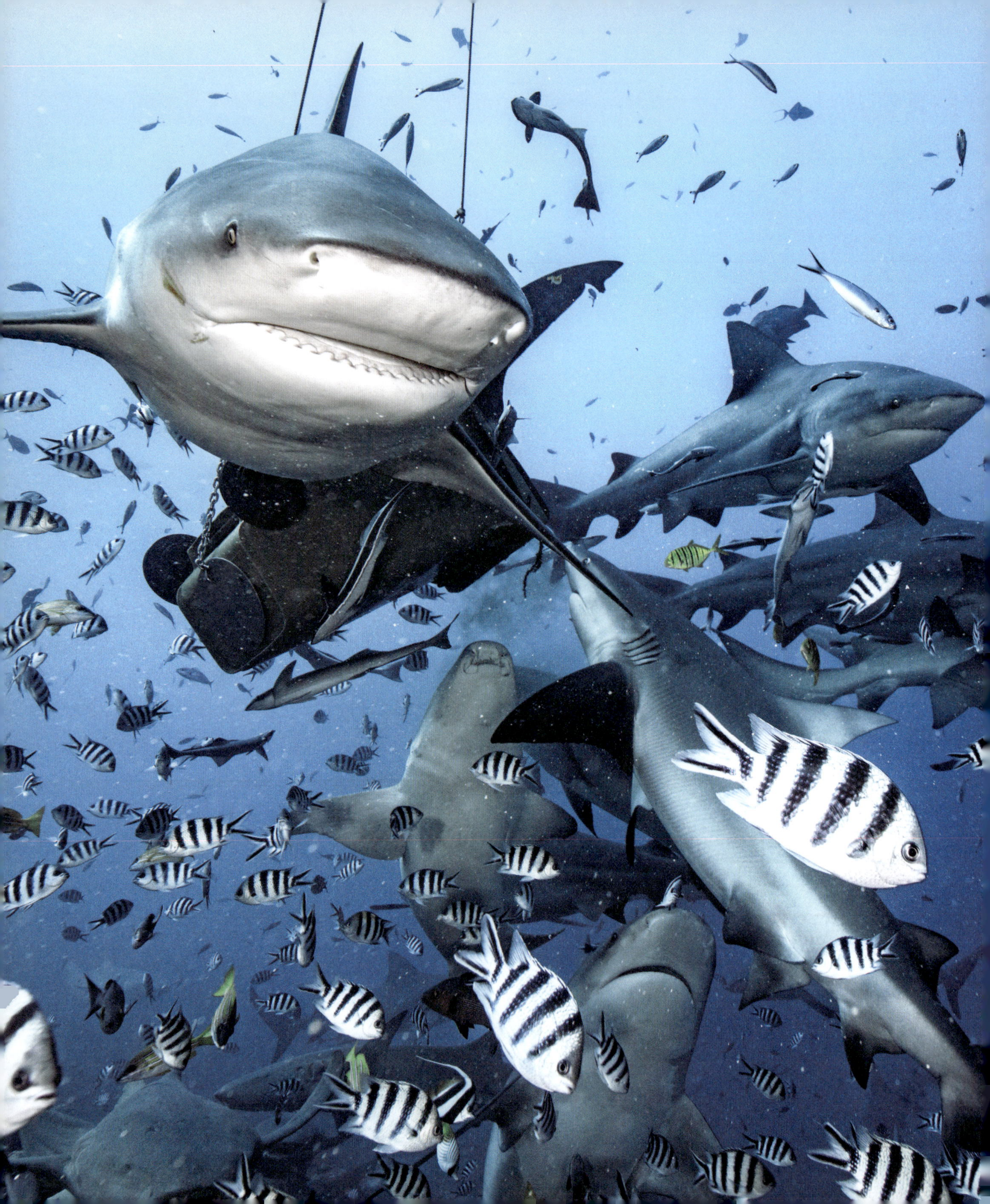

Beqa Lagoon, Fiji
Get up-close to a bull shark feeding frenzy

Why it's special

While many Westerners have an irrational fear of sharks, largely thanks to sensationalist media, in the Pacific Islands the locals have a different perception of them altogether. Sharks are highly revered in Fijian culture, where they're commonly found in folklore and totems. The ancient shark god, Dakuwaqa, is a protector spirit, believed to provide protection to seagoers. In the waters surrounding Fiji's islands, many different species of sharks thrive, including one that lures divers year after year for a very unique encounter; the bull shark. In Beqa Lagoon, you can get very close to huge, feeding bull sharks within the constraints of a well-organised dive operation, while feeding money back into the local community and ensuring the continued management of a marine protected reserve.

Best time to dive

This tour runs year-round, though there are two distinct seasons in Fiji. November to April are the summer months, characterised by warmer water temperatures 29–34°C/84–93°F), calmer seas and better visibility. During the winter months of May to October, water temperatures can drop down to 20°C (68°F), but there's more shark activity.

Gear
- Although you're diving in tropical waters, on the shark dive you'll be stationary while watching the action take place, so I recommend a 3-5mm wetsuit
- The operators prefer plain black – nothing white or bright

Photography tip
A wide zoom will allow you to capture those up-close toothy grin portraits. Whilst zooming out and shooting really wide will allow you to capture all the chaos of the whole scene.

Strobes are a must, for the 30m (98ft) reef.

Qualification
- Open Water

Beqa has a number of ledges where different levels of certified divers can be immersed in the action. With that said, outside of having the right certification, divers should feel confident with being face-to-face with large sharks. If you're feeling apprehensive, tell your dive guide when booking.

Getting there
It's a 2.5-3-hour drive from Nadi international Airport to Pacific Harbour via the coastal road (Queens Highway).

Opposite Bull sharks, lemon sharks and the occasional tiger shark all work up a frenzy at Beqa Lagoon, Fiji

Dive in

As diving increases in popularity and, in recent times, the fear of *Jaws* is gradually replaced with a respect for these apex predators, an interest in shark encounters has grown amongst divers, including diving with the 'big three' great white, tiger and bull sharks. In the clear waters of Fiji's Beqa Lagoon, you can get up close with one (possibly two) of the big three, in what will likely be one of the most unforgetta-bull dives you'll ever do.

Beqa Lagoon comprises over 100km² (24,700ac), protected by a 30km (19mi) long barrier reef and it is home to over 450 fish species. But what lures divers here are the sharks that patrol its waters, with eight main species identified here. These are whitetip, blacktip and grey reef sharks; tawny nurse; sicklefin lemon; silvertip; tiger and, of course, bull sharks.

Shark Reef Marine Reserve, nestled within Beqa Lagoon in the Pacific Harbour area of Fiji's main island, Viti Levu, was established in 2004 and was Fiji's first protected reserve for sharks. In 2014 it went on to become Fiji's first national marine park. The area of the reserve was being overfished and the Traditional Owners of the reef, the Wainiyabia and the Galoa Peoples, were offered a unique incentive by the Department of Fisheries (with support from a local dive operator); relinquish your traditional fishing rights on this patch of reef in exchange for a monthly fee paid to the village. The Galoa people now fish outside of the protected reserve which has become a diver's hotspot, and each month they receive the Shark Reef Marine Reserve Levy that's paid by divers to local tourism operators.

My own visit to Beqa was a 'research trip'. We were travelling the world on a private yacht and as we approached Fiji, my shark-loving employer flew me ahead to capture footage of the famous shark dive, and report back about it. On our voyage we'd already had some fantastic shark encounters, such as the hammerheads at Cocos Island (*see* p. 68) and, comparatively,

Beqa was a very different scene. The main difference is the use of tuna baits to attract the sharks, which can alter their natural behaviour. The feeding frenzy that ensues is completely different to the peaceful aggregation of hammerheads circling over us at Cocos. So, this is a choice for individual divers prior to planning a trip to Beqa, and ultimately you may decide it's not for you. Upon looking at my footage of getting close to dozens of bull sharks (plus one large tiger shark), my employer decided that it was definitely for him so we steered the yacht in the direction of Pacific Harbour. As it happened, his dives were pretty different to mine with fewer bull sharks and no tiger. Nevertheless, he loved it.

If you do decide to get amongst the sharky action at Beqa, here are the basics of the operation. There are four shark feeding attractions in Beqa Lagoon, managed by different operators, and each has strict guidelines for divers. This includes a pre-dive safety briefing and assigning a Dive Master to divers with less than 30 dives under their belt. You can't wear white or bright colours – it's dark, full body wetsuits only – and you must remain in a fixed position behind a coral or rock ledge; you can't just float around and explore. Leading you down a depth of between 25-30m (82-98ft), the action happens in an underwater amphitheatre, where your Fijian dive guides will attract sharks with tuna baits. Any sharks that get too close are redirected by dive guides with a metal prod.

Ninety-nine % of the time, the Fijian shark whisperers keep the sharks under strict control – and let's face it, it's a free snack for the sharks and that's all they're interested in. Very occasionally they get too close or too frisky – most famously in an incident in 2019 when a diver had his head grazed by a tiger shark, losing his mask and hoodie (but otherwise unscathed). Never forget these are apex predators, so follow your guide's instructions carefully and keep a low profile. For the thousands of people who have dived here since 1999, the reported incidents have been few.

Each shark dive experience is slightly different. With Beqa Adventure Divers (BAD) you'll descend to a depth of 30m (98ft) to watch the big shark action, in 'The Arena', and after 15 minutes watching a cyclone of swirling sharks getting their fill, you'll ascend to shallower depths where your guide will feed reef sharks and other smaller shark species before you surface (fijisharkdive.com).

With Aqua-Trek, you'll spend around 20 minutes watching the big shark action in 'The Bistro' before slowly ascending, exploring a nearby wreck along the way. The wreck and surrounding reef provide shelter for a few opportunistic residents, including one of the largest moray eels you'll ever see (aquatrek.com). The Bistro can also be dived while basing yourself at Waidroka Bay Resort on the Coral Coast (waidroka.com).

Coral Coast Divers (coralcoastdivers.com), also in Pacific Harbour, established Fiji's newest shark dive a few years ago, called 'The Colosseum'. With a maximum depth of 18-20m (59-66ft), suitable for divers who don't have an advanced certification.

Beqa Lagoon Resort, located on Beqa Island, manages a third shark dive called the 'Cathedral' which, located closer to the barrier reef, attracts more tiger sharks than the others (beqalagoonresort.com).

A large bull shark takes the bait during a feeding session at Beqa Lagoon

Wolf and Darwin Islands, Galápagos

Pregnant whale sharks and schools of hammerheads in the legendary northern Galápagos Islands.

Why it's special

Marine iguanas, giant tortoises, flightless cormorants, blue footed boobies ... the Galápagos Islands are renowned for their many weird and wonderful residents. For divers, these waters offer some truly unique encounters with marine animals, one quarter of which is endemic. In the isolated, northern part of the archipelago, two ancient volcano peaks form the islands of Wolf and Darwin. Here, strong oceanic currents bring a range of marine species together, with schooling hammerheads and giant, pregnant whale sharks grabbing the attention of divers from near and far. What also grabs divers are the strong currents – you'll often find yourself hanging onto boulders underwater or caught in a mix of converging currents. Novice divers, add this to the list for later on. Advanced divers, prepare for some of the best diving you'll ever do.

Best time to dive

The prime diving season in Wolf and Darwin is the 'garúa season' or the 'dry season' months of June to November, when the weather is cooler, the sea is generally calmer and the visibility better. During this time, the nutrient-rich Humboldt Current flows strongest, attracting schools of hammerhead sharks, whale sharks, and other pelagic species. In the dry season, currents are stronger and water temperatures are cooler, ranging from 18-24°C (64-75°F). December to May is the wet season with warmer weather warmer and occasional rain. The warmer waters (ranging from 20-30°C/68-86°F) bring in different marine life, such as manta rays, but visibility might be slightly reduced compared to the dry season.

Gear
- A 5 and 7mm wetsuit for 18-24°C (64-75°F) water temperatures. Temperatures can really fluctuate from the southern region to the north, so be prepared
- Hood
- Booties
- A reef hook, if allowed
- A reliable dive computer

Given the strong currents and remoteness, a surface marker buoy (SMB), whistle and any other signalling device such as a Personal Locating Beacon are recommended.

Photography tip
A wide-angle zoom will have you capturing all of the Galápagos marine megafauna.

Be prepared both mentally and physically for photographing the Galápagos. There's a lot of action here, and with strong currents and a large camera in hand, it tends to be a lot of work.

Qualification
- Advanced open water

Open ocean, shifting currents and a lack of shelter make these waters best suited to advanced divers with a great deal of previous experience diving in strong currents.

Getting there
Liveaboards depart from San Cristóbal or Baltra in the Galápagos. The airports in both towns have flights that connect to mainland Ecuador.

Opposite A school of jacks shoot pass me, in a kind of 'welcome to the Galápagos' moment

Wolf and Darwin Islands, Galápagos

Pacific

Dive in

In the far reaches of the Northern Pacific, about 1000km (621mi) from Ecuador's coast, lies the volcanic archipelago that is the Galápagos Islands. Home to flora and fauna that's found nowhere else on Earth, the Galápagos are famous for influencing Charles Darwin's theory of evolution after he visited the islands in 1835, spending 19 days here identifying individual species, collecting samples and making notes.

Having learned about the Galápagos in school, from a young age I dreamt of visiting the islands and exploring their watery realm. In my early 30s, my wildest dreams played out when we sailed into Galápagos waters and spent almost a month there. Working on a private yacht, my lodgings were decidedly more comfortable than Darwin's sleeping hammock on the HMS Beagle, and with access to modern dive gear and a submersible, we were able to thoroughly explore the underwater world of the Galápagos. Parking the sub on the sea floor amongst schooling hammerheads and curious seals was an experience that I'll hold onto forever!

The incredible diving in the Galápagos is largely due to it three converging ocean currents, the Humboldt Current, the Panama Flow and the Cromwell Current. Sea currents are the drivers of the ocean, with each current having a different characteristic like nutrients, velocity, temperature, even saltiness. The mixing of nutrient rich, cold and deep upwelling waters means that the waters of the Galápagos house a plethora of large and sometimes unique marine life not seen anywhere else. Migratory marine megafauna, including whale sharks, use and rely on these ocean currents.

Every year at the start of the Garúa Season, whale sharks arrive in the northern part of the Galápagos Marine Reserve and they can be reliably spotted around the small, far northern islands of Wolf and Darwin. It's an incredible sight, as many of them are large females with swollen bellies, appearing to be pregnant. The famed Darwin's Arch (now collapsed and

Opposite Manta ray at a cleaning station *Below* Awestruck by a school of hammerheads

Pacific

looking more like pillars) is a popular site to observe them filter feeding. One of my all-time favourite photographs was captured after waiting for a long period of time underwater for a whale shark to drift by. It was one of the last dives of our trip and my body was tired from enduring ripping currents and gripping onto rocks underwater, patiently watching and waiting. Then, appearing from nowhere and leaving me in total awe, a massive whale shark slowly cruised past, like a huge bus. Her body wore the scars of time and adversity; a shark bite on her dorsal fin, about a metre in diameter, proved both scale and misadventure. It really is an incredible feeling to be dwarfed by such a beautiful, big whale shark.

Wolf and Darwin are stars of the Galápagos dive scene for more than their whale shark visitors. In the waters surrounding these two extinct volcanoes, there's an unparalleled variety of species of marine life, in large numbers, to be discovered. Boasting the largest shark biomass globally, these islands are a haven for shark enthusiasts. Galápagos sharks, scalloped hammerheads, whitetip and blacktip reef sharks, dusky and silky sharks, and more, coexist in these waters, creating a spectacle rarely seen elsewhere. Dolphins are regularly spotted, as well as clouds of tropical reef fish. And then there's the rays – mantas, golden rays, eagle rays and stingrays – frequently seen around the islands.

Separated from the main group of islands in the Galápagos, Wolf and Darwin are more susceptible to illegal fishing. At Wolf Island, national park staff operate from a floating station to monitor visitors to the islands. Their remote location also means that the islands aren't visited by conventional Galápagos cruise operators. Dive operators such as Galápagos Sky, Humboldt Explorer, Tiburon Explorer, Galaxy Diver and Aggressor Fleet offer seven to ten night trips. It's essential to note that diving at Darwin and Wolf demands significant experience, often requiring an Advanced Open Water Diver certification.

A pregnant whale shark emerges from the depths. One of my most memorable diving experiences

Tufi, Papua New Guinea
Go critter crazy in the land where the term 'muck diving' originated

Why it's special

Despite the lack of roads and being bordered by thick jungle and sea, the local villagers around Tufi are no strangers to foreign faces. From British ships in the 18th century, to Anglican missionaries, then Aussies during the colonial era and the ships and planes of WWII. Nowadays, the remote outpost of Tufi in Papua New Guinea's (PNG) so-called 'tropical fjordland' plays host to a steady stream of divers who come to encounter its stunning scenery, reefs and rich local culture. Formed by ancient volcanic activity, the fjords, with their steep, sponge-covered walls, harbour a myriad of macro life. Beyond the fjords, Tufi's outer reefs boast hard and soft coral gardens and a diverse range of pelagic species, thanks to the nutrient-rich equatorial current that flows past. This unspoiled region, coupled with its warm, clear waters, provides an underwater journey that's both visually stunning and rich in marine biodiversity.

Best time to dive

While you can dive here year-round, the months between May and November offer clear skies, good visibility (up to 30m/98ft) and the water temperature remains at a comfortable 26–29°C (79–84°F). The doldrum months of October and November are best, due to calmer seas and light winds, while July to September are the windier. The north-west monsoon season from December to March can bring wet weather and decreased visibility.

Gear
- 3mm wetsuit for 26-29°C (79-84°F) water temps
- Reef smart sunscreen
- Sun protective clothing and polarised sunglasses
- For wreck dives, a dive light is recommended to illuminate hidden corners

Remember, Tufi is very remote. Take what you need, plus spares.

Photography tip

There aren't many places that provide such a wide array of options for underwater photographers as PNG does. For starters you'll want a wide angle for reefscapes and wrecks. Then, you'll most definitely need a macro lens for the muck in the fjords and macro on the reefs. Strobes are a must.

Qualification
- Open Water

Divers of all levels can enjoy Tufi, with a range of sites from easy, shallow fjord dives to more challenging wreck and reef dives. While beginners can explore the fjords and nearshore reefs, advanced certification is advisable for deeper wrecks and offshore sites.

Getting there

There are twice-weekly flights from Port Moresby to Tufi, which takes an hour via a charter plane with Tropicair. Due to the smaller aircraft, luggage is restricted. Check current weight limits at the time of booking with Tufi Resort.

Opposite Pink anemonefish

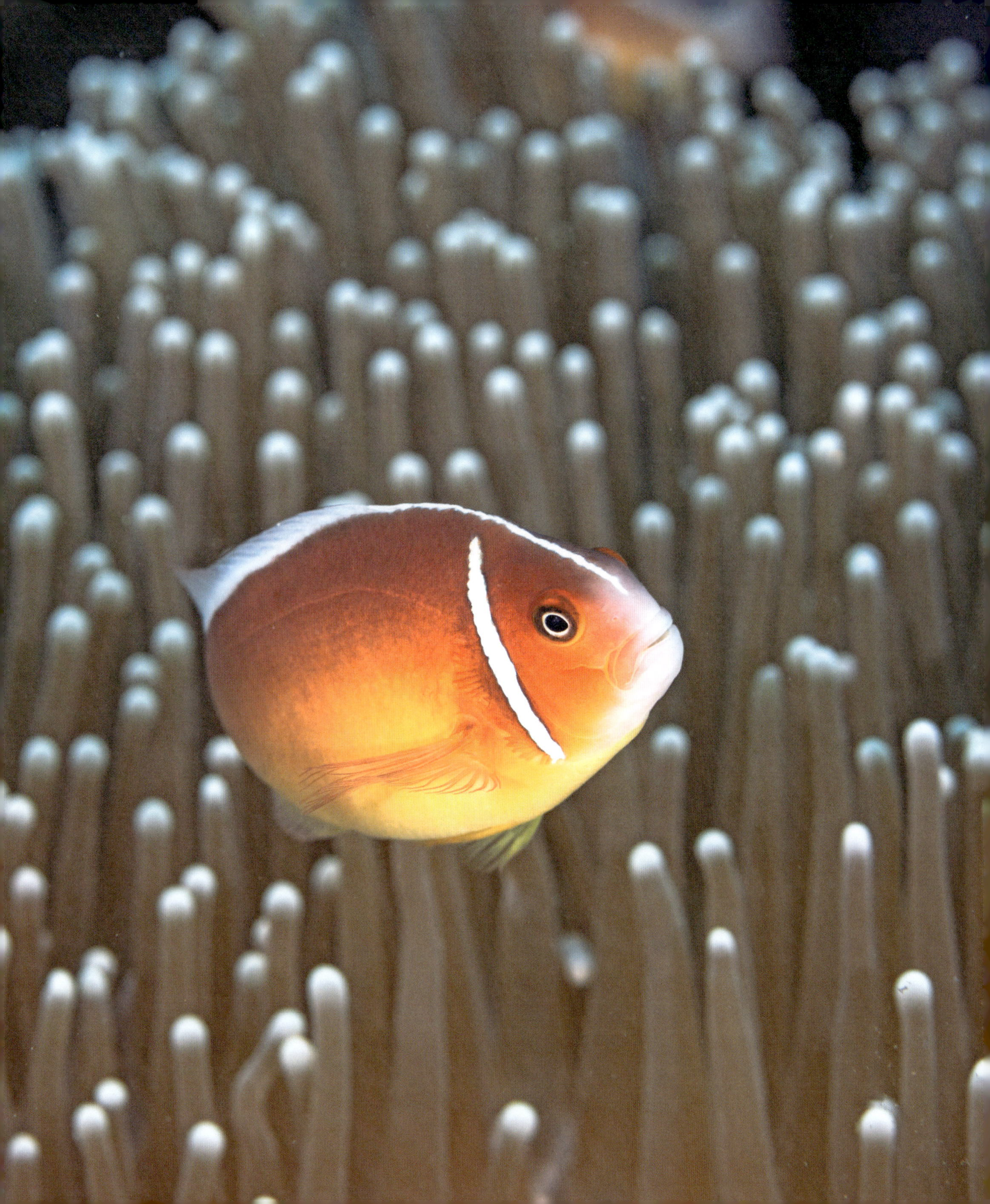

Pacific

Dive in

The words 'tropical fjords' are an odd combination; formed by glaciers, fjords are found in cold places like the Milford Sound or Norway. PNG's Cape Nelson region is unique in its tropical topography, with big coastal valleys partly submerged by water, fjord-like in appearance but labelled by geologists as 'rias'. However, 'ria-land' doesn't quite have the same ring to it as 'fjordland'. Whatever you call them, there's no denying that the dramatic landscape around Tufi is spectacular. Imagine mountains rising 150m (492ft) from the water, covered in mosses and a thick jungle full of rare orchids, exotic birds and giant insects. Then beneath the surface, walls sloping down as far as 90m (295ft), serving as an underwater time capsule for WWII relics and a kingdom for critters.

Growing up in Cairns, PNG was closer to us than any Australian capital city, and yet this huge island – the second biggest in the world – was a mystery. My brother Toby has been operating as a commercial pilot in PNG for over ten years now. We've shared countless dive adventures over the years, all over the world, and he'll tell you straight up that 'nowhere compares to PNG'. For sure, no dive list is complete without PNG on it and Tufi, an hour's flight from Port Moresby, has some unique offerings that set it apart.

In Tufi, there are two contrasting dive scenes – the fjords and the reefs. The fjords, calm and protected, are a haven for muck and macro enthusiasts, with the resort's jetty and the public wharf hosting some great dives in shallow water. (Interestingly, the term 'muck diving' was first coined by PNG diving pioneer, Bob Halstead). From vibrant nudibranchs and pygmy seahorses to mandarin fish, crocodile fish, ghost pipefish, and other weird and wonderful critters, Tufi's macro life can be found hiding among the junk around the jetties and the fjord's sloping walls. For those with a taste for history, there are some WWII wrecks to be found beyond the jetties including a Jeep and two torpedo boats. For diehard critter hunters, jetty dives in the afternoon or night will reward with the chance to see nocturnal critters, too.

Venturing out into the Solomon Sea, Tufi's outer reefs and offshore sites offer big seamounts and healthy, vibrant coral gardens that stretch as far as the eye can see. There are over 25 reefs within an hour's boat ride from the resort, with plenty of pelagics to be found such as barracuda, trevally, manta and eagle rays, black and whitetip reef sharks and even hammerheads. There's also some fantastic WWII wreck diving, including Black Jack, a largely intact B-17F bomber. Visit nearby Boga Boga village, you may be lucky enough to hear elders recanting stories of how their village rescued the ten crew members from the sinking plane back in 1943.

Engaging with the local villagers is a quintessential part of what makes this diving holiday so special. Witnessing ceremonial dances and sing-sings, watching canoes being handcrafted from sago palms and clothes being made from tapa all adds depth to the Tufi experience. If you're feeling adventurous, you can even stay in a village guesthouse for a few days – ask resort staff for recommendations (tufiresort.com).

Part of Tufi's charm is its primitive state. There are no roads; arrival is either via plane or canoe. The region is sparsely populated and rarely visited by liveaboards. The accommodation, Tufi Resort, was originally a hotel and pub for the expat community when it was under Australian administration. The fjord views from the resort are spectacular, and the dive shop by the jetty will organise everything for your dives, both in the fjords and on the outer reefs. Tufi's combination of stunning natural beauty, big and small marine life, and rich indigenous culture make this not just a diving destination, but an immersive and deeply memorable experience.

Opposite (clockwise) Hawk fish; coral grouper; the rias of Tufi

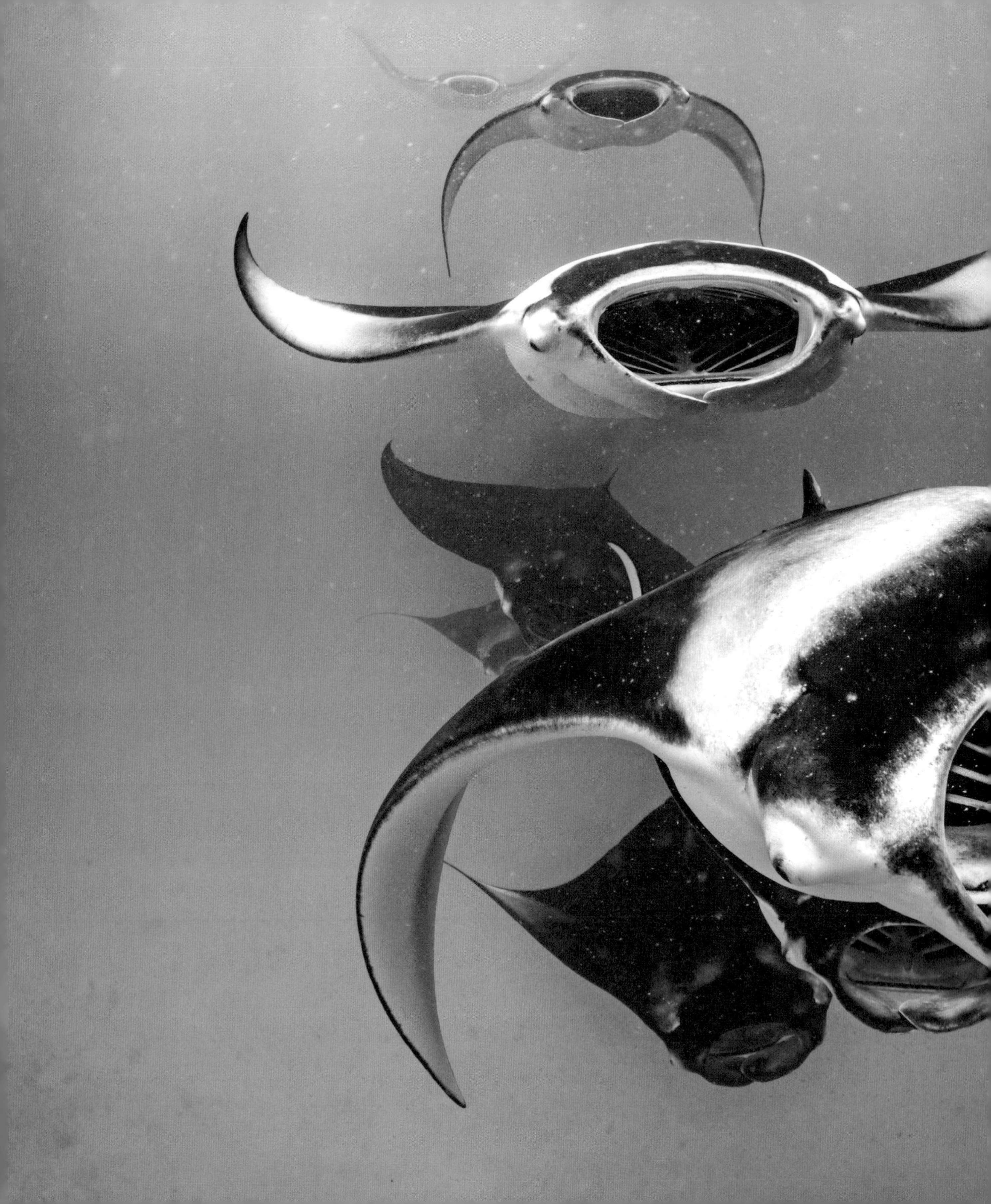

Indian Ocean and Africa

1. Fuvahmulah, Maldives 214
2. Baa Atoll, Maldives 218
3. Trincomalee, Sri Lanka 223
4. KwaZulu-Natal coast,
   South Africa 227
5. Southern Red Sea, Egypt 231

Fuvahmulah, Maldives
The Maldives' shark island, where diving with tigers is guaranteed

Why it's special

The volcanic island of Fuvahmulah is completely different to other islands in the Maldives. Forget turquoise lagoons and overwater bungalows; here you wake each day to the local mosque's call to prayer and you'll spend your diving time with huge tiger sharks in the harbour, and many other shark species that call this island home. Between dives, you can explore the island's lush interior, with freshwater lakes (kihlis) and farms of mangoes and pineapples, or go surfing with locals. With at least 20 dive sites, there's amazing diving here year-round including pristine reefs, steep drop-offs and volcanic seascapes. But it's the sharks that'll bring you here.

Best time to dive

For tigers, visit anytime year-round. For threshers and scalloped hammerheads, September to December are best due to the thermocline being closer to the reef. Oceanic mantas' mating season of March to May is best for spotting these beauties, and for whale sharks, January to April is your best bet.

Gear
- Water temperatures can range between 27-30°C (80-86°F), but can drop down to 25°C (77°F) in deeper waters. It's worth packing a 3mm suit for the diving days and a few rashies or exposure suits for snorkel sessions

Photography tip
A wide zoom will allow you to capture those up-close toothy grin portraits.

Go as wide as possible, to capture the chaos of the whole scene.

Qualification
- Open Water

Fuvahmulah has a number of dive sites, accommodating different levels of certified divers.

With that said, outside of having the right certification, divers should feel confident being face-to-face with large sharks. If you're apprehensive, that's ok, just tell your dive guide when booking.

Getting there
Access to Fuvahmulah is via daily flight from Malé with Maldivian Aero.

Opposite With woodlands, wetlands and freshwater lakes, Fuvahmulah is different to other Maldivian islands
Previous A manta train cruises past me in Baa Atoll

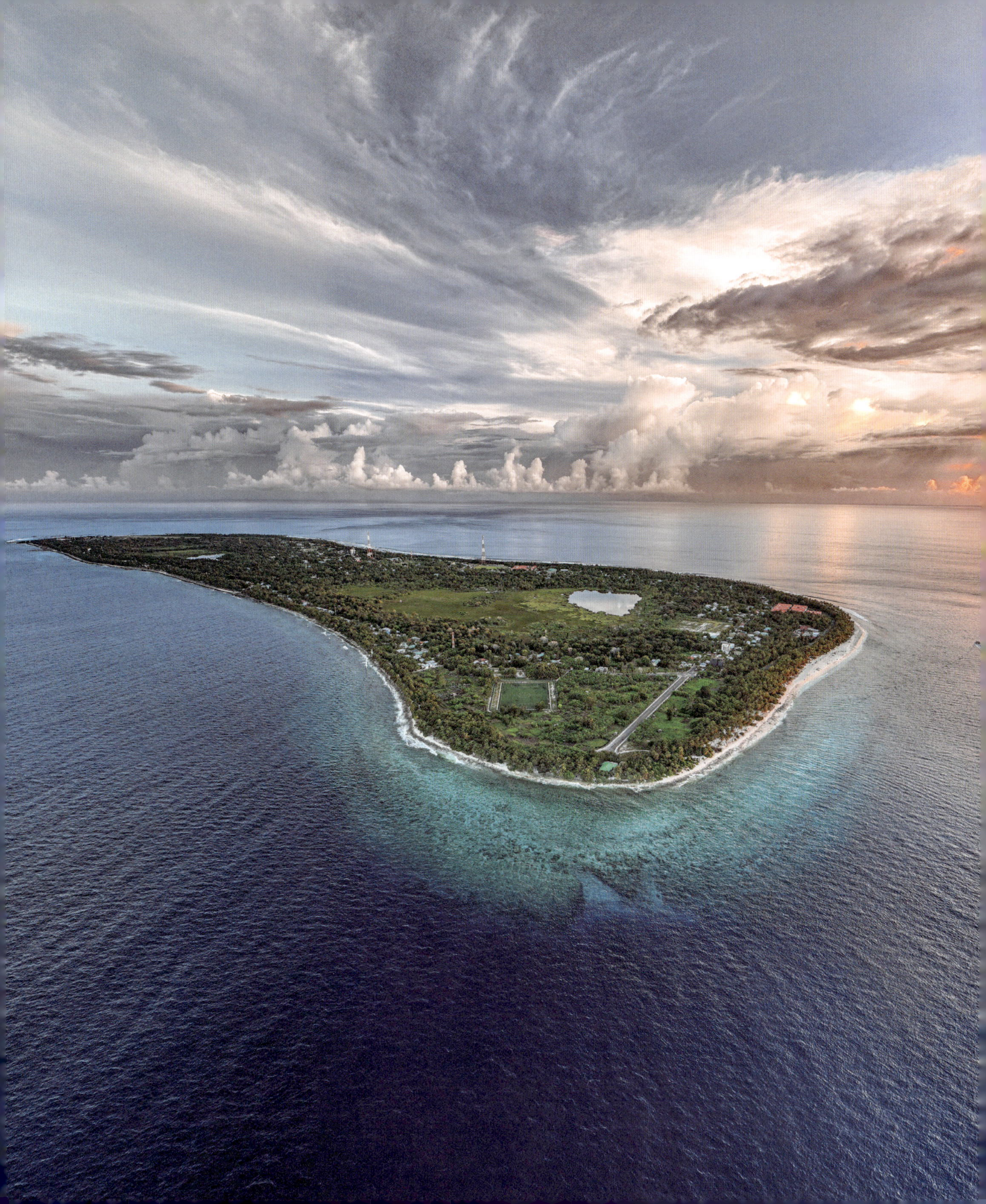

Indian Ocean and Africa

Dive in

Positioned in the north-central expanse of the Indian Ocean, the Maldives is a nation comprised of 20 natural atolls and some 1190 islands: what divers' dreams are made of. I've been fortunate enough to travel here a few times while working on European-owned yachts, and it's somewhere that I'll happily return to again and again. While the picture-perfect archipelago has long been on the radar of divers and snorkellers for its warm tropical temperatures and thriving reefs, nowadays some sites are extremely overcrowded, with throngs of snorkellers finning each other in the face to get close to whale sharks and other megafauna. The far southern atoll of Fuvahmulah (pronounced foo-mullah) opened to tourists fairly recently, grabbing the attention of divers – well, shark lovers, specifically. Among the seven species of sharks that you can spot here, one is luring divers from near and far – the tiger shark.

Just 33km (20.5mi) from the equator (a 1.5-hour flight from the capital Malé), Fuvahmulah is the third-largest island in the Maldives. Unlike the Maldive-typical picture of calm, white sand beaches fringed by turquoise lagoons, the waters surrounding Fuvahmulah are dark blue with drop-offs that plunge 2000m (6560ft) into the Indian Ocean. The island also has a great surf break, the only beach break in the country. Being subjected to deep-water, nutrient-rich currents invariably means Fuvahmulah attracts a variety of pelagic life and, in particular, oceanic megafauna such as threshers, hammerheads, oceanic mantas and whale sharks. Oh yes, and tiger sharks.

Known as 'shark island', you'll find at least seven different shark species at Fuvahmulah. The star attraction are the tigers, with operators guaranteeing, 100%, that you'll see them. The tuna fishing industry is what keeps the 160+ resident tigers (plus many more migratory ones) close to the island's harbour. For Maldivians, tuna is a staple of their diet and you'll find it in most meals (I recommend mas huni for breakfast – a mix of tuna, onion, coconut, and chilli. Delicious!) Located within the deep Equatorial Channel, tuna is plentiful and the islanders sustainably fish them using pole-and-line, before gutting the fish and throwing the unneeded parts back into the ocean, a gift that's enthusiastically received by the waiting tiger sharks.

Considered by many Maldivians as the most beautiful island in their archipelago, Fuvahmulah is well cared-for by its proud residents and in 2020 UNESCO declared it a biosphere reserve. It's only in recent years that its tourism potential has been realised, when local man Lonu, the owner of Shark Island Dive, pioneered shark diving on the island in 2015. Prior to that, the island was very much just a working community, with fishing and agriculture being primary revenues, and not much infrastructure to accommodate tourists. Unlike the other glamorous atolls of the Maldives which attract honeymooners and wealthy tourists with luxe accommodation and fine dining, on Fuvahmulah there are schools, mosques, traditional foods and a refreshing lack of beachfront hotels due to the council's designated 'green zone' along the coastline.

The 4.5 x 1.2km (2.8 x 0.7mi) island has over 20 dive sites but the most popular is at the entrance to the harbour where scraps from the local fish market ensure that tiger sharks stick around all year. On your dive, expect to see a handful of tigers, sometimes up to five metres (16ft) long, in 10m (33ft) deep water. The usually deep-water thresher sharks can also be found at a few sites around the island in waters as shallow as 12–15m (39–49ft). From late September to the end of December, it's common to see schools of scalloped hammerheads, or solitarily year-round, though they're found in deeper waters where currents can be strong. Oceanic mantas can be found at cleaning stations around the island year-round, but March to May (mating season) is your best chance of seeing them. Whale sharks also make an appearance between January and April.

There are a range of small, family-run hotels and guesthouses, offering some of the most affordable accommodations (together with delicious homemade foods) in the Maldives. It's also worth mentioning that Fuvahmulah is very much a local island so alcohol is prohibited and will be confiscated by customs on arrival (visitfuvahmulah.mv).

Opposite Tiger shark. One of at least seven species of sharks you may find at Fuvahmulah

Baa Atoll, Maldives
Experience manta madness at the world's largest manta ray feeding station

Why it's special

There are few marine creatures more graceful than the manta ray and it's an absolute privilege to encounter these often-solitary creatures come together in large numbers. Each monsoon season, this phenomenon occurs at tiny Hanifaru Bay in the Maldives' Baa Atoll, where winds and tides sweep zooplankton into the bay and reef mantas travel from near and far to join the plankton party. This is the place where you may be lucky enough to encounter them in chains as they cyclone feed together, gorging on plankton. There's no scuba here; this one's for freedivers and snorkellers as the bay is small and no deeper than 20m (66ft) in places.

Best time to dive

Manta season at Hanifaru Bay spans from mid-May to November, during the south-west monsoon/wet season, with the best time being from late July to early October. For higher chances of witnessing the manta madness, consider visiting around a full or new moon, when tides capture more plankton in the bay.

Gear
- A long-sleeved rash shirt or 1mm exposure suit is perfect, as the water is 26-29°C (79-84°F) and you'll spend all your time on the surface
- As scuba has now been banned in Hanifaru, you'll just need to pack your snorkelling and freediving gear (mask, snorkel, fins)
- Reef smart sunscreen
- Sun protective clothing and polarised sunglasses

Photography tip
Pack a wide-angle lens, and there's no need for strobes here as the light is beautiful and the action is fast paced.

Hanifaru's holy grail is to photograph the elusive manta train. This is by no means an easy or guaranteed event. If you are lucky enough to see lots of mantas, pay attention and watch for signs of the mantas becoming uniformed and feeding in an organised manner. This is your moment to get into the right position and hopefully capture the magic.

Qualification
None needed (snorkel/freedive)

Getting there
You can reach Dharavandhoo from Malé International Airport via a half hour domestic flight. From here, Hanifaru Bay is a short speedboat ride from your resort.

Opposite A reef manta 'working it' for my camera

Baa Atoll, Maldives

Dive in

Each year seasonal weather patterns dictate life over a small coral atoll nation in the middle of the Indian Ocean. As winds push from west to east, new ocean nutrients find their way to the shores of these remote atolls and an astonishing natural event begins. Beneath the turquoise waters of Hanifaru Bay, situated within the UNESCO Biosphere Reserve of Baa Atoll in the central Maldives, reef manta rays arrive in their thousands to feast on zooplankton, heralding the start of one of the world's greatest animal feeding migrations.

This mass gathering can be attributed to Hanifaru Bay's unique, elongated shape and geographical location which serve as a natural funnel, gathering plankton brought up from the deep sea. During the south-west monsoon season (mid-May to November), the Indian Ocean's currents push nutrient-rich water into the bay. Additionally, the lunar tide counters the oceanic current, trapping plankton inside the bay. This results in a thick soup of zooplankton such as copepods, shrimp, fish eggs, crustaceans and mollusc larvae. If you're lucky, you could spot over a hundred mantas feeding here at one time; a very unique opportunity given the incredible presence of one manta, let alone many altogether.

Averaging up to 3.5m (11ft) in length and weighing up to 700kg (1540lb), it's a magical experience to share the water with a manta. In Hanifaru Bay, they fly past you like giants, their wings spread wide and their mouths agape. It's a real spectacle to behold as they glide and roll, inhaling as much plankton-rich soup as possible, though it's an icky feeling when your ears and hair get clogged up with millions of tiny zooplankton (there's no word that describes it better than 'icky'). The diving gets exciting when you see the mantas 'cyclone feeding', with 50 or more forming a chain and swimming in synchronised rows with their mouths wide open. The head of the chain eventually catches up to the tail, creating a manta whirlpool of synchronised dance.

While mantas steal the show at Hanifaru Bay, there's plenty more to see under the waves with the area being known as a nursery for grey reef sharks, and the whale sharks that arrive each season for the same reason as the mantas (to fill their bellies with plankton). Though scuba diving is now prohibited in the bay (freediving and snorkelling only), with a maximum depth of 20m (66ft) you'll always be close to the action. While in the past, tourism activities got a little out of hand here, there are now rangers that patrol Hanifaru Bay, doing a great job of minimising the impact of tourism. They impose a strict limit of five boats at a time, accompanied by certified guides, and a maximum of 45 minutes per session. They also ask divers to remain at least three metres (10ft) away from the mantas, and refrain from using flash photography.

A few years ago, I was a guest photographer for just over a month at Amilla Fushi Villas in Baa Atoll (amillafushimaldives.net), an opportunity that allowed me to spend a solid amount of time with the reef mantas at Hanifaru Bay (a 15 minute boat ride from the resort). Being positioned so close to the action allowed me to be in the water every day and, most importantly, when the moon cycles were right. In the days leading up to a full moon, I witnessed first-hand the rise in zooplankton and the beautiful spectacle of the legendary manta feeding chains. The whole exercise of getting there, having the right gear, etc, was easy thanks to friends that run Dive Butler Amilla, the dive centre based at this luxury resort. Of course, staying at Amilla for a month (or even a few nights) is out of reach for most people, including myself if I wasn't there working. Thankfully, there are other options. Just across the channel from Hanifaru is the island of Dharavandhoo and Aveyla Manta Village (aveyla.com). This boutique beachfront resort overlooks Hanifaru Bay, is affordably priced and owned by two local divers. Liquid Salt Divers, a PADI 5 Star Dive Centre, is just around the corner and there are 20 great dive sites within 15 minutes of cruising. In terms of liveaboards, there are many in the Maldives, most having at least one or two Baa Atoll itineraries on their schedule each year.

Manta Expeditions operate trips in the Maldives and in other manta hotspots globally. They are reasonably priced and work closely with The Manta Trust, with a focus on education and manta conservation on each trip (mantaexpeditions.com).

Opposite Mantas feasting in plankton rich waters
Above Manta train

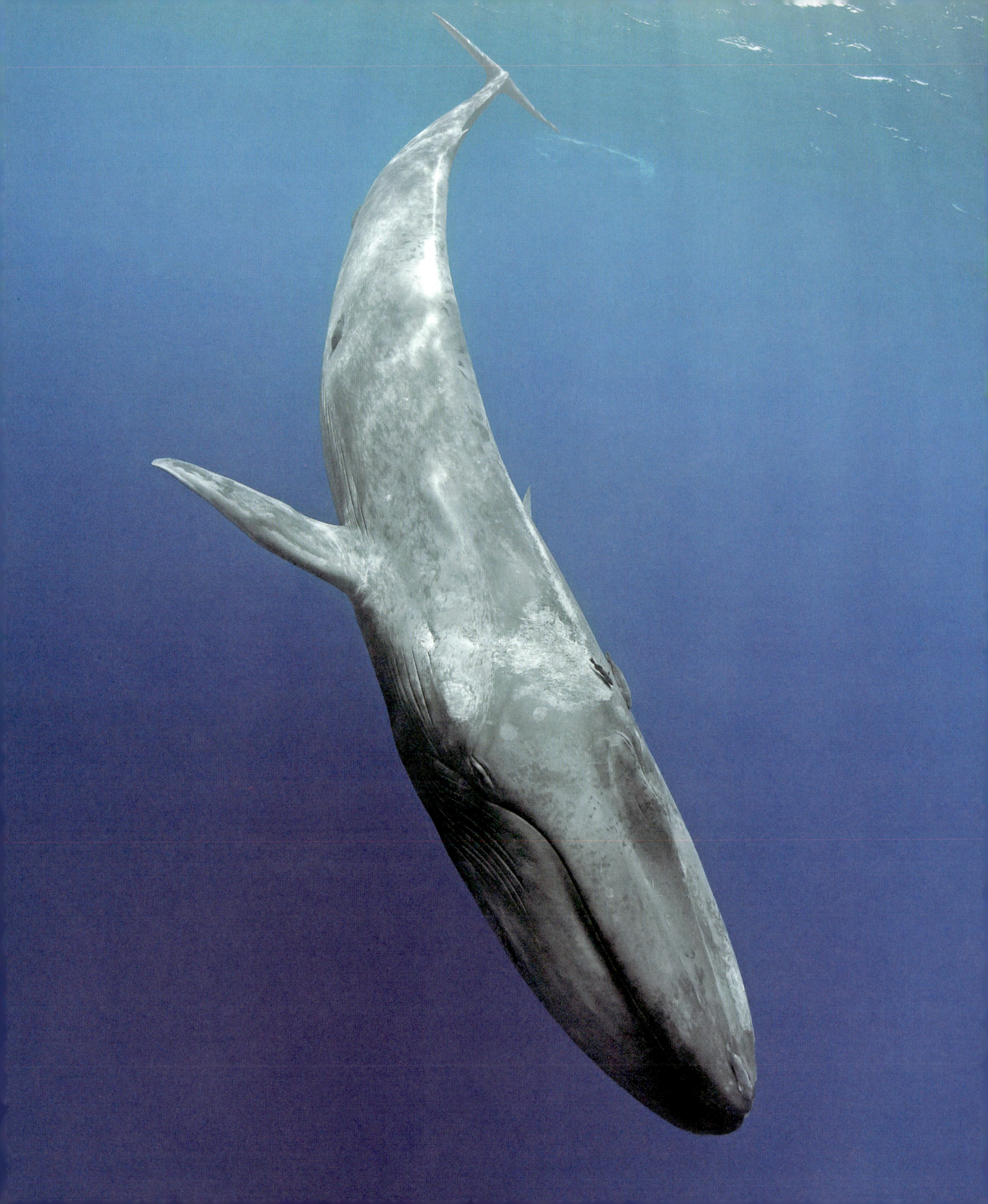

Trincomalee, Sri Lanka
Eyeball giants of the deep in the tropical waters of northern Sri Lanka

Why it's special

Though modest in size, the island nation of Sri Lanka is home to some giant animals. Asian elephants roam the jungles topside, and just beyond its shorelines are blue whales. Located on Sri Lanka's north-east coast, the port city of Trincomalee serves as a gateway to the most mega of underwater experiences; freediving with blue whales. In Trinco's historic harbour and just beyond, marine megafauna come to feast on an abundance of microorganisms, including a resident population of pygmy blue whales. Though swimming with these giants is illegal in Sri Lanka, a few licensed operators are authorised to offer in-water experiences, offering you the chance to potentially come eye-to-eye with the planet's largest animal species.

Best time to dive

March and April are the prime months to witness blue whales in Trincomalee. During this period, the increased number of whales, favourable water temperature (averaging 25–26°C/77–79°F), and great visibility create an optimal setting for potential blue whale sightings.

Gear
- A 3mm wetsuit for 25-26°C (77-79°F) water temps
- A hat and sun protective clothing for spending hours out on the open sea
- Freediving gear snorkel, mask, fins and weights
- Reef smart sunscreen
- Dry bag to keep your gear protected
- Warm clothes for after your swim

Photography tip
Capturing a blue whale on camera is no small task. Not only are you shooting as wide as possible, you also need to be poised, settings ready to go, as you're likely only going to have time to compose one passing shot. If possible, it's good to include elements of the surrounding marine environment to provide context and scale, for example your dive buddy.

Qualification
- Freediver (no dive qualification needed)

While freediving with blue whales doesn't require certification, comfort in open water and good swimming abilities are necessary. A good knowledge of marine mammals' behaviour and local regulations are imperative to ensure a responsible and respectful experience with the whales.

Getting there
The are regular flights to Sri Lanka's Colombo (Bandaranaike) International Airport. An overnight stay may be required before the 5-hour road trip to Trincomalee.

Opposite Pygmy blue whales are some of the largest creatures on the planet

Dive in

When the 26-year civil war with the Tamil Tigers ended in 2009, tourists began to flock back into northern Sri Lanka. In Tamil culture, the ancient port city of Trincomalee (nicknamed Trinco) is a place of great significance. The city has many sacred Hindu sites and its deep-water harbour, the world's fifth largest natural harbour, has attracted seafarers, pilgrims and traders since 400 BC. Today, Trinco's 17th century Fort Frederick is a tourist hotspot and also a vantage point for spotting one of the region's most famous residents, a pygmy species of the blue whale.

Just offshore from Trinco is one of the world's largest submarine canyons with 1350m (4400ft) high walls, dropping down to 3350m (11,000ft) further out to sea. Having this giant underwater canyon so close to the mainland means that blue whales (and other deep-water species) can venture unusually close to shore. For divers and animal lovers, this presents a unique opportunity to observe them close up. And for travellers, Trinco's rich history and culture provides the perfect place to encounter local Tamil culture.

Sri Lanka's pygmy blue whales are unique in their behaviour. Unlike other blue whales that migrate to colder waters, these ones remain in this region year-round forming a 'resident population'. Venturing out onto the water, there's a chance that you may come face-to-face with one, if you're lucky. Coming to the surface for brief intervals, small groups of snorkellers and freedivers can quietly slip into the water in the path of an oncoming whale, watching as it glides by. This encounter is considered a 'fly-by'; a brief moment with the whale as it swims by. Furthermore, these giants are shy and will deep dive if they're spooked. For this reason, a quiet approach is employed, and scuba gear isn't used. After the whale flukes its tail in the air and goes into a deep dive, it will then pop up again ten to twelve minutes later in another location. Even for seasoned operators, there's difficulty in calculating the blue whale's next location, timing and placement for swimmers, all the while trying not to interrupt its behaviour. But, when all the elements align, to have the opportunity to slip into the water with an animal that's twice the size of a school bus is truly a thing of wonder.

Meanwhile, other cetaceans may be spotted like sperm whales, Brydes whales, big pods of spinner dolphins and, if you're lucky, false killer whales. I've been lucky to get up close to a pod of false killer whales and it still stands as one of the most amazing underwater experiences I've ever had. But of course, the blue whale steals the show in these waters, given the extreme rarity of an encounter anywhere in the world.

While the word 'pygmy' implies small, this particular species of marine megafauna is anything but little. 'True' blue whales, the biggest animals on Earth can reach up to 30m (98ft), while pygmies can reach up to 24m (79ft), with their shorter tails giving them a stumpier look than their bigger cousins. Their subspecies was only discovered during the '60s, a terrible time to be alive, if you were a whale. In just 50 years, a shocking 239,000 blue whales were slaughtered, leaving just 360 remaining when the International Whaling Commission (IWC) finally banned whaling in 1972. Before harpoons, a blue whale's lifespan stretched beyond 90 years.

These days, the main threats are ship strikes and entanglement in fishing gear. But unregulated tourism is now becoming problematic. While it's illegal to swim with whales in Sri Lanka and a permit is required to do so, the industry isn't being properly regulated and lots of dodgy operators have popped up. For this reason, it's important to only choose authorised operators. Another way that you can help is by contributing photos of whales and dolphins to conservation organisations who monitor cetacean populations. A good local organisation to send photos to is Oceanswell (oceanswell.org).

Opposite Nilaveli beach, just north of the port city of Trincomalee

Trincomalee, Sri Lanka

Indian Ocean and Africa

KwaZulu-Natal Coast, South Africa
Dive into a highway of sardines off South Africa's wild east coast

Why it's special

Each winter in South Africa, billions of sardines depart from their spawning grounds at the Agulhas Bank to follow a nutrient-rich seasonal cold current up the coast. Naturally, this many sardines making a pilgrimage together is not ignored by their predators, both animals and fishermen, and by divers and photographers who travel great distances to get amongst the action. The captivating KwaZulu-Natal coastline is the heart of it all, where fishermen cast their nets from the shore and divers take to the seas, looking for Cape gannets as their 'eyes in the sky' for bait balls below. The sardine run offers a dynamic and unpredictable adventure for those willing to brave chilly temperatures and long days in choppy seas for the chance to get amongst one of the planet's greatest animal migrations.

Best time to dive

While the sardines usually begin their journey north around May, the peak of their run along the Wild Coast is during June and July. Their exact route can vary from year to year, depending on where the cold current is. Though it's a reliable annual occurrence, there have been some years when they haven't been spotted at all, perhaps due to warmer waters near the coast that season.

Opposite Long-beaked common dolphins creating a network of air bubbles to trap sardines before launching their attack

Gear
- A 5-7mm wetsuit including a hood for water temperatures ranging between 15-21°C (59-70°F)
- Gloves
- Booties
- A hat for spending hours out on the open sea
- A waterproof windbreaker coat for on the boat
- Dry bag, to keep your gear protected

Be ready with scuba gear when the action is contained and below, and with snorkelling/freediving gear when the action is on the move and fast-paced.

Photography tip
Shoot wide and ensure your camera has fast autofocus abilities.

When scuba diving, strobes are a must to adapt to the fading light.

Qualification
- Freediver (no scuba qualification needed)

If you want to scuba dive, an advanced dive certification is recommended, as the action can be full on.

Divers should have experience with blue water diving/freediving and be comfortable with open ocean conditions. The ability to manage strong currents and rapidly changing underwater scenarios is crucial, as is the strength and endurance needed for long days in the water and for climbing in and out of the boat all day long.

Getting there
Halfway along the famed Wild Coast, Port St Johns is accessible via a 4-hour drive south from Durban.

Dive in

There's a Zulu proverb, 'Isikhathi sibuye ngokubili,' which translates to 'time returns as a circle'. In South Africa, there are few annual occurrences as reliably cyclical as the sardine run. While it may not be as renowned as the Serengeti's wildebeest stampede, the sardine run far eclipses the wildebeest in numbers. It's even earned the nickname 'the greatest shoal on Earth!'

The action usually begins in May as billions of sardines slowly leave the deep, cold water of Africa's southernmost point, Cape Agulhas, and swim north in the direction of Mozambique. During this time, cool winds blowing off the land combine with upwellings of the nutrient rich Agulhas Current, allowing for the passage of the pilchards as they travel in the cold current. By June, the beginning of winter in the southern hemisphere, the run is in full swing with giant shoals of silvery fish, sometimes kilometres long, swimming along the KwaZulu-Natal Coast. Upon reaching Durban area, any that haven't been caught, eaten or beached will gradually descend to cooler depths, eventually returning to their southern spawning grounds. And so, the cycle continues.

You can spot the action above the surface with gannets and other seabirds swooping and diving into the choppy water. When pods of dolphins show up, the scene turns into a well-organised chaos. Common and bottlenose dolphins will peel away parts of the shoal, pushing them up to the surface and corralling them into tight bait balls. Then other predators arrive, like bronze whalers and Bryde's whales, hoping to get in on the bait ball buffet. Amidst the swirling chaos, Cape gannets propel themselves through the water, embodying their Zulu name 'isicibamanzi' which means 'the spear into the water'. It's said that these birds can plunge into the ocean at a speed of up to 120km/hr (74mi/hr) when hunting sardines.

For dive boats seeking bait balls, swooping gannets are a good sign. After launching from the beach, the hunt begins, bouncing around the sea and then speeding towards gannets, knowing that the sardines will be close by. If your crew give the nod, you'll jump into the water faster than you can say 'isicibamanzi,' throwing on your mask and snorkel as you go. In the case of static bait balls that seem to be hanging around for a while, you may jump into scuba gear instead. On some days you'll jump in multiple times, on others it can be a non-event. The unpredictability is part of the adventure; with fast-paced underwater action, sudden changes in direction, and the possibility of a surprise visit by a marine giant such as a humpback or Bryde's whale.

Divers and underwater photographers aren't the only ones who look forward to the sardine run. In Zulu legend, the sardines are a gift from the sea god. For local communities, they're food on the table. And for commercial fishermen, they're money in the bank. Sometimes locals can get lucky, with predators chasing fish into the shallow water, allowing fishermen to cast nets close to shore. This creates a real spectacle for beachgoers.

The stretch of coastline that runs adjacent to the ephemeral sardine highway is known as the 'wild coast'. There are various towns that you can base yourself at, with Mbotyi and Port St Johns being popular choices. The coast here is rugged and dramatic; sitting in your small inflatable the coastline seems to continuously change with towering cliffs and pristine beaches, along with a real sense of isolation. There are a few companies to choose from and I recommend supporting locally owned. Offshore Africa have a great reputation and they also have their own spotter plane, which is a huge advantage when looking for bait balls (offshoreportstjohns.com). When booking your trip, commit to as many days as you can, in case the weather prevents you from going out on some days. In any case, prepare for long days of bumping around on choppy seas; this one's not for the faint-hearted, but the rewards are great. In the words of another old Zulu proverb, 'you cannot cross a river without getting wet'.

Below The ocean boils with activity as Cape gannets plunge for sardines

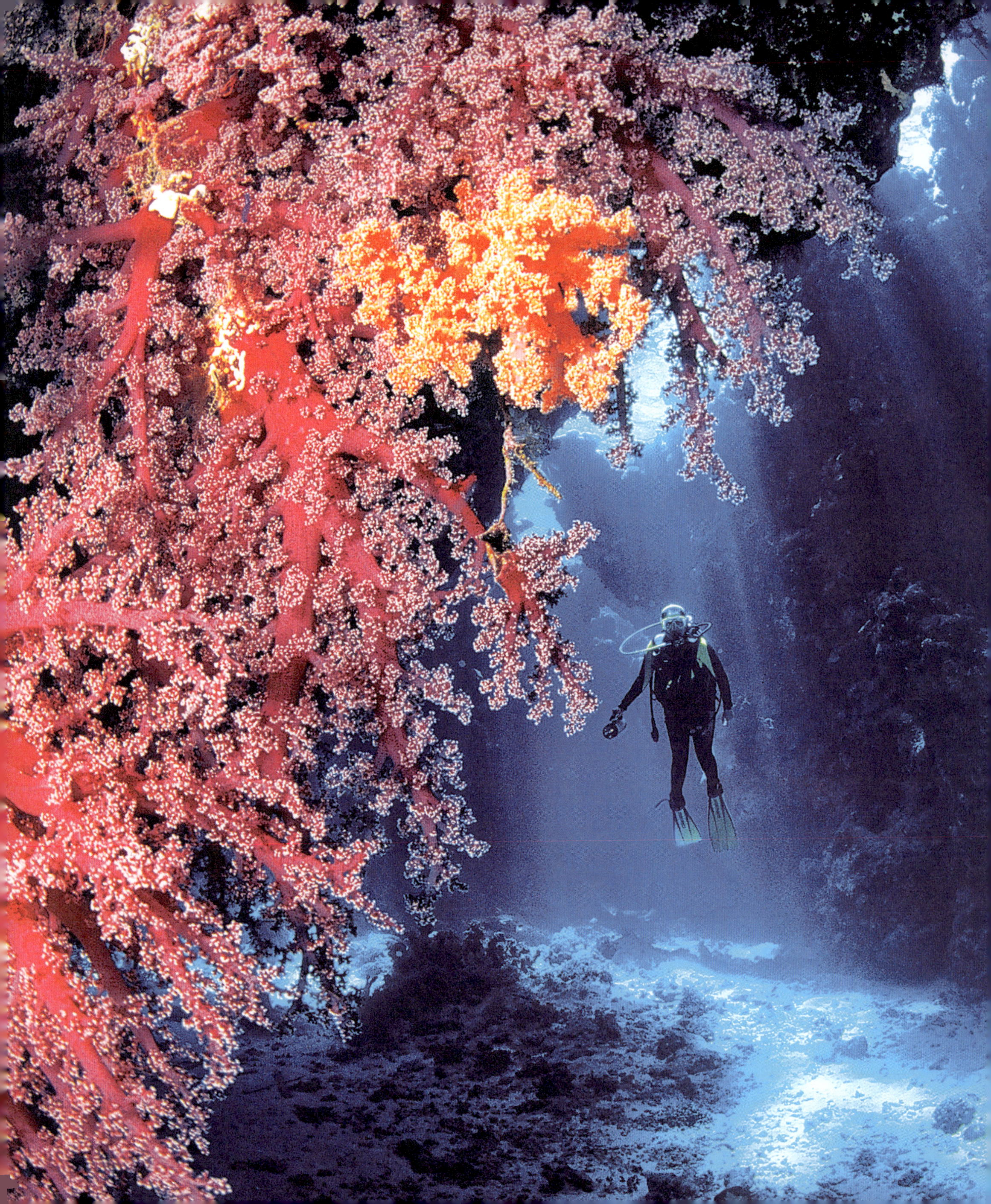

Southern Red Sea, Egypt

Whitetips in a red sea, south Egypt is the place to be!

Why it's special

With one of the world's busiest shipping lanes and a coastline of sprawling resort towns, Egypt's Red Sea gets its fair share of activity. The world's northernmost tropical sea is renowned for its incredible coral reefs and marine life, though many dive sites are becoming overrun. For those that prefer their dives crowded with fish, not people, southern Egypt is the place to be. About 100km (62mi) south of the Egyptian Riviera town of Marsa Alam you'll find the quieter section of Egypt's Red Sea. Imagine pristine reefs, incredible visibility, dramatic wall drop-offs and ripping currents that keep advanced divers on their toes. Beginning with the Fury Shoals and stretching down to St John's Reef near Sudan, the offshore dive sites here offer Egypt's healthiest reefs and plenty of pelagics, including the elusive oceanic whitetip shark.

Best time to dive

The optimal diving season in Egypt's Southern Red Sea spans from March to May and then again from September to November. These months promise the clearest waters, calmest seas, and an abundance of marine life. As the south can be a little unpredictable, your liveaboard itinerary may be rerouted in the case of strong winds.

Gear

Slightly warmer than the north, the water temperatures of Egypt's southern Red Sea sit between 28-30°C (82-86°F) in the summer and autumn as low as 23°C (73°F) in winter. A 3mm wetsuit for summer and a 5mm in the middle of winter should be ideal.

Photography tip

For photographers, the Red Sea has a lot to offer. One of the main drawcards, for me, are the incredible coral seascapes and, if you're lucky, a close encounter with an oceanic whitetip. With these two in mind, I would be shooting wide with strobes. Not too wide, though; maybe something around 35mm.

Qualification

- Advanced Open Water

Several liveaboard operators enforce a specific minimum dive requirement. Current Egyptian regulations state that scuba divers must have logged a minimum of 50 dives to explore the four offshore island marine parks: The Brothers, Zabargad, Daedalus, and Rocky Island.

Getting here

You can join a liveaboard from Marsa Alam, which has an international airport. Alternatively, EgyptAir offers a 1-hour flight from Cairo to Marsa Alam.

Opposite The soft corals of the Red Sea are legendary

Dive in

Egyptians have a long history with diving. An Egyptian named Ahsan-ul-Ghawasin is credited with creating the first dive apparatus back in the 12th century, using bellows (a pump) and a heavy stone. Carvings in the 3500-year-old temple of the female Pharaoh Hatshepsut show dugongs, rays and pelagic fish from her Red Sea expedition to Punt. From pearls to coral, the jewellery of ancient Egypt also offers evidence of freediving in the distant past.

Nowadays, the Red Sea is famous for its reefs, wrecks and ruins. These waters are home to over 1200 species of fish, including 44 shark species, and since about 40% of the Red Sea is less than 100m (328ft) deep, dive sites are plentiful. The Red Sea's brilliant corals, which have proven to be remarkably resistant to rising sea temperatures, delight divers in their various forms including gardens of fire coral, towering pinnacles swathed in soft corals, and various hard corals. Other marine habitats of the Red Sea include mangroves, salt marshes and seagrass beds. With its high salinity, and in the absence of other oceanic currents and big rivers running into it, the visibility here is known to be incredible. But along with the Red Sea's notoriety come the crowds. Dive sites in the north (around the Sinai Peninsula) and any places that are accessible via day trips are getting more and more crowded, causing divers to head further south and further offshore.

The section of the Red Sea from Marsa Alam down to Egypt's deep south near the Sudanese border, has some amazing diving, however its ripping currents make it best suited to fit and advanced divers. With incredible walls and reefs, the south is a pelagic playground attracting mantas, schooling fish and plenty of sharks, including whale sharks and the elusive oceanic whitetip. With their distinctive rounded fins and bold curiosity, this is one of the few places in the world where divers can still reliably find them. Listed as 'Endangered' on the IUCN Red List, oceanic whitetips fall victim to commercial fishing, and their fins are especially valuable. Slow to reproduce, their numbers are quickly declining and drastic action is required to save them from extinction.

Your best chance of seeing an oceanic whitetip is on a liveaboard trip that visits the outer sha'abs (reefs) of the Red Sea in southern Egypt. During May and June, they're often spotted at St John's Reef. A popular spot on liveaboard itineraries, this reef presents a submerged maze of caves and overhangs, swathed in soft corals and teeming with life. The Fury Shoal system is great for seasoned divers, with intricate labyrinths, drop-offs, wrecks and sprawling coral gardens.

The best time to see whitetips here (and at the sites mentioned below) is October until December. The Rocky Islands and Zabargad are also worth a mention; Zabargad has a great wreck dive known as 'The Russian Wreck' and it's also known for whitetips. Meanwhile, the strong currents at the nearby Rocky Islands bring in pelagics including mantas, dolphins, giant barracuda and feeding sharks.

It's worth spending a few days in Marsa Alam either side of your trip, or, for a quieter alternative, head further south to the village of Hamata. Both places have fantastic beaches and great dive sites nearby. While many tourists participate on snorkelling day tours of the nearby 'dolphin house reefs' (Samadai and Sataya), it's worth doing your research before joining in. Researchers have found that the large pods of spinner dolphins visiting these reefs come here to rest after hunting, and boatloads of tourists distress them. Bottlenose and spinner dolphins can often be spotted during tender rides to and from dive sites during your liveaboard. This is the best way to enjoy these beautiful animals, rather than interrupting their valuable chill time.

Above Oceanic whitetip shark *Overleaf* Schooling bannerfish, Maldives

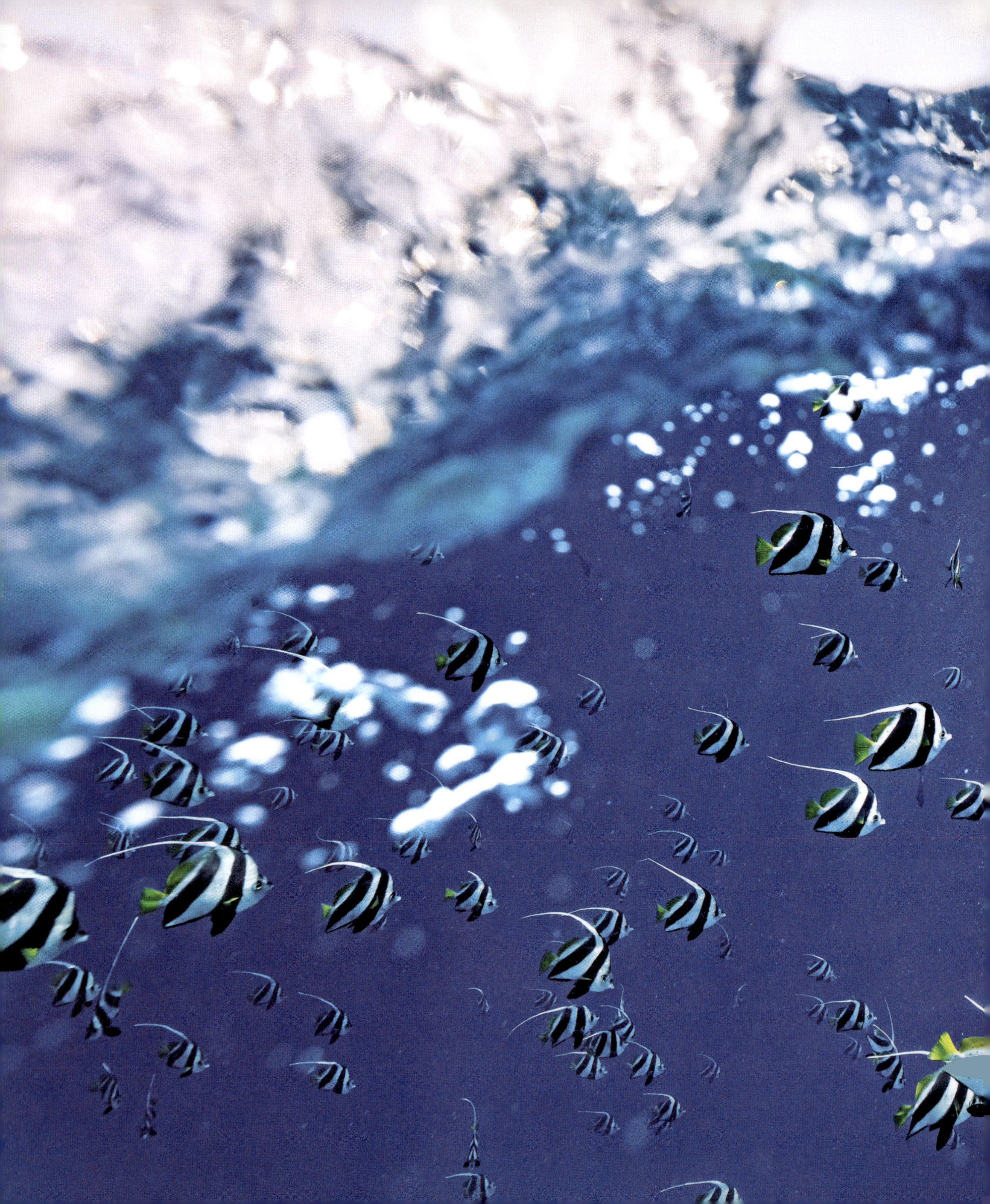

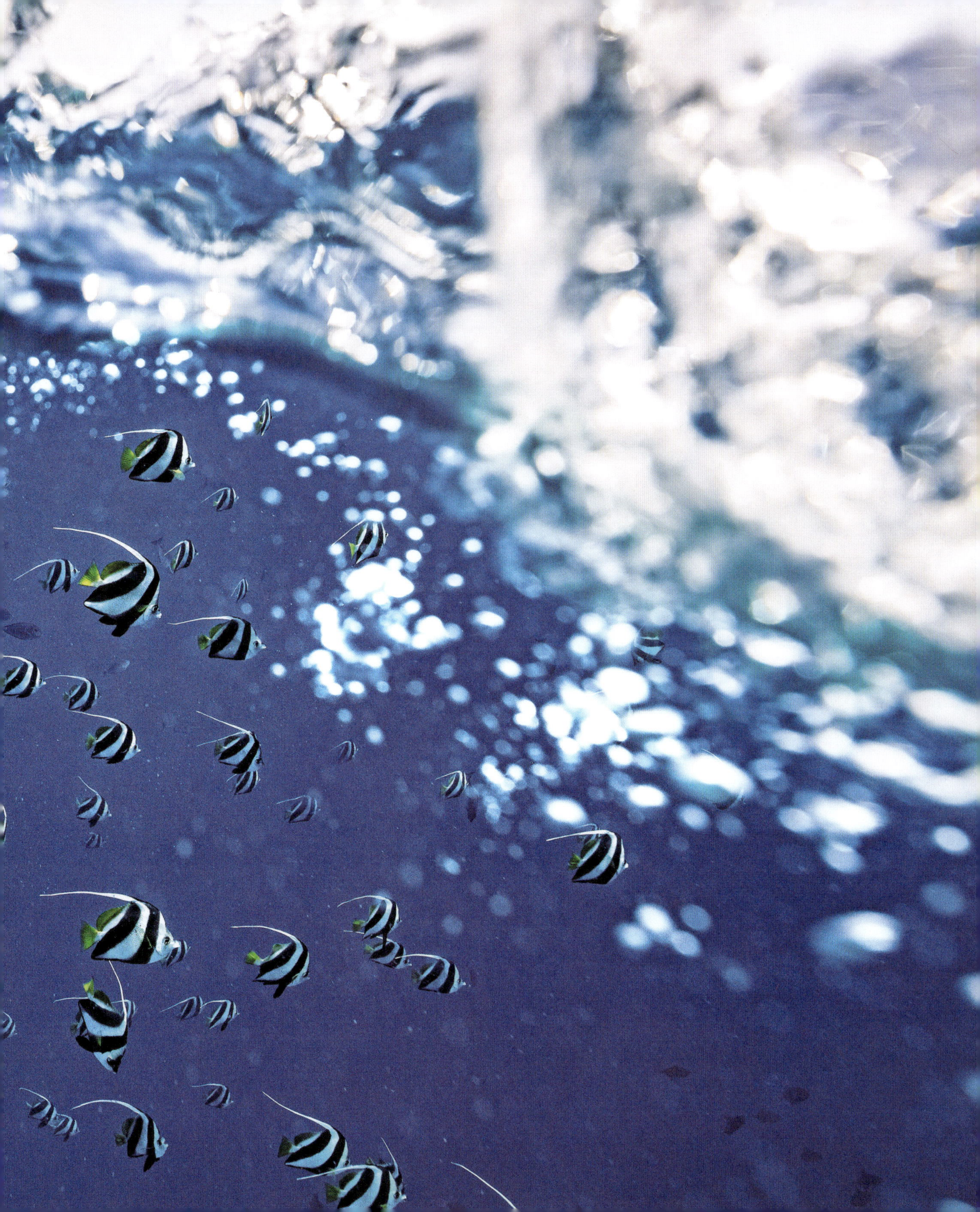

INDEX

A
Admiralty Islands, Lord Howe Island, NSW 15
advanced open water diver vii
American saltwater crocodiles 74, 76, 99
anacondas 60, 63
Andaman Sea 136–45
anemonefish 16,
anemones 16, 50, 144
angelfish 15, 20, 70, 76, 197
Anhumas Abyss, Bonito, Brazil 63
Anilao, The Philippines 172–5
Antarctica 49–53
Aotearoa New Zealand 44–7
Arctic char 116
Arctic Circle 104–9
Atlantic grey seals 130
Atlantic spotted dolphins 59
aurora borealis (Northern Lights) 108, 115, 117
Australia 2–43
Australian sea lions 35

B
Baa Atoll, The Maldives 218–21
Bahamas, The 56–9
Ballina angelfish 15
Balls Pyramid, Lord Howe Island, NSW 15
Banco Chinchorro, Mexico 99–101
barracudas 68, 120, 155, 165, 166, 170, 171, 181, 184
Barrel of Butter (skerry), Scapa Flow, Scotland 127, 129
basking sharks 123–5
Bedwell Island, Rowley Shoals, Western Australia 39
belugas 111, 112
Beqa Lagoon, Fiji 199–201
big-eye trevally 165
Bimini, The Bahamas 56, 59

bioluminescent jellyfish 172, 175
black coral 44, 46
Black Rock, Mergui Archipelago, Myanmar 144
blacktip butterflyfish 155
blacktip reef sharks 139, 144, 150, 154, 184, 200, 207, 211
blackwater diving 172–5
blotched stingrays 144
Blue Corner, Rock Islands, Palau 181
Blue Holes, Rock Islands, Palau 181
Blue Magic, Raja Ampat, Indonesia 155
blue-ringed octopus 161
blue whales 224
bonfire diving 175
Bonito, Brazil 60–3
bottlenose dolphins 39, 47, 59, 78, 184, 228, 233
Bougainville Reef, Coral Sea 6
boxfish 161
Brazil 60–3
Bristol Channel, Devon, UK 130–3
bronze whalers 228
Bryde's whales 92, 224, 228
bull sharks 199–201
bumphead parrotfish 178
butterflyfish 12, 15, 20, 70, 155, 197
Byron Bay, NSW 23–5

C
cabbage corals 181
California, USA 87–9
Californian sea lions 87, 90
Cape gannets 227, 228
Cape Kri, Raja Ampat, Indonesia 155
Caribbean, The 83–5
Caribbean reef sharks 76
carpet sharks 46–7

cave diving vii, 63, 95–7, 166, 181
Cayo Centro, Mexico 99
cenotes, Yucatan Peninsula, Mexico 95–7
Chandelier Cave, Rock Islands, Palau 181
Citizens of the Reef 11
Clerke Reef, Rowley Shoals, Western Australia 36, 39
climate change 11, 16
clownfish 12, 139
Cocos Island, Costa Rica 68–73
Colombia 64–7
common dolphins 228
Coolidge, SS (wreck) 190–3
coral atolls 36–9, 99–101, 170–1
Coral Bay, Western Australia 20
Coral Nurture Program 11
Coral Sea 6, 9–10
Coral Triangle 150, 153, 166, 170
Costa Brava, Spain 120
Costa Rica 68–73
creole fish 76
Cromwell Current 205
Cuba 74–7
cuttlefish 40–3, 158

D
Darwin and Wolf Islands, The Galápagos 202–7
deep diving 190–3
Dive Master diver vii
diver safety xii
dog sharks 46–7
dolphins 15, 20, 39, 59, 83, 124, 150, 155, 171, 181, 184, 196, 207, 224, 228, 233
Dominica, The Caribbean 83–5
Dominican Republic 78–81
Dos Ojos National Park, Mexico 96
double-header wrasse 12
drysuit diving viii, 44–7, 49–51, 111–12, 115–17, 127, 130

dugongs 20
dusky gropers 120
dusky sharks 207
dwarf minke whales 6, 9

E
eagle rays 25, 76, 100, 120, 171, 181, 184, 207, 211
East Australian Current (EAC) 12, 15, 24
East of Eden, Similan Islands, Thailand 139
ecotourism 90–3, 150
Egypt 231–3
Elephant Rock (Hin Pusar), Similan Islands, Thailand 139
elkhorn corals 74–6
England 130–3
Espiritu Santo, Vanuatu 190–3
ethical encounters with marine life xiii
Eurasian tectonic plate 116
Everest Sea Mount, Cocos Island, Costa Rica 73
Exmouth's Naval Communication Station, Western Australia 20

F
Fakarava atoll, The Tuamotus, French Polynesia 182, 184, 185
false killer whales 83, 224
Fiji 194–201
freediving vii, 20, 36, 40, 90–3, 104–7, 123–4, 187–9, 218–21, 223, 227
French angelfish 76
French Polynesia 182–5
frigatebirds 92, 93
frogfish 158, 161
Fury Shoal, Red Sea, Egypt 232
fusiliers 9, 139, 140, 144
Fuvahmulah, The Maldives 214–17

G

Galápagos 202-7
Galápagos sharks 64, 71, 207
Galápagos whaler sharks 15
Gardens of the Queen (Jardines de la Reina), Cuba 74-7
garibaldis 87, 88
Garuae Pass, Fakarava atoll, The Tuamotus, French Polynesia 185
geological landscapes 115-17
German Channel, Rock Islands, Palau 181
ghost nets 144, 145
ghost pipefishes 139, 140, 154, 161
giant black sea bass 87
giant groupers 20, 67
giant trevally 171
glass fish 140
golden rays 207
gorgonian fans 10, 76, 120, 139, 144, 150, 157, 171, 181, 197
Grand Bahama, The Bahamas 56-9
Great Barrier Reef, Qld 6-11
great hammerheads 56, 59, 184
great white sharks 15, 30, 33
green anacondas 60, 63
green turtles 20, 100, 165, 166, 171, 181
grey nurse sharks 24, 25
grey reef sharks 144, 150, 171, 184, 185, 200, 220
groupers 20, 67, 185, 197
guitar sharks 1771

H

half-banded angelfish 15
Hammerhead Triangle, Colombia 64, 67
hammerheads 39, 56, 59, 64, 67, 68, 70, 165, 171, 184, 202, 207, 211, 214, 217
Hanifaru Bay, The Maldives 220-1
hard corals 39, 139, 149, 150, 181, 232
hawksbill turtles 20, 25, 100, 165, 166, 171, 181, 196
Hebrides, The, Scotland 123-5
Heron Island, Great Barrier Reef, Qld 6
Holmes Reef, Coral Sea 6

horse-eye jacks 76
Humboldt Current 205
humpback whales 19, 20, 24, 39, 67, 78-81, 83, 187-9, 228

ice diving 111-13
Iceland 115-17
Imperieuse Reef, Rowley Shoals, Western Australia 36
Indonesia 149-55, 158-63
instructor viii
Island Four (Koh Miang), Similan Islands, Thailand 139

J

jacks 67, 68, 71, 76, 181
jellyfish 50, 172, 175, 181
Jellyfish Lake, Eil Malk Island, Palau 181
Jessie Beazley Reef, Tubbataha, Philippines 170
Julian Rocks, Byron Bay, NSW 23, 24, 25

K

kelp bass 88
kelp forests 87-8, 130
Koh Bon, Similan Islands, Thailand 140
Koh Tachai, Similan Islands, Thailand 140
Kuhl's stingrays 139
KwaZulu-Natal coast, South Africa 227-9

L

Lady Elliot Island, Great Barrier Reef, Qld 6
Langjökull glacier, Iceland 115, 116
leafy sea dragons 2-5
leatherback turtles 100
Lembeh Strait, Indonesia 158-63
leopard seals 49, 50-1
leopard sharks 23, 25, 87, 139
loggerhead turtles 20, 25
Lord Howe Island, NSW 12-17
Lundy Island, Devon, UK 130-3

M

McCulloch's anemonefish 16
mackerel 9, 39
Magdalena Bay, Mexico 90-3
Malaysian Borneo 165-7

Maldives, The 214-21
Malpelo barnacle-blenny 67
Malpelo Island, Colombia 64-7
Malpelo wrasse 67
Mangrove Jacks 20
manta rays 6, 9, 15, 20, 25, 64, 71, 136, 143, 144, 150, 154-5, 171, 207, 211, 217, 218-21, 232
Manta Ridge, Raja Ampat, Indonesia 155
Manta Sandy, Raja Ampat, Indonesia 155
Maori wrasse 39
marbled grouper 185
marine biodiversity 20, 50, 59, 67, 68, 70, 88, 120, 124, 150, 153, 172
marine debris 146
Master Reef Guides 11
Meda Grande, Spain 120
Meda Perita, Spain 120
Medes Islands, Spain 119-21
Mergui (Myeik) Archipelago, Myanmar 143-7
Mermaid Reef, Rowley Shoals, Western Australia 36, 39
Mexico 90-101
Milford Sound, Aotearoa New Zealand 44-7
mimic octopuses 154, 158
Misool, Raja Ampat, Indonesia 149-51
mobula rays 71
Moorish idols 20, 178
moray eels 67, 120, 201
muck diving 158-63, 208, 211
Myanmar 143-7

N

napoleon wrasse 139
nature-based tourism 150
neon flying squid 172
Neptune Islands, South Australia 33, 34, 35
Nesgjá, northern Iceland 117
New South Wales 12-17, 23-9
New Zealand fur seals 47
Ngedebus Coral Garden, Rock Islands, Palau 181
Ningaloo Reef, Western Australia 19-21
Nitrox viii, 158, 161, 178
North American tectonic plate 116

North Atlantic humpback whales 78-81
North Atoll, Tubbataha, Philippines 170, 171
North Equatorial Counter Current 197
northern Norway (Arctic Circle) 104-9
nudibranchs 5, 15, 20, 46, 87, 88, 139, 140, 154, 158, 169, 171
nurse sharks 99, 100, 101, 144

O

Ocean Census 124
oceanic whiptail sharks 232
octopuses 20, 46, 120
open water diver vii
orange garibaldi 87, 88
orange spine unicorn fish 178
orcas 50, 92, 93, 104-9
Orkneys, Scotland 127-30
ornate ghost pipefish 139, 140
Osprey Reef, Coral Sea 6, 9, 10
Öxarárfoss Waterfall, Iceland 117

P

Palau 178-81
Panama Flow 205
Papua New Guinea 208-11
parrotfish 20, 39, 139, 178
Philippines 169-75
photography 157, 162
planktonic creatures 172-5
Port Lincoln, South Australia 30-5
prickly shark 73
puffins 130
pygmy blue whales 223-4
pygmy cuttlefish 161
pygmy seahorses 140, 150, 154, 157, 171

Q

Queensland 6-11, 26-9

R

ragged-toothed sharks 64, 67
Raja Ampat, Indonesia 149-55
Raja Ampat epaulette (walking) shark 150
Raja Ampat (Santa Claus) pygmy seahorse 150
Rangiroa atoll, The Tuamotus, French Polynesia 182, 184

Rapid Bay, South Australia 2-5
rebreathers viii
red coral 120
Red Sea, Egypt 231-3
red snapper 178
Reef Restoration Foundation 11
reef sharks 76, 181, 196
  see also blacktip reef sharks; grey reef sharks; whitetip reef sharks
ribbon eels 139
Ribbon Reefs, Great Barrier Reef, Qld 6, 9, 10
Richelieu Rock, Similan Islands, Thailand 140
Rock Islands, Palau 178-81
Rocky Islands, Red Sea, Egypt 232
Rowley Shoals, Western Australia 36-9
Russia 111-13

S
sailfin snapper 178
St. John's Reef, Red Sea, Egypt 232
salema porgy 120
Santa Catalina Island, California, USA 87-9
sardines 227-9
scalloped hammerheads 67, 70, 165, 207, 214, 217
Scapa Flow, Scotland 127-30
scorpionfish 144
Scotland 123-70
SCUBA vii-viii
sea angels 111, 112
sea ice diving 111-13
sea snakes 120
seahorses 140, 150
seals 127, 129
Shark Airport, Tubbataha, Indonesia 171
shark cage diving 30-4
short-fin pilot whales 83
sicklefin lemon sharks 200
Silfa Fissure, Iceland 115-17
silky sharks 64, 67, 71, 76, 171, 207
Silvan Bank, The, Dominican Republic 78-81
silvertip sharks 200
Similan Islands, Thailand 136-41

sinkholes 95-7
Sipadan Island, Malaysian Borneo 165-7
snappers 71, 140, 144, 165, 170
snub-nosed dartfish 76
soft corals 10, 15, 20, 39, 50, 112, 136, 139, 144, 149, 150, 154, 166, 181, 194-7
South Africa 227-9
South Atoll, Tubbataha, Philippines 170
South Australia 2-5, 30-5, 40-3
South Equatorial Current 197
Southern Red Sea, Egypt 231-3
Spain 119-21
sperm whales 83-5, 224
spinner dolphins 39, 224, 233
spotted eagle rays 76
Sri Lanka 223-5
SS *President Coolidge* (wreck), Santo (Vanuatu) 190-3
SS *Yongala* (wreck), Qld 26-9
stingrays 139, 144, 207
striped marlin 90-3
submersibles xi, 52, 73
sunfish 120
surgeonfish 197
Surin Islands, Thailand 136
surviving when things go wrong 166-7
sweetlips 171

T
tawny nurse sharks 200
Thailand 136-41
The Bahamas 56-9
The Caribbean 83-5
The *Coolidge* (wreck), Santo (Vanuatu) 190-3
The Hebrides, Scotland 123-5
The Silvan Bank, Dominican Republic 78-81
The Tuamotus, French Polynesia 182-5
The White Sea, Russia 111-13
Thingvellir National Park, Iceland 115, 117
three-stripe butterflyfish 12, 15
thresher sharks 214, 217
Tiger Beach, Grand Bahama, The Bahamas 56, 59
tiger sharks 20, 56, 59, 71, 171, 184, 200, 214, 217

Tiputa Pass, Rangiroa atoll, The Tuamotus, French Polynesia 184
Tonga 187-9
trevally 9, 39, 144, 165, 171, 197
triggerfish 139, 171
Trincomalee, Sri Lanka 223-5
Tuamotus, The, French Polynesia 182-5
Tubbataha, Philippines 169-71
Tufi, Papua New Guinea 208-11
Tumakohua Pass, Fakarava atoll, The Tuamotus, French Polynesia 185
tuna 39, 67, 139, 171, 217
turtles 9, 20, 25, 93, 100, 139, 165, 166, 171, 181, 184, 196

U
Ulong Channel, Rock Islands, Palau 181
UNESCO Biosphere Reserves 99, 185, 217, 220
UNESCO World Heritage sites 66, 68, 71, 117, 169, 170, 181
USA 87-9

V
Vanuatu 190-3
Vatu-i-Ra, Fiji 194-7
Vava'u, Tonga 187-9

W
Waigeo, Raja Ampat, Indonesia 153-5
Washing Machine, Tubbataha, Philippines 171
Wayag Lagoon, Raja Ampat, Indonesia 154
West of Eden, Similan Islands, Thailand 139
Western Australia 19-21, 36-9
Western Rocky, Mergui Archipelago, Myanmar 144
whale sharks 15, 19, 20, 64, 67, 100, 136, 143, 144, 150, 169, 171, 181, 202, 205, 207, 217, 220, 232
whip corals 150, 171
whip rays 144
White Cave System (Sistema Sac Actun), Mexico 95-7
White Sea, The, Russia 111-13

whitetip reef sharks 139, 144, 150, 200, 207, 211
Whyalla, South Australia 40-3
wobbegongs 23, 25, 150, 155
Wolf and Darwin Islands, The Galápagos 202-7
wreck diving 26-9, 59, 100, 101, 127-30, 132, 133, 171, 181, 190-3, 196, 201, 211, 232
wunderpus 154

Y
Yongala, SS (wreck), Qld 26-9
Yucatan Peninsula, Mexico 95-7

Z
Zabargad, Red Sea, Egypt 232

Opposite Rowley Shoals, Australia

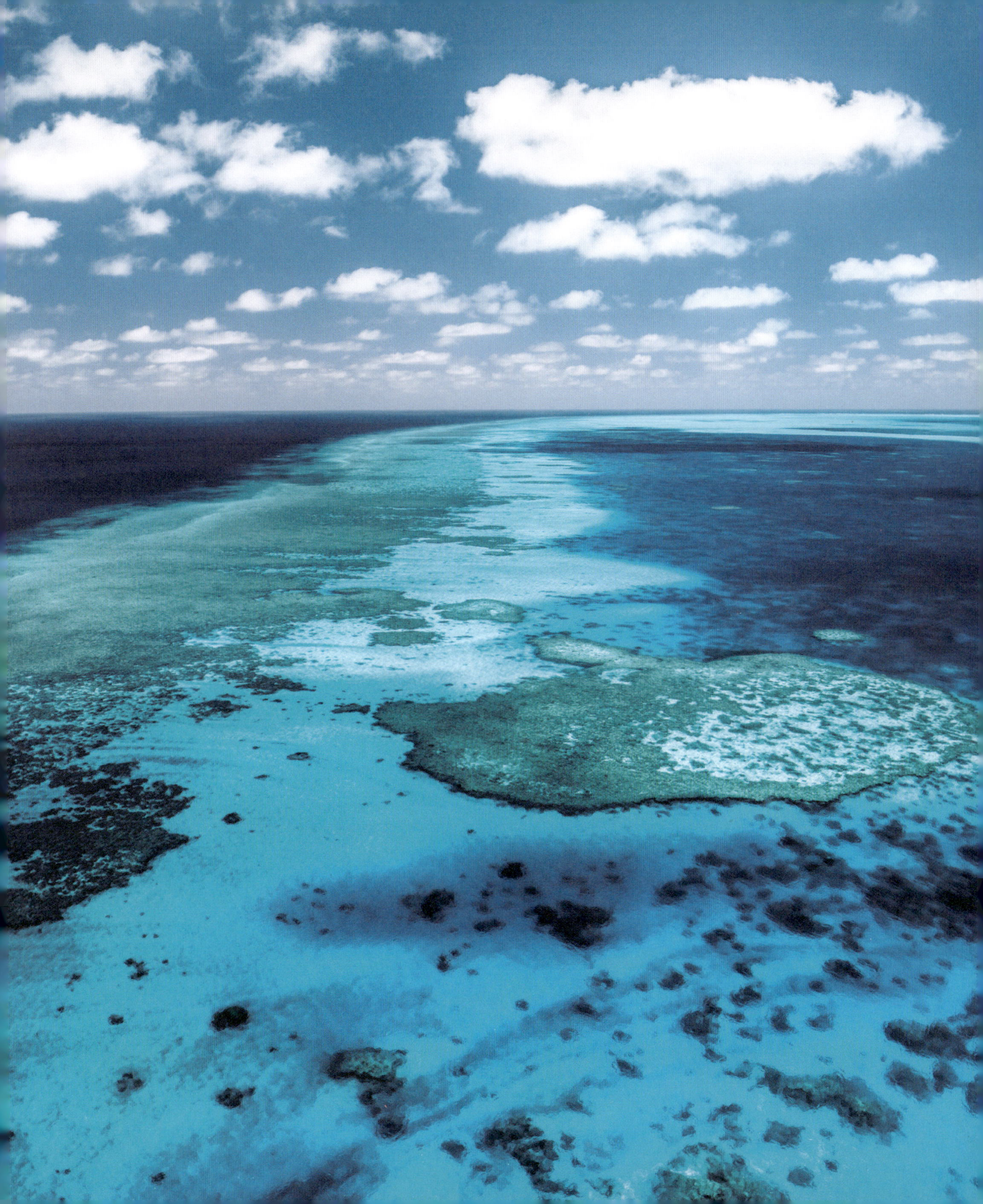

ABOUT THE AUTHOR

Todd Thimios is a self-confessed dive tragic. A technical diver with a degree in Marine Science, Todd has completed more than 3500 dives since becoming a Dive Master at age 16. Growing up in Queensland, Todd had an adventurous childhood exploring the Great Barrier Reef on his family's boat. With dreams of diving the world, Todd became an instructor at age 20, working on Lord Howe Island throughout his twenties before flying to the French Riviera to work on private superyachts.

In the following years, Todd became a sought-after dive guide for billionaires and celebrities, circumnavigating the planet twice and diving the remotest of locations. He helped to niche out a job previously (and still now) unheard of, a 'Dive Scout'. Flown ahead of guests to new destinations, Todd would find, film and curate ultimate dive itineraries before guiding and filming for guests underwater, including diving with orcas in the Arctic and exploring virgin reefs in the South Pacific. In a profile piece published by Get Lost Magazine, the journalist described Todd's unique job by saying, 'It's the type of resumé that wouldn't seem out of place in a Bond film.' Adding to his skillset, Todd has also trained as a submersible pilot, diving to depths of 1000 metres with clients in their submersibles.

After decades of dive travel, Todd met his wife, Melissa (a travel writer and fellow diver) after she saw one of his orca photos featured by National Geographic. Together they founded Thimios Media, where they partner with ethical, high-end dive brands and tourism operators to create media that focusses on the world's finest diving experiences. Todd is now based in Byron Bay with his young family and continues to dive and travel, but these days he takes his little dive crew along for the ride.

ACKNOWLEDGEMENTS

Putting this book together over the past two years has been a wonderful experience. I've dived new places, revisited some favourites, rummaged through an ever-growing tower of hard drives and, best of all, reconnected with old friends in amazing places. The diving community is a passionate one, full of colourful characters. Maybe it's the salt air or the excessive nitrogen, but it's fair to say we're a rather quirky mob and I love it.

Firstly, thanks Mum and Dad for encouraging me to pursue what I love. You made it simple from a young age. "You like to dive, well then Todd, you should dive the world, the rest will fall into place". Thank you for putting me on such a wonderful path, I love you both.

I've been blessed to have some wonderful mentors over the years. Ofer Ketter, Bob Cranston, Brian Busteed, Bob and Robbylee Phelan and my uncle Terry. Without you guys I wouldn't be where I am today

To the lovely Megan Cuthbert and the crew at Hardie Grant, Ethan Patrick, Andy Warren, Susanne Geppert, Megan Ellis and Simone Wall, thanks for all your professionalism and guidance and, most importantly, for offering me the great privilege that is writing a book about diving the world. I'm forever grateful.

To my editor, Deborah Dickson-Smith. Thank you for not only bringing your in-depth knowledge of dive travel to this project, but also for being an amazing editor. And thank you for being the wonderful, likeminded diver that you are; I look forward to our future diving escapades.

Above all, no words will ever summarise my love and appreciation for my beautiful wife, Melissa. You made this project happen and you made sure it stayed on track over the past few years. For this reason, it's you that has worked the hardest on this book. You're the most generous and supportive person alive. The girls and I are in very good hands.

To my two amazing little girls, Piper and Tia. I hope you are both ready for a lifetime of diving adventures. I think we have officially mapped out every future holiday that we're all going to take together. You both inspire me beyond words and I just can't wait to show you how beautiful this world is.

Lastly, to all my dive buddies over years, thank you for making this wonderful adventure possible. It's been a hell of a lot of fun and I will never underestimate what a luxury it is to spend my days exploring the planet underwater. Discovering new worlds, along with their unique inhabitants, has been nothing short of epic. I hope this book not only inspires readers to get underwater, but ultimately has you diving faraway and exotic places that were once beyond your wildest oceanic dreams.

Photo credits

All photographs ©Todd Thimios with the exception of: Pages xii, xiii, 52 Triton Submersibles; 4, 48, 50–51, 65, 66, 75, 76, 82, 84–85, 86, 89, 91, 94, 96–97, 98, 101, 110, 113, 114, 116–117, 122, 125, 132, 162–163, 173, 210 (bottom), 222, 226, 228–229, 232–233 Alamy; 10 Michelle Barry; 35 (top right) Jayne Jenkins; 37, 38, 239 Jampal Williamson; 38 (below) Scott Portelli; 41 Nathan Godwin; 54, 61, 62 (top/below) Daniel de Granville; 57 Epic diving Bahamas; 58 (below),70 Ofer Ketter; 67, 88, 92, 93, 100, 129, 131, 151 (top left), 155 (right), 161 (top left), 174, 225, 230 Shutterstock; 126,128 Torbjörn Gylleus; 133, 140, 171 iStock; 152 Grace Picót; 183 Bernard Beaussie; 185 Frédérique Legrand; 192 (below) South Pacific WWII Museum; 198, 200 David Robinson; 215, 216 Paul Maloney.

Published in 2025 by Hardie Grant Explore,
an imprint of Hardie Grant Publishing

Hardie Grant Explore (Melbourne)
Wurundjeri Country
Building 1, 658 Church Street
Richmond, Victoria 3121

Hardie Grant Explore (Sydney)
Gadigal Country
Level 7, 45 Jones Street
Ultimo, NSW 2007

www.hardiegrant.com/au/explore

All rights reserved. No part of this publication may be reproduced, stored in a retrieval system or transmitted in any form by any means, electronic, mechanical, photocopying, recording or otherwise, without the prior written permission of the publishers and copyright holders.

The moral rights of the author have been asserted.

Copyright text © Todd Thimios 2025
Copyright concept, maps and design © Hardie Grant Publishing 2025

Maps in this publication are made with Natural Earth. Free vector and raster map data @ naturalearthdata.com.

A catalogue record for this book is available from the National Library of Australia

Hardie Grant acknowledges the Traditional Owners of the Country on which we work, the Wurundjeri People of the Kulin Nation and the Gadigal People of the Eora Nation, and recognises their continuing connection to the land, waters and culture. We pay our respects to their Elders past and present.

For all relevant publications, Hardie Grant Explore commissions a First Nations consultant to review relevant content and provide feedback to ensure suitable language and information is included in the final book. Hardie Grant Explore also includes traditional place names and acknowledges Traditional Owners, where possible, in both the text and mapping for their publications.

Ultimate Dive Sites

ISBN 9781741179026

10 9 8 7 6 5 4 3 2 1

Project editor Megan Cuthbert
Editor Deborah Dickson-Smith
Proofreader Ethan Patrick
First Nations consultant Jamil Tye, Yorta Yorta
Cartographer Emily Maffei
Design Andy Warren
Typesetting Susanne Geppert
Index Max McMaster
Production manager Simone Wall

Colour reproduction by Megan Ellis and Splitting Image Colour Studio

Printed and bound in China by LEO Paper Products LTD.

The paper this book is printed on is certified against the Forest Stewardship Council® Standards and other sources. FSC® promotes environmentally responsible, socially beneficial and economically viable management of the world's forests.

Disclaimer: While every care is taken to ensure the accuracy of the data within this product, the owners of the data do not make any representations or warranties about its accuracy, reliability, completeness or suitability for any particular purpose and, to the extent permitted by law, the owners of the data disclaim all responsibility and all liability (including without limitation, liability in negligence) for all expenses, losses, damages (including indirect or consequential damages) and costs which might be incurred as a result of the data being inaccurate or incomplete in any way and for any reason.

Publisher's Disclaimers: The publisher cannot accept responsibility for any errors or omissions. The representation on the maps of any road or track is not necessarily evidence of public right of way. The publisher cannot be held responsible for any injury, loss or damage incurred during travel. It is vital to research any proposed trip thoroughly and seek the advice of relevant state and travel organisations before you leave.

Publisher's Note: Every effort has been made to ensure that the information in this book is accurate at the time of going to press. The publisher welcomes information and suggestions for correction or improvement.